THE
HONOURABLE
ALECK

Love, Law and Tragedy
in Early Canada

IAN BRUCE ROBERTSON

ABOUT *THE HONOURABLE ALECK*

What goes into the making of a judge? Although Aleck Robertson's time as a justice of the Supreme Court of British Columbia was cut tragically short by his untimely death, his career as a community leader and successful barrister aptly prepared him for that role. Yet as this book shows, it was his deep devotion to his beloved Maggie and his family that undeniably shaped the man he was. A unique and fascinating look at the life of a judge who initiated a long running family tradition of judicial service.

Justice Paul Williamson, Supreme Court of British Columbia

This totally engaging, true account of a wondrous love affair is also a rich history of life in gold rush British Columbia, filled with fresh insights into the personalities, places, and politics of the period to 1880. The letters which are the foundation for the book also offer extraordinarily rare glimpses into the everyday activities and concerns of this far away time. Ian Robertson brings Alexander and Maggie Robertson, and the lions of the era –Amor de Cosmos, Joseph Trutch, George Walkem, and many others famous and obscure – back to life. His writing weaves the stories of the Robertsons and the tragedy that cuts the letters off, through the main events of their era in a compelling narrative that I could not put down.

Prof. John Lutz, History Department, University of Victoria

Ian Robertson has a unique and charming way of taking what some may see as a rather mundane set of correspondence and documents and breathing a vibrant and very readable life into them. The love story of Alec and Maggie will not only entrance local readers from Southwestern Ontario, who will thrill in the story of two of their most famous families being brought back to fascinating life, but readers everywhere who enjoy life, love, romance and tragic loss. In short, it is a book for everyone.

Jim Gilbert, Author & Historian, Chatham-Kent, Ontario

This book is proof, if proof be needed, of the value of personal correspondence in building a picture of the past. Such letters not only document the domestic side of the most public of lives, but they often reveal facts about, and perspectives on, the politics of the day that may not be preserved in archived government documents. Given how people communicate now, one fears for the historians of tomorrow.

BC's legal history remains largely unwritten, and *The Honourable Aleck* – although a work of creative non-fiction rather than academic history – does a wonderful job of bringing a life in the law to life. But it does more than this. Alexander Rocke Robertson was, among other things, a lawyer, a judge, a member of BC's first provincial government and the founder of a legal dynasty. He was also, as this book so abundantly shows, one half of a loving partnership. And this is the true subject of this quite delightful story.

Hamar Foster, QC, Professor of Law, University of Victoria

ALSO BY THE AUTHOR

While Bullets Fly

A soldier is badly wounded in a mobile, fast-moving theatre of war. Without rapid surgery, he will die. There are no helicopters to move him out to a hospital.

This was the problem faced by the military medical authorities in the Second World War. Their solution: take the medical services to the wounded! They set up mobile ambulance units, field dressing stations and blood transfusion units, all based on trucks so that they could move swiftly to keep up with the troops.

They also set up field surgical units, which were mobile operating rooms based on three trucks and managed by the surgeons themselves. Working often in conditions that would be condemned in modern hospitals, they did whatever they could to save lives.

This is the story of one such unit, the 2nd Canadian Field Surgical Unit under the command of the young surgeon Rocke Robertson. Written by Rocke Robertson's son, this is a vivid and intimate account of a field surgical unit in action-saving lives *while bullets fly*.

Produced by:

FriesenPress
Suite 300 – 852 Fort Street
Victoria, BC, Canada V8W 1H8

www.friesenpress.com

Distributed to the trade by The Ingram Book Company

Cover image A-03023 courtesy of Royal BC Museum, BC Archives

Image on pages I, 1, 159 and 281, "The Birdcages", courtesy of the Royal BC Museum Corporation (A-02776)

To Bonnie,
my inspiration

CONTENTS

INTRODUCTION

This is the story of Alexander Rocke Robertson and Margaret Bruce Eberts Robertson, or 'Aleck and Maggie'. They were first cousins who loved each other from early days in Chatham, Upper Canada, married and moved to Victoria, British Columbia. There they had a devoted family life, and Aleck was a recognized and highly respected lawyer, politician and then Supreme Court Judge in pioneering British Columbia. These were the exciting formative years of BC, and Aleck played an important role in the evolution from two divided colonies, Vancouver Island and British Columbia, to a unified province in the Confederation of Canada.

Aleck and Maggie were apart for long periods during their lives, and they wrote to each other constantly. Their letters were passionate and beautiful, ending only when cruel fate tore them apart forever with Aleck's untimely death in 1881 at the age of 40. Their letters to each other started in 1852 and ended in 1881. They were preserved by their descendants in a cache of old family letters, and these letters are the key source of information and inspiration behind this book. I have supplemented that source by drawing on numerous texts on the history of Canada, both printed and on-line.

Is this a love story, or a non-fiction history? It is both, for love is a vital part of our history. History is made by people living their lives, doing things and loving, and love in turn helps guide them in what they do. In this case, the love between Aleck and Maggie buoyed them up through lives as important as they were dramatic.

Thus I have made *The Honourable Aleck* a work of creative non-fiction. The main events and activities took place when and where indicated, and I have provided the creative touches, mainly the conversations, family and love scenes, to add texture and enjoyment to the story.

I am dedicating this book to my wife Bonnie, who has been a tremendous source of inspiration and support to me over the years it has taken to read the letters and write the story. My thanks go to her, and also to my brother Stuart. Like our great grandfather, Stuart is an eminent lawyer, with the added attribute of having a passion for family history. It was Stuart who started me down this road, and he has been a wonderful coach.

I am also most grateful to our American cousins Diane Plesha, Roxanne Robertson-Moore and Joan Byers. They guarded the letters for years, and then helped us bring them out into the open. They have also given us many useful facts and stories from their own family experiences.

Thanks go to Glenys Galloway for her thoughtful editing. Finally I acknowledge the support and guidance I have received from Justice Paul Williamson of the Supreme Court of British Columbia, Professors John Lutz and Hamar Foster of the University of Victoria, and Jim Gilbert, a Chatham historian. They have helped to turn me into a history addict.

Ian Bruce Robertson

A Note on the Families

The story of *The Honourable Aleck* involves the mingling of two families that were centred in Chatham, Upper Canada (now Ontario) in the mid-1800s: the Eberts family that started with the arrival of Count Hermann Melchior von Eberts in Canada in 1777, and the Robertson family that started with the arrival of Dr. Alexander Rocke Robertson in Canada in 1830.

Count Hermann Melchior von Eberts was a surgeon who came to

Canada with the Hanau Regiment of Austria, engaged by the British government to participate in the American revolutionary war. He married Marie Francoise Huc of Montreal where, having left the regiment, he set up his practice. They had eleven children, four of whom died in infancy. They moved to Detroit and then Sandwich (now Windsor), across the Detroit River in Upper Canada.

Their fourth child Joseph married Ann Baker, daughter of William Baker, in 1810. William Baker was one of the founders of Chatham, having been sent to its location by the government to establish a blockhouse and start building gunboats. Joseph and Ann had seven children. Their oldest was William, and their fourth was Euphemia (Effie).

William Eberts, an important businessman in Chatham, married Mary Bell McEwen in 1840. They had ten children: Hermann, Margaret (Maggie), Melchior, Anne, David (Dide), Walter, Wilhemina (Winnie), Duncan, Henry and Jessie.

Dr. Alexander Rocke Robertson (Rocke), a surgeon with the British Navy, came to Chatham in 1830 as it was in dire need of medical services. Upon his arrival he befriended the Eberts family which by then was well-established in that town, with extensive business interests. He married Effie Eberts in 1839. This was the first joining of the Eberts and Robertson families. Rocke and Effie had eight children: James, Alexander Rocke (Aleck), Ann, Tate, Elizabeth (Lizzie), Margaret, Charles and Frances Ellen (Pet).

The Honourable Aleck tells the story of the love affair and life together of Aleck Robertson and Maggie Eberts.

PART 1
1852-1868

Love

1

FIRST LETTERS

Although he didn't know it, Aleck Robertson was writing his first ever love letter.

It was a warm fall day in 1852 in southern Upper Canada, and he was supposed to be studying. The Caradoc Academy at Strathroy stressed discipline and hard work, and he was surrounded by his classmates bending seriously over their books. But Aleck was not thinking about his work. Instead he had in mind a delightful girl who lived nearby his home in Chatham, Upper Canada. Her name was Margaret Bruce Eberts, and everyone called her Maggie. Their two families were very close as neighbours and relatives, and Aleck and Maggie were first cousins.

Ever since she had been old enough to talk and to read, Maggie had been good company, and in spite of their age differences (he was now 11 years old, she 8) they had become friends. To Aleck's surprise he could talk and laugh with Maggie almost as if she were his age. She was a cute, lively and chatty girl with sparkling blue eyes and a grin that made Aleck chuckle.

Aleck was the top student in his class at the Academy, and a competent athlete. He was also a popular boy, with a ready smile and good humour, always willing to help a friend with his homework. He sang in the school choir and took lessons on the violin. Even though he had his older brother

James and his cousin Joseph Eberts there with him, he did miss his family. Strathroy, although only 50 miles distant, seemed an awfully long way from Chatham. To his surprise he also missed Maggie. He actually felt like writing her a note, just to be in touch. After all, she had asked him to tell her everything.

He had thought about doing so from the time he first arrived at the Academy, but he found it a surprisingly complex challenge. First of all, she was a girl, and he wasn't too sure that he should be writing girls, at least not yet. Second, she was his cousin, which made the idea even more absurd. Well, perhaps. Or perhaps it made it more explainable! A friendly note to a cousin might be more easily explained than one to an unrelated young girl. Then there was the problem of simply finding the time and place to write. He could not write his letter in the common room, as the other boys would see him and make fun of him. And when else was there time?

Finally he decided that he would do it during study period, when nobody would notice. So with only a slight tinge of conscience Aleck put several books on the side of his desk to provide some cover, took out a clean sheet of paper, and checked to be sure that the master was snoozing at the front desk. The coast was clear.

Caradoc Academy
November 1st, 1852

My dear Cousin Maggie

This is the first opportunity I have had of writing you a letter. I have not time to write you a long letter for it is in school that I write this. James and Joseph are both well. I am also. It is with a great deal of joy that I can inform you of the approaching vacation for I assure you that I have been homesick long ago. It is only 7 months next Thursday. Give my love and kind regards to your kind parents and tell your mother I have got the money and pocket book she sent me. Give my love to Grandma, Aunt Phillis, Aunt Maggie, Aunt Frank & Co and to Hermann Melchior Annie and David. I have to conclude with hopes of receiving a better answer.

Believe me
Your aff't Cousin
A R Robertson

Maggie's mother Mary Bell Eberts handed Maggie the letter the evening of the day it had arrived at the post office in Chatham, still not knowing who had sent it. Maggie opened it, exclaiming "oh, how exciting" as she did so. "Mamma, it's from Aleck Robertson! How wonderful! I asked him to tell me all about the Academy, and here he's written me!" Her face glowed as she turned back to the letter and read it through, slowly and seriously.

Then she looked up at her mother. "Oh Mamma, here, read it! He hasn't said very much about the Academy, but he's already looking forward to next summer holidays! Surely we'll see him at Christmas time?"

"Oh I'm sure we will" said Mary Bell as she took the letter and read it quickly. Maggie was right, it didn't say much, but something stirred in Mary Bell's heart as she re-read the letter. It was unusual for an eleven year-old boy to be writing a letter to his eight year-old girl cousin. But then again, why not? They discussed what Maggie should say in reply, and then the girl ran upstairs to write it.

Seated at her desk, she felt warm and excited, as if launching into a new adventure. She wrote a brief note thanking Aleck for his letter, saying that her brothers and sisters were well, and expressing the hope that he would be in Chatham for Christmas. Mary Bell told her that the letter was just fine, and they sent it off in the next post.

2

YOUNG LOVE

That brief exchange of letters between the two cousins signaled the start of a relationship that moved gradually from laughter and fun to interest, then to serious interest, and then to love. In spite of the age difference between them, there were many occasions when they were together, whether at family gatherings and visits, or simply in the course of day-to-day life when Aleck was home from school.

Aleck was employed by the Eberts & Eberts Company in the summers, so had even more reason to be closely involved with Maggie's family. This work was interrupted when, on the afternoon of August 15, 1854, the Eberts Building and several surrounding buildings burned to the ground. The Eberts family fortunes suffered a reversal from which they never fully recovered, but the fire had no effect on the flourishing romance.

Maggie was entranced by her wonderful cousin, drawn strongly to his wit and friendliness and good looks. She was a lively girl with many friends, but it was always to Aleck that her thoughts turned, waking and in her dreams.

Aleck, three years her senior, always found Maggie interesting and fun, attractive in a way that he did not fully understand and could not describe. He did, however, have other social priorities to be attended to. As the years went by he had an ever-increasing fondness for the shapely presence of his teenaged female friends. His relationship with Maggie was important, but could not match his attraction to the swelling busts of the girls in his group.

This situation had an important evolution when Aleck returned to Chatham for the summer of 1856. Maggie was then 12 years old, and mature for her years. As always they met as friends, but starting that summer there was a new sense of – something – in their relationship. Aleck was entranced by the change he saw in her. Dressed in her light summer clothes, Maggie was the very image of the young maiden emerging from the cocoon of childhood into the first wonderful blush of womanhood. Her face was mature and lively, her eyes a sparkling blue that blended intelligence with a constant zest for life. She was nicely tall, and her figure had developed to a smooth and graceful curve, with a soft bosom fit for the eye of any young man.

Often he would just gaze at her and she, sensing his gaze, would look back at him, directly into his eyes. He would feel a rush, a lifting of his senses into unknown territory.

That Christmas their relationship took an exciting step forward. They had seen little of each other during this holiday, with Aleck home from Upper Canada College in Toronto where he was completing his schooling. Thus it was with a mutual sense of pleasure and relief that they greeted each other at the Eberts home at the annual family Christmas party. At one point after dinner they found themselves standing beside the dining room table where the plates of dessert sweets had been laid out. They were alone, and they did not miss the opportunity.

"I haven't seen very much of you this holiday, Maggie. I really am sorry. I would have liked to have had more time with you."

"Oh Aleck, that is so nice of you to say. And I agree. I have wanted to see you more often, but there just hasn't seemed to be the time for it."

Aleck reached out and took her hand in his. "Maggie, you are a great girl, you know. And I really enjoy our times together. Do you?"

For the first time in her life, Maggie was speechless. He was holding her hand, for goodness sake! Holding her hand! Then with a desperate but unsuccessful effort to staunch her blush, "Oh yes Aleck, I enjoy being with you so much." She looked directly into Aleck's eyes with a slow and mysterious smile that spoke of happiness and promise, a look he would long remember.

With the sound of approaching footsteps, Aleck abruptly released her hand and stepped back just as Maggie's father walked into the room. William looked at the young couple standing guiltily by the table, hesitated, then gave them a quick nod and turned his attention to the desserts.

Back at school, Aleck lay awake amidst the snores of his three room-mates. He had much on his mind, but this and the other sleepless nights were not caused by his studies or his considerations of future career. They were caused by his preoccupation with Maggie Eberts.

Aleck had to admit to himself that he loved Maggie Eberts, his dear sweet cousin Maggie Eberts! Somehow she had moved from being a close, enjoyable friend to a position at the centre of his being, of his heart and his mind. His soul. His head had finally come to understood what his heart had known for some time.

It was wonderful, but oh so complicated! She was his cousin, and so young! What would their parents think? One way or the other he wanted to be sure that Maggie was aware of his feelings. He could write her and tell her, but how on earth do you write a love letter? And surely it would be dangerous to send it to her, where her parents might read it? Finally, in a desperate effort to resolve the problem and get some sleep, Aleck decided to send her a Valentine card.

After Aleck had returned to Toronto for his last spring at UCC, Maggie had missed him more than she would have believed possible. Her world was different now. Aleck had held her hand. That was not a thing that friends do, it's what lovers do! And the way he had looked at her!

She was at her desk when her mother knocked on her door, and then looked in. "Working, dear? My, you are the studious one these days. So quiet and thoughtful! Well, you can take a break because you have a letter, and I'll bet it's a Valentine. And it's from Toronto!" Maggie stared at her mother with her mouth open. Mary Bell put the letter on her desk, stroked her hair and smiled kindly at her, and then turned and closed the door gently behind her.

Maggie sat staring at the small envelope on her desk. She was filled with a sense of excitement so strong that she felt frozen in her chair. Then she took a deep breath and opened it, and withdrew a simple card in which there was a slim piece of paper. It was of course from Aleck – who else? She knew his handwriting. He had written out a poem to her.

May God's mercy preserve thee, His power protect,
His goodness uphold thee, His wisdom direct.
May your life be a happy one, may sorrow or care
Never sadden your heart nor find a place there.
This little emblem may discover traces of regard from me.
May feebly show myself thy lover seeking love's return from thee.

Maggie read the poem six times, each time more carefully than the last. But there was no mistaking it. No getting around it. He had told her that he loved her! He loved her! Oh, Aleck loved her! She pressed the paper to her heart, stood up and waltzed around the room, humming parts of different songs as they came to mind, all out of order and as confused, yet happy as she was herself.

At a family party in May of 1857, Aleck and Maggie had a chance for a brief discussion uninterrupted by relatives. They agreed that it was wonderful to see each other again. Aleck suggested that later that day, around 4 pm, they both attempt to escape their families and take a walk on the footpath along the Thames River. She agreed, and then they turned to other guests, feeling both guilty and elated.

Shortly after 4 pm, they met just south of the Third Street Bridge as planned. They stopped and exchanged polite greetings and then, glancing about and finding no witnesses, they strolled together into a grove of trees off the trail on the river side. They stopped and faced each other. The rain was less here under the branches, but their faces were still cold and damp as they stood silently, gazing awkwardly into each other's eyes.

Aleck finally broke the silence. "It's lovely to see you again Maggie. Um… how are you? You look well."

Although just 13 years old, Maggie knew that she would have to take the lead with her tall, lovely man, who was suddenly so awkward. She reached out and took his hand. "Oh Aleck, I'm just fine. And it's lovely to see you too. And thank you for the Valentine. It was beautiful."

Aleck smiled and blushed. "I'm glad you liked it, Maggie. I so wanted to send it to you. I hope it was appropriate to do so. I…I…"

"Yes Aleck, it was appropriate. It said everything that I would have said to you had I the courage to do so."

"Oh Maggie, you are so sweet. So thoughtful. Maggie, I do love you, just as I said in the poem. You are wonderful, and I love you."

"I love you too, dear Aleck, with all my heart. I dream of you, and I think of you always."

They embraced gently, tentatively, still looking into each other's eyes. Aleck leaned down and kissed her softly on the lips, and then they hugged each other hard and long, standing immobile in the light rain. When they finally parted, they agreed to keep their love secret.

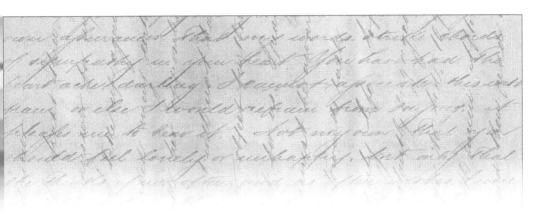

3

DISCOVERIES

Aleck arrived home from Toronto in early June of 1857, finished forever with school. He had topped his class and was proud of it, as were his beaming parents. They welcomed him home and toasted him at his first dinner back, and then he had a brief time when he could see friends and prepare for work.

On Monday, June 22 at 9 am sharp, Aleck walked into the offices of Wilson & McLean to start his career in the law. Mr. Mclean greeted him, told him that there was much to be done and that he would report directly to the senior clerk. His pay would be $13 per week to start. It was all just fine.

Maggie had one more year at Chatham's Central School. She had many good friends in her class of 22, and was always pleased to be amongst the top 3 or 4 in exams. She also took piano lessons at the school, and was becoming fluent in French. Maggie had a quiet summer planned, and although she had many friends to enjoy, with Aleck in town all the time now there was no question where her real interest lay. They exchanged notes whenever they could, generally brief ones planning their rendezvous.

Even though they were extremely careful about these meetings, they were observed once by Mary Bell Eberts. Passing by a park in downtown Chatham, she glanced briefly at a flash of color in the wooded area, and saw to her surprise that it was her daughter Maggie and young Aleck Robertson, standing very close together, hugging and starting into a kiss. Her intuition sang to her, and she overcame her initial urge to call out and greet them. She hurried on, her mind racing.

Two days later Mary Bell and Effie Robertson met at the Rose Tea Room for afternoon tea. Their conversation started with the usual social niceties, but it didn't take long for Mary Bell to come to the point. "Effie, to change the subject for a moment, I would like to have a word with you about Aleck." Effie stopped smiling, raised her eyebrows, and gazed expectantly at her friend. They often discussed their children, of course, but there was something different in Mary Bell's tone that put her on alert.

"Have you noticed that he seems to be rather fond of Maggie? They are great friends, naturally, but I mean, well, that they may be a bit more than just friends?"

Effie paused for a brief instant as a whirling collage of images raced through her mind's eye: Aleck and Maggie laughing together at family picnics; Aleck mooning through uncharacteristically quiet times. She had never connected these images together, but now – what? "I really hadn't noticed, I must admit." She folded her hands together and rested her chin on them, casting her eyes down to stare at her cup. "But I must say, now that you mention it, I have noticed a few things that might indicate some sort of special relationship. Why? What do you think?"

"My dear, I must be absolutely frank with you. I have wondered for several years about them. He has sent her Valentine cards, and I have seen them often talking together, thick as thieves. Even William noticed them at one of our Christmas parties, talking and standing very close together. He laughed about it and passed it off as their just being good friends, and of course I agreed with him. But I think he may have had other thoughts, as did I. Then two days ago I was walking to the shops and happened to pass by the park in Wellington Street, and I saw them in among the trees. And…and…they were embracing and kissing!"

Effie blanched. "What? Right there, out in the open?"

"No, no, they were quite well hidden, but I just happened to be in the right place to see them as I walked by. I can tell you, I was shocked! I didn't know whether to rush over and confront them, or carry on. I just kept walking, but as you will imagine I was very upset and confused."

"Oh Mary Bell, so you must have been! Oh my heavens! Two cousins kissing in public! Our children doing such a thing!" Effie barely contained herself from tears with the help of the napkin that she took from her lap. Mary Bell dabbed her own damp eyes with her napkin, and then reached out and took her friend's hand.

"Effie, don't worry about them being seen. It was just by chance that I happened to be there. But we must talk about them, and what we should do."

Effie clutched Mary Bell's hand. "I know, Mary Bell. I know. Oh, it's not the public display that distresses me so. It's the fact that our darling children are in love, and they are cousins! Oh dear!" She withdrew her hand and folded the napkin back on her lap.

The women talked at length about their dilemma, in hushed tones with their heads close together. They were in full agreement on all accounts: they loved and admired their own child, loved and admired the other's child, and would be pleased if the two were really in love and would eventually marry – except for the cloud of family relationship. They were cousins, and that meant that some people would frown upon the relationship, and could make it difficult for them and for their families.

"But of course they know that, and they will have thought long and hard about it. So the fact that they still carry on means that they are very attached to each other, and will be badly hurt if they are forced to part." Effie spoke quietly but with great feeling, her eyes again glistening with tears.

Then Mary Bell asked the question that they had both been mulling over. "What will our husbands think? I know William will not be happy, and I'm afraid he might make a terrible fuss that could hurt poor Maggie very badly."

They stared into each other's eyes, concentrating on that question. Then they started to smile. Their smiles broadened to grins, and then they laughed with relief. As mothers, they could deal with it. They laughed with joy at the thought of such love between two young people. They laughed at the thought of their husbands harrumphing and fretting and not knowing what to do. When they stopped laughing, they agreed that they would not tell their husbands about it. If the men found out for themselves, then they, the mothers, would support the young people.

Aleck and Maggie met as often as they could, wherever they could. The winter weather constrained them, but in the springtime warmth of 1859 they were once again able to meet in more secluded places. It was in mid-May, in their favorite place in the woods by the river, that they took another bold step forward.

After their usual chattering and laughing, Aleck took Maggie in his arms and kissed her firmly on the lips. It was so simple, so easy, so wonderful! It was always wonderful when he kissed her, and this time there was also something different and tantalizing. Aleck opened his mouth slightly while kissing her, and put his tongue softly onto her lips. She was momentarily startled and almost pulled back, but the warmth of his tongue and his delicious taste overcame her in a wave. Within seconds their mouths were open and they were exploring each other's lips and mouths with their tongues.

The kiss lasted for a long time, with brief pauses for breath. Their mouths were like magnets, drawn to each other with irresistible force. With the kiss still raging, Aleck moved his hand from her back and caressed her breast. The moment was electric – a smooth, pulsating yet soft caress! Although he was in fact holding her cotton blouse, the curve of her breast was passionately wonderful to him. How often had he gazed at it, longing to touch, and now here it was! His senses were inflamed, and were then heightened even more when he felt her hand on his thigh. She placed it there for but an instant, moved her fingers in a slow circular motion, and then moved her hand away to stroke his cheek.

For both of them the moment opened a floodgate of emotion. They were dissolving all of the barriers between them! But then, panting with sexual arousal and love, they knew that they must stop. Hands removed from bodies, they pulled their lips apart and gazed silently into each other's eyes. Maggie turned away and gazed into the clearing. Her thoughts were a triumphant jumble of joy and excitement.

Aleck felt the same way as he stood up and adjusted his clothing. Their relationship, so steeped in love and understanding, was now complete with the promise of sexual joy and fulfillment.

4

THE ENGAGEMENT

1860 came in with a harsh wintery blast, but the love between Aleck and Maggie continued at its high temperature. As the winter turned to the spring and then summer, Aleck and Maggie once again met as often as they could out of doors. Without ever discussing it they had come to an agreement that if they were assured of privacy they could kiss passionately and hug aggressively, and Aleck could stroke her breasts and she could stroke his thighs. In the warmer weather of summer, when clothing was lighter and more open, Aleck even managed to stroke her breasts inside her clothing, skin on skin. This drove them both almost wild with suppressed excitement, but the iron rules of society stopped any further explorations. They would part from these occasions hot and flushed, aching with desire.

With this affair whirling around her, Maggie felt very grown-up and worldly. She had wondered at first about his advances, but then had found that her own responses were so immediate and genuine that it must be all right, as long as they stayed within the strict limits demanded by society. She wasn't sure how his fingers caressing her nipples fit into society's rules, but when he did it, such waves of sensual joy coursed through her body that she was prepared to accept it – indeed, could not resist it.

Aleck was developing extremely quickly and well in his work at Wilson & McLean. Many of his friends now called him 'Lawyer Aleck', a nickname that he liked although it was still far from accurate. But something else tugged at him – his taste for adventure. He felt the lure of travel to new places, the excitement of the unknown. He had done little travel to date, but he had read a lot about life out there in the big world, and he knew in his bones that adventure had to be part of his future life.

Thus Aleck became increasingly interested in the news from out west. The gold rush in British Columbia was in full cry, and there were frequent stories in the press about fortunes won and lost, and thefts and murders and all sorts of violence surrounding the prospecting and mining activities. It sounded like a world of high adventure and opportunity, and his interest was stoked by discussions with his uncle John Waddell, who shared his enthusiasm for new horizons such as this.

It was unfortunate that this sense of adventure conflicted with his love for Maggie. He would have liked to travel and be away, but he found himself tied to Chatham because Maggie was there.

Maggie always enjoyed her summers up at Georgian Bay on Lake Huron. She visited with family in Collingwood and Owen Sound, where she stayed with her Aunt Frances Eberts Smith who was married to the legendary steamship builder, owner and Captain William Henry Smith. This took her away from Aleck, which was most unfortunate, so that summer, for the first time, they began to write to each other seriously and at length. Maggie's early letters were filled with passion and romantic language.

July 25, 1860

My own darling

It seems so long since I have seen you. My heart longs for thee my own, my own dearest L…

…I am stealing the time to write to thee. There are two or three young people spending the evening here. I would like to hear from thee but I am afraid I might not as I know not what minute I may go. I must not write any longer as they will be surprised at my long absence.

I love thee my own passionately, fondly, truly and only. Does't thou love me, Mon Mignon? I hear thee say "yes, my own".

Thine own, L.

Aleck liked the way Maggie signed herself 'L', meaning 'your Love' in Maggie shorthand, and referred to him as 'my L' as well, and decided to adopt it. He also enjoyed her use of the formal 'thee', which came from a mixture of her churchgoing and her love of romantic novels.

When letters came from Aleck, Maggie would take them quietly and innocently to her room, close the door, and then devour them. His letters were a joy to her. Aleck would mix in expressions of love with news about family and friends in a most interesting way.

September 3, 1860

My L.

…My own darling L., I often think with melancholy fondness of pleasant scenes in the last 3 years. They are gone and mingled with the past but the recollection of them now sings to me yet, and is a secret source of pleasure at many a time which otherwise might be lonely. My L. my own darling do you love me as fondly and exclusively as you did then?…

…I took tea with Mr. Armstrong Saturday night. I wish I were boarding with him. It's such a beautiful and well furnished house, fine library and piano, and in addition to all this 2 young ladies quite pretty and who are fine musicians.

Mr. Armstrong says they sing sometimes old songs familiar
to him, which bring home so powerfully to his mind that he
retires to his room. Oh Darling L. how holy the ties must be
that bind one to his wife, his children and his home ...

Yours in truth my loved L.

L.

Valentine's Day of 1861 was on a Tuesday. Aleck and Maggie had agreed on the Sunday before that they would meet in their usual spot near the Third Street Bridge to express their love for each other, taking a break from sending cards. It was miserably cold and they were bundled up in their winter coats, making intimate hugging and kissing impossible.

Their conversation started, unusually, not on love but on war. It now appeared inevitable that there would be a civil war in the United States. The prospect of such a war was very disturbing to Canada, and they discussed the various implications of it, depending on which side was victorious.

They sighed and clung closely, arm in arm, and turned the talk to themselves. When Aleck completed his training with McLean in June, he might well go back to Toronto for more study. The prospect was upsetting to both of them. "But you know, darling, we could at least make it even more certain that we are meant for each other if we were to be engaged." Aleck said this with a serious look on his face, stopping and turning to Maggie and taking her hand in his.

Maggie gasped. "But Aleck, we can't be engaged yet. Well, we can, but surely we have agreed that it's best to hold off being engaged and telling the world of our love until we are truly ready to marry! I know that you are determined to be established and earning sufficient to take care of me before we would consider marrying, and that won't be for several years at least!" Maggie was close to tears, the frustration palpable in her voice. "What are you thinking, my dearest love?"

Holding both of her hands, Aleck looked into her eyes. "Well, my darling

Maggie, I hereby ask you to love me and, when the time is right, to marry me. If you say 'yes', then we shall be secretly engaged. We shall be engaged in the sight of God, and in our own hearts. Let us pledge ourselves to be true to each other, and to work ceaselessly towards that happy day when we can declare our love to the world, and be married and live together forever."

"Oh Aleck" said Maggie, reaching up to kiss him softly on the lips. "Yes. Oh yes. Let us be engaged. And let the world learn of our love when we are ready to tell them, and let them be happy for us. Oh yes Aleck. Oh yes!" He swept her into his arms, and their chilled lips met and warmed each other as they celebrated the first moments of their secret engagement.

5

CAREER MATTERS

On Friday, June 21, 1861 Aleck completed his articles with Wilson & Mclean of Chatham. In their final conversation McLean told him that, as previously discussed, he had made arrangements for Aleck to take a position with the firm of Prince & Blain of Toronto. This would take him away from Chatham and his Maggie, but Aleck saw it as the best possible way to put in the year before he would be old enough to write his Bar exams.

Aleck's room on the upper floor of the impressively named 'Brown's Fine Lodgings' on Bay Street in Toronto was big enough and quite comfortable, with a rent that he could afford as long as he was careful in his living expenses. It was a ten minute walk to the offices of Prince & Blain in Queen Street.

His first walk since arriving and finding his lodgings had been to the post office in Front Street, and had been rewarded with a letter from Maggie. Bless her soul! She had the same sense of urgency that he did, the feeling that they must be in contact all of the time, whether together or apart, whether in person or by letter.

August 6, 1861

My Darling

…I've thought of you today so much – I've thought of how you've loved me, how you have held me up during the long years that are past, how you kept me in your heart, how you've held me to it. A gushing tenderness meets these thoughts – a tenderness which says there was not one look, not one word which was not thought with deep love – with passionate affection…

I love you Aleck. I love, love you. J'aime…

Prince & Blain were prospering in the burgeoning market of Upper Canada. Albert Prince, the senior partner, was at 36 years of age an eminent member of the Upper Canada Bar. His practice was based in Windsor, where he had lived since 1833 when his family moved there from England. He was well connected politically, a strong supporter of the Liberal cause and known to have political aspirations of his own. These connections brought to him a growing clientele, requiring that he have offices in Toronto as well as Windsor.

His young partner David Blain was well into his stride in Toronto, and between him and Prince there was a heavy load of work handed out to the three junior lawyers and clerks and secretaries in the office. To Aleck this was a welcome and exciting move in his legal career. His work days were full, often stretching into the evenings. Other evenings were taken up studying in his room or attending the Bar admission courses given at Osgood Hall. His Saturdays were also times for study, for long walks, and for occasional social outings. On Sundays the main event was always church in the morning, and sometimes religious events later in the day or the evening. Aleck went to church not out of habit, but out of strong religious conviction.

He and Maggie wrote each other frequently. In one letter he listed the reasons that he loved her.

September 26, 1861

My own Pet

... Can I tell you how much I do love you? Your letter contains several interrogatories. Let me then answer them. You ask will a year's absence...ever estrange us or change our treasured way of testifying our affection? I am persuaded never. I love you because I respect you. I love you because you share my feelings, desires, hopes, yearnings and I love you L. (would I could throw my arms around you this moment) because there is sympathy between us that I cannot account for except on the old Platonic theory which you doubtless remember.

This latter remark almost seems wrong for it seems like attributing a lesson of God to such preposterous causes. I think humbly yet confidently that I love you because I am permitted to do so and that you love me for the very same reason. I feel happy that there are no other influences to bring us together but the sincere affection of our hearts. This I believe with the divine blessing will continue always and as long as it does our hearts will ever be young...

For Maggie, life was busy and full of people and issues to deal with, but the missing ingredient, her beloved Aleck, dominated her thoughts. She found his letter of September 26 of particular interest with its list of reasons why he loved her. She liked and agreed with the elements that he listed, but they were not enough. She knew there was more to it, at least for her.

Aleck always seemed larger than life; out of the ordinary; a rare being who had his eyes on the whole world, above the flow of normal life and being. Everyone respected him and liked him, but he seemed to feel no sense of superiority or advantage. And somehow, for some reason, he loved her and was her best friend. In fact, he needed her, and was unhappy when he was not with her and could not draw strength from her.

Why was that? Was he, perhaps, uncertain of himself in spite of his very obvious talents? Did he need a mentor, a loving mentor, to help him in this complex world?

This was hardly a question that she could pose to him, but in her heart she knew that there was something in it. Perhaps God had sent her to support him in this life that included not just great events and moments, but also a myriad of small issues that must be dealt with. Perhaps the Lord had brought them together through the magic of love to form a perfect team.

Maggie smiled at this thought, writing furiously in her diary.

That Christmas John Waddell, Maggie's adventuresome uncle, announced plans to go west to the colonies of Vancouver Island and British Columbia, there to make his fortune in the gold rush. He was not a miner, but he had all sorts of business skills that he was certain would serve him well in those exciting western colonies. He planned to leave in February, and then bring his family out when he had become properly established.

"Tell me Robertson, what are your plans once you've passed your examinations next month? Would you wish to continue working here in Toronto, or back in Chatham? Or perhaps elsewhere?"

Albert Prince sat relaxed in his office chair, gazing at the young Aleck Robertson who had become something of a star in his office in the eight months since his arrival. It was April 24, 1862, just a few weeks before Aleck and all other aspirants of that year would sit their Bar admission examinations. Prince had his own agenda for this meeting. He was determined to keep the young man in his firm, and this was not just for the purpose of maintaining the high quality of the legal work handled by the firm. Prince had serious political aspirations, planning to run for office on the Liberal side when the opportunity arose. In Aleck he saw a potentially strong political supporter and ally.

Aleck's reply to his question did not surprise him. "Well Sir, I've been assuming that I would be going back to Chatham to continue my preparations for the Bar. I'm sure that Mr. McLean will have me back, and it would be nice to complete my studies while living at home."

"Did you find the work there stimulating? How did it compare to the cases you have worked on here?"

Aleck had suspected for some time now that the Toronto firm might want him to continue on with them, and naturally that presented him with a dilemma. Were it not for Maggie being in Chatham, he would not hesitate to seek the more challenging employment here in Toronto. But now, well, he just didn't know what to do. Heart versus head is always a tough competition.

"Oh, we had some very interesting cases in Chatham. Mr. McLean seems to know a lot of people and to be well plugged in to the political scene there, so we had a good list of clients. Not like here though, I must say. Your firm is a very exciting place, Sir."

Prince knew in an instant what his strategy should be. "You're absolutely right, Robertson. We do have an exciting practice here. I must admit, I would hate to see you leaving us to return to a more limited practice in Chatham. I fully understand your wish to return to your home, at least until you have been admitted to the Bar. Perhaps we can find a way to kill two birds with one stone."

"Sir?"

Prince reminded Aleck that the other base of his practice was in Windsor, now a significant town close to Chatham by train. His two-headed law practice was starting to be of concern as he could not be in both Toronto and Windsor at once, but both demanded his attention. When he was in Windsor he knew that his Toronto business was in Blain's strong hands, but when he was in Toronto his Windsor work lost its momentum.

He needed to have a junior partner there.

"I would like you to consider coming to Windsor to continue your work and your preparations for the Bar. Just as I have Blain here in Toronto, I need a partner in Windsor to keep things moving along there. I think you would find the work there stimulating – somewhat more challenging than in Chatham and, of course, Windsor is a mere stones-throw from Chatham. You could go home for weekends if you wished!"

Aleck was staggered – a partnership with Albert Prince? He, a young aspiring lawyer not even yet accepted by the Bar of Upper Canada, part-nering with this star? Aleck looked down at the floor to hide his blush of excitement. Prince smiled quietly.

Aleck spent his 21st birthday, May 12, 1862, studying for the Bar exams. Two days later he wrote the exams, which he found engaging but not difficult. On May 19 Prince called him into his office, shook his hand and told him that he had passed the exams with flying colors, and could therefore now describe himself as a Solicitor and Attorney at Law.

One week later, on the strength of his work at Prince & Blain, his splendid showing in the Bar exams and an interview with a panel of three senior lawyers, he was admitted as a Solicitor of Her Majesty's Court of Chancery. During these final weeks at the firm he had several discussions with Prince about the proposed partnership arrangement in Windsor, and finally accepted the offer "with great pleasure and thanks".

On the last weekend in May he said goodbye to his colleagues at the office and took the train back to Chatham. His family welcomed him home and congratulated him on his partnership with Albert Prince. His welcome at Riverside was somewhat more complex.

On his arrival he entered the parlour where Maggie and her mother where sewing. He paid his respects to Mary Bell first, and then hugged Maggie and kissed her on the cheek. Mary Bell smiled and gazed out the window.

They had just sat down and started talking about his return when

William strode into the room. There was a moment's pause as he stopped and looked at Aleck, clearly surprised that he was there. His face registered a fleeting frown, and then a distant smile of welcome. "So, Aleck, you've returned to Chatham! Mary Bell tells me that you've done well in your examinations. Well done. I congratulate you."

"Thank you Sir. Yes, I have finally done my Bar exams, and with a bit more work and study I hope to be called to the Bar within a year or so."

William sat down. "You lawyer fellows seem to take an awfully long time to get your education. Tell me, where exactly do you stand now? What do we call you, and what are you allowed to do with your present credentials?"

"Well Sir, having passed the Bar admission examinations I am now, formally, a Solicitor and Attorney at Law under the auspices of the Law Society of Upper Canada. But I am not yet a Barrister, which means that I am not yet permitted to appear in court except in support of a lawyer who is a member of the Bar. My next task is to do whatever studying and practical work is required to be accepted formally by the various courts in Upper Canada. I have already been accepted as a Solicitor of Her Majesty's Court of Chancery. That was the easy one as it deals more with common sense solutions to disputes than with complex legal issues. The others are more complex and also fussier as to whom they will accept. They are Her Majesty's Courts of King's Bench and of Common Pleas in Upper Canada. I am told that it will likely take about a year to gain acceptance by them, and then I will be invited to join the Bar of Upper Canada."

"My goodness Aleck" said Mary Bell, "what a long time it takes to be a lawyer!" She then moved diplomatically to the question they all had on the tips of their tongues. "Your mother has mentioned to me that you are thinking of perhaps going to Windsor to work your way through this next round of studies. Is that true?"

Aleck squirmed in his chair. He glanced at Maggie as he replied, his heart churning as he saw her tense, anguished look, her eyes staring at him. "Yes Auntie, it is. Albert Prince has offered me a partnership with him in Windsor, where he has a thriving practice – so much so that he must also keep his office in Toronto to serve his clients in the senior courts there. I have accepted his offer. I see it as a great opportunity to move ahead in the profession, and of course, it is much closer to Chatham than Toronto." This latter point was aimed at Maggie, but she didn't seem particularly happy about it.

But William was, and showed it with his warm smile and congratulations to Aleck on such an excellent prospect. Just as Aleck had noticed William's frown on his arrival in the room, so now he noticed William's delight that he would be working in Windsor, and not in Chatham. "Windsor is a fine town, I know. I'm sure you'll do very well there, my boy."

On June 11, 1862 Aleck moved by train to Windsor, accompanied by two large valises of clothes and two trunks of books. He was met at the Windsor railway station by his senior partner Albert Prince.

DR. ALEXANDER ROCKE ROBERTSON, MD 1801-1864

EUPHEMIA "EFFIE" EBERTS ROBERTSON 1818-1875
PICTURES OF CHATHAM COURTESY OF JIM & LISA
GILBERT HISTORIC PICTURE COLLECTION

OLD CHATHAM

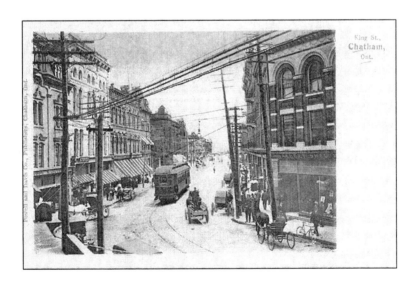

KING STREET WEST, CHATHAM CIRCA 1860

ALEXANDER ROCKE ROBERTSON IN 1864

MAGGIE EBERTS IN 1867

6

PRINCE & ROBERTSON

On June 18, 1862 Maggie sat in her room late in the afternoon, devouring her second letter from Aleck since he had left Chatham for Windsor. She had finally settled down to the realization that he really was away from her, starting the next stage of his career in Windsor, not Chatham. She had pondered their dilemma from every angle, and had to agree with Aleck that this was the best course to follow.

She gazed for a moment out of her window at her favorite tree, leaves rippling in the summer breeze. It reminded her of their glade in the woods by the river. Their soft words, their kisses, his searching hands – oh! She smiled quietly and returned to the letter. He was well settled in a place called 'Hirons House' in Windsor, and there seemed to be reasonable prospects for work there.

June 16, 1862

My darling Maggie

...I ought to mention before proceeding farther that my office is in that brick building nearly opposite the "Hirons House" – a nice light airy room but although as comfortable as offices usually are – yet minus some little things – I hope in time to

add.

I have a very excellent room at the Hirons House – and can enjoy the quietness of retirement as oft as I please – a pleasure is it not Pet? I have made but one call yet, and that upon Prince – agreeably to his repeated invitations – I spent last evening there, and in fact the whole night for it being dark at 10:30 when I was thinking of leaving, and the distance of four miles of in part not very good walking – I accepted his proffered hospitality and slept there...

Windsor, formerly 'Sandwich', was established as a village in 1854, the same year that it was connected to the rest of Canada by the Great Western Railway. It became a town in 1858. It was larger than Chatham, and with its close proximity to Detroit it had a thriving commercial base. It was the county seat of Essex County, which brought substantial legal work to it from the surrounding area.

This did not, however, translate into a heavy workload for Aleck. Some of Prince's work required his assistance, but his own slate of clients grew slowly. He had an irregular flow of civil cases and a few criminal cases, but nothing dramatic. Thus even with his studies for admission to the courts he still had time for visits around the town and the area, did some sailing on the lake nearby, and was invited to a round of social evenings that quickly grew tedious and repetitious.

In mid-July he paid a brief visit to Chatham, but to his intense frustration did not see Maggie. He still had the nagging feeling that Maggie's father was not pleased with their relationship, so he did not wish to push too hard.

His concerns about William's discomfort over their relationship were dispelled somewhat with a visit later in July from Maggie's mother, who came through Windsor to visit friends.

July 23, 1862

My Maggie

Quite unexpectedly I met your mother at the station on Monday evening and after the train left saw her across the river and got a cab. We found your Uncle John at the store, and then I left her. When I met her in the station she said with a roguish kind of look, "I've a letter for you. When we get on the boat I'll give it to you." She said this with such good nature, and that smile she always wears when not displeased, that I looked upon it as a very good omen.

On the boat she said "now I'll give you the letter if you promise to behave yourself". Of course, I was ready to give the requested promise, and so Mignonne I received your billet. I mention this little incident Darling because you will be pleased to know that your note was handed to me with such good feeling...

Maggie spent the month of August at the family house in Owen Sound, seeking to escape the terrible summer heat of Chatham, but finding little relief in the Sound. September brought cooler temperatures and easier tempers for all concerned.

With the ending of summer Aleck's work picked up somewhat, but it was still not what he had hoped for. One meeting of exceptional interest occurred in October, when the eminent S.S. Macdonnell paid a surprise visit to his office. Aleck's secretary Mrs. Quinn announced Macdonnell's arrival in hushed tones, and Aleck hurried to the door to greet the great man and escort him to seats around the table.

Samuel Macdonnell was one of Windsor's most distinguished citizens. He graduated from law school and was called to the Bar in 1847. Later, he received the degrees M.A. and L.L.D. By 1849 he was practicing law in Amherstburg. A year later he was made clerk and solicitor for the Western

District, and moved to Sandwich. He held the office of Warden of Essex County in 1855 and 1856. When Windsor was incorporated as a town on January 1, 1858, Macdonnell was elected as its first Mayor, while he also served as Crown Attorney for Essex County. He resigned as Mayor two years ago to pursue his legal career, but it was widely assumed that he would run for the position again in the future. In addition to his legal and political careers, Macdonnell was an important land developer.

"I am pleased to have the opportunity to meet you here in your lair, Robertson. We have of course met a few times, but it's always good to see a man on his home turf. Prince tells me that you are doing good work. But tell me…how is it going for you? Are you well settled in? Are the clients flocking to you as they surely must?"

They exchanged polite smiles. "Well Sir, I wouldn't say 'flocking', but fortunately a few poor souls have found their way to my door. It is of course helpful having Prince as a partner. I'm finding Windsor extremely interesting, and am meeting enough people that I'm sure the business will improve in due course."

Macdonnell burst out laughing. "My dear Robertson, I am a politician by nature, a lawyer by profession and a businessman by inclination, and I can tell you, in any of the languages of those three pursuits, your answer could be more simply put as 'no.'"

Aleck frowned and gazed at him, awaiting the explanation that was due.

"Oh, please don't get me wrong. I mean no disrespect when I say that. Indeed, I used your very words on a number of occasions when I was starting my own career, trying to say that while I was in business and happy to be so, I could use a bit more work if I was going to make ends meet. It is a common condition, even when in partnership with a man like Prince. The problem that I found, and perhaps this will sound familiar to you, is that an important partner puts your name on the door in a positive way, but you still have to find most of the work yourself. You do sometimes get a few scraps from your partner's table, but they are generally at the lower end of the spectrum, not very interesting and not very rewarding. I hope I'm not too far off the mark?"

It was Aleck's turn to laugh. "My dear Sir, you are right on target, I assure you. A bulls-eye! It will of course be easier when I have my Bar, but even so, I thought I would have more to do now. I know I must be patient, but, well, I am not."

"Of course you're not. You have a brilliant future ahead of you, and you want to get on with it. Well now, this brings me to the purpose of my visit."

Macdonnell said that he was deeply involved in politics, had a large clientele craving his legal services, and an extremely large land development business to oversee. He needed help in all three areas of his work, and he insisted that the help be of the highest quality. After hearing Prince sing the praises of his young partner on several occasions, Macdonnell had decided that Aleck would be ideal to help out in his legal work, and possibly on the political side as well.

"If you are interested, I will send some legal work your way to get it off my desk, and to help get you more in the swim of things. It will of course be better when you have your Bar so that you can take cases right through to conclusion, but even now there is lots to be done that is well within your professional realm. On the political side, I would like to call upon you occasionally to help me sort through issues that have legal implications. I have a couple in mind as we speak. But first, tell me, are you interested?"

Aleck managed to reply with a reasonably steady voice.

"I am Sir. Thank you. I look forward to it."

On November 15, 1862 Aleck received notification that he had been admitted as an Attorney of Her Majesty's Courts of King's Bench and of Common Pleas in Upper Canada. This was all very well, but he still had to wait for his Diploma of Barrister at Law to be awarded by the Law Society of Upper Canada. With it would come his license to practice in all the courts in Ontario. Then, finally, he would be invited to join the Bar of Upper Canada. There would inevitably be long delays and then oral examinations. The process was all very frustrating.

An important part of Aleck's ongoing education in Windsor was his interest in politics. While he did not become directly involved, his work with men like Prince and Macdonnell inevitably drew him into the flow of debate and discussion surrounding the political process. This put him in the public eye more than he had reckoned for, and helped his legal career. He became increasingly known for his articulate presentations on the issues of the day.

While interested in the political process, he had little respect for partisan party politics. He preferred to think that politicians would support issues because they made sense, rather than simply taking the party line.

March 25, 1863

My beloved

If I were to relate the views of the place, beyond doubt the first topic would be the election…

…You ask me Darling – which side I take. I have not given much consideration to political matters – that I think necessary before identifying myself with either party. Perhaps from the fact of my venerable father having been conservative, my predilections are in favor of that party, but I am of opinion that an honest, conscientious man would sometimes have to sacrifice principles and honour if he resolved to follow the tortuous and often grossly inconsistent course of either party. I think it would be more congenial to my feelings and views to support any measure I deemed to be pro bono publico, no matter by which party it was introduced, and opposing anything of an opposite character no matter if my own party (if I belonged to any) advocated it. I should like to be an independent…

Aleck's sense of apolitical politics reflected his broader sense of political purpose as he became increasingly involved in the business and political life of Windsor and, therefore, of Canada. Canada at that time consisted of Upper and Lower Canada, soon to be renamed Ontario and Quebec.

Now there was excited talk of the idea of joining the far-flung colonies to the east and west into a Confederation with Canada, giving a country with a geographical base to rival that of the United States. Ideally it would be tied together by a railway that would facilitate the movement of people and goods from coast to coast, and make the entire country easier to defend. Aleck saw this as a grand design to be supported vigorously, and he did so in his conversations and statements, public and private.

It also fed on Aleck's lust for adventure – he would like to play an active role in the development of this huge new country. How he would do so was not yet clear to him, and this mingled sense of political force and adventure had not yet surfaced enough as to enter into or affect his relationship with Maggie. It soon would, but for now their letters continued to stress the importance of patience, while at the same time dwelling on the love and longing that bound them together.

In late August Aleck was summoned to Toronto for the oral examination for Bar admission. He passed with ease, and then on September 1 received his Diploma of Barrister at Law from the Law Society of Upper Canada, and with it license to practice in all the courts in Upper Canada. On October 1, 1863 he was called to the Bar of Upper Canada.

S.S. Macdonnell now started to turn to him more and more, and in late October Aleck formed a separate partnership with Macdonnell, increasing his work stream. He was certainly well established in Windsor, recognized and admired, and he could probably do quite well for himself over time. But now that lure of adventure, mingled with his sense of the destiny of Canada that had lingered in his mind through the discussions with his Uncle John Waddell, burst into life. British Columbia – Vancouver Island – the Cariboo – gold! Aleck was drawn to the thought of travelling to that far side of the continent to seek his fortune in the gold-driven economy, and at the same time to perhaps play some role in the political future of Canada.

He posed the idea in a letter to Maggie in early November. His thought at that point was that they would be married and go out to the west together. Maggie was not in favour, and dealt with it as just another of her excitable fiancée's passing fancies.

November 7, 1863

> *...My Darling, you wrote something about our going to BC. We'll not say anything about it for it would affect our marriage and I would like it to be free from the thought of such a parting from all whom I love. I feel so unsettled. I suppose nothing will restore my accustomed gaiety but seeing you...*

Aleck received this message and understood it fully, but in his own mind the matter was more or less settled. Why, for heaven's sake, should he and Maggie wait for years while his practice here in Upper Canada grew to the level that they could afford to be married, when he could in a much shorter time make a substantial nest egg out in BC, and then they could live wherever they wished?

This led to a second line of thinking. Rather than have the two of them go out there together, perhaps he should go first, make his money, and then either bring Maggie out to live there, or return in triumph to Upper Canada. As he worked this idea around in his mind, it was helped along by yet another letter from John Waddell, writing from Victoria in the colony of Vancouver Island. Uncle John had now been in the colony since March of 1862. Typical of this inveterate adventurer he had already tried several things, and was now manager of Macdonald & Co., the first bank in Victoria. He urged Aleck to join him, and said that if he did so, it might be convenient for him to accompany the Waddell family on their move to join him in Victoria.

January 27, 1864

My Maggie

> *...I want to tell you something about myself and a project I have in view, first of all saying that what I write is for you*

only. I have been thinking very seriously of going to Vancouver
Island. Some reasons that I have mentioned to you, and some
that I have not spoken about lead me to think this a judicious
step. I am satisfied that progress in Canada would be a slow
thing for one situated as I am. Were I with you I would like
to tell you more of the motives that influence me. Meantime
dear Pet you must tell me what you think about it. Mother
and father are quite willing, and the main difficulty seemingly
now is to get sufficient funds. This I hope to accomplish in
some way or other. Do you know for a certainty whether the
Waddells think of going this year and when?...

Maggie did not like being angry at Aleck, but she very definitely was now
as she read this letter. Oh, what a stubborn man he was! Could he not see
that leaving Chatham and going out west would separate them once again,
at such a distance and probably for a long time? How could he suggest it so
calmly, so decisively? How long had he felt this way? How could he say that
he loved her, and then leave her once again? Why was it always head over
heart, logic over passion, when he was concerned?

Did he really love her? Really? Or was this perhaps his way of saying
good-bye, his way of getting out of a cloying relationship with a much
younger person? Tears of anger and frustration flooded her eyes and
stained the letter. She threw it down and moved to her window, arms firmly
crossed. She stared blearily at the snow falling gently through the trees, her
mind filled with unhappy images: Aleck with another woman in Windsor;
Aleck in a ship on the high seas, walking the deck arm in arm with another
woman; Aleck in wild, far-off Victoria, living free of the entanglements of
Chatham.

But slowly, slowly the soft fall of the snow did its magic. She calmed
down and began to think more rationally. There had been no sign ever,
in any way that his love for her had faltered since he moved to Windsor.
Indeed, over Christmas they had managed to have two wonderful, intimate

meetings. He would have had to be totally false, a charlatan even, to say those words to her and do those things with her if he was withdrawing his love for her at the same time. No, Aleck was not a charlatan. His iron-clad idea of earning enough money before they could be married was also reasonable.

It confirmed to her how important the prospect of adventure was to her fiancée. Give him some rein when he yearned for it, or face the prospect of living with a caged animal.

But then she became agitated again. Was this good enough for her? Was his declared love for her really strong enough to hold out through a long stay out west? Should she take the chance? What if it meant leaving Chatham, away from her parents and family and friends, and moving to the west only to find that her man was forever having some adventure or other away from home? These were troubling thoughts, restless thoughts. Almost as long as she could remember she had been confident in her love for Aleck, and in his for her, but did she really know him that well?

She stared out the window, her thoughts whirling. These were not questions that she wanted to worry about, but she had to. They were real questions! Well, so was life real and full of risks, but also rewards! She clenched her hands and closed her eyes and tried to organize her thoughts, but all she could do was conjure up his face, smiling at her. Here indeed was reward! Risk, yes, definitely. But oh, the reward! She knew, she just knew that she had made her choice years ago, and there was no way around it. She would have to live with it, and manage it as best she could.

Although they still dwelt on their love for each other in their letters, their preoccupations moved to the practical matters of his leaving his practice in Windsor, making travel arrangements to coincide with those of the Waddell family, borrowing money from relatives to make the trip, and having as much time as possible in Chatham before he left.

By the end of the first week of March the arrangements for Aleck to travel to Vancouver Island with the Waddell family were in place. They would leave Chatham for New York by train on March 31, and on April 4 they would take ship for Panama. They would cross the Isthmus by train, and then travel by steamer up to San Francisco. After a brief rest there they would take another steamer for the final run north to Victoria. The trip would take around six weeks. As the American Civil War was still raging, they were told that their voyage down the eastern coast of the continent would take place under the protection of the United States Navy.

Aleck had originally thought that leaving Windsor would be the easiest part of the exercise, but he was wrong. He was an active, outgoing man, certainly not self-effacing, but he had underestimated the impact that he had made during his relatively short stay in Windsor. He had developed a substantial network of friends and colleagues, most of who liked and admired him. The news that he intended to leave spread quickly, and was met with dismay.

On March 12 at 2:30 pm as pre-arranged, S.S. Macdonnell arrived at the office and, after a brief chat, asked Aleck to come with him to attend an important meeting that had cropped up unexpectedly. They walked several blocks to the centre of town and, turning the corner at the courthouse, they saw a small crowd of people gathered around its front steps. The people turned toward them as they approached, and there were cries of "here they come" and "here he is now". To his bewilderment Aleck saw that they were all smiling at him, and several patted his back as Macdonnell led him though a parting in the crowd and up the steps, where County Court Judge the Hon. J.R. Watkin awaited them.

The judge came forward and shook Macdonnell's hand, and then turned to Aleck and shook his hand warmly. Macdonnell stepped over to the side, and the judge leaned forward and, over the murmurs of the crowd, said to the wide-eyed Aleck "well Mr. Robertson, if you insist upon leaving us, then we must insist upon giving you a fine Windsor send-off, now mustn't we?"

"Well your Honour, I…"

The judge had already turned to the crowd and called for silence. "Ladies and Gentlemen, we are here to deliver to our colleague Alexander Rocke Robertson a formal message of regret that he has decided to leave our fair city for the wilds of the west. You have all, I hope, seen and signed this statement, which I will now read."

Address of Regret from the Citizens of Windsor
To Alexander Rocke Robertson
Presented at the Court House, Windsor, by the County Court Judge
March 12, 1864

We, the undersigned, having learned with deep regret your intention of leaving Windsor for a distant part of the British Dominions, desire to express, on the eve of your departure, the high esteem in which you are held not only by your personal friends but also by your fellow townsmen generally - an esteem which we beg to assure you is founded on our knowledge and appreciation of the stable and valuable elements of your character, your many good qualities, your eminent abilities, and your irreproachable deportment.

It is with much satisfaction, on this occasion, that we bear testimony to the fact that the professional labours in which you have been engaged during your residence here, while they led the public to place a high estimate on your talents and legal acquirements, and justified your friends in hoping for you a highly useful and honourable career, established, at the same time, unbounded confidence in your integrity, and gained for you the respect of all with whom you came in contact in the relations of business.

But it is mainly because your sympathies and exertions were ever easily called forth on behalf of whatever was right and good – because your outward life afforded manifestations of liberal culture, high principle, and gentlemanly and Christian conduct, that your departure will be felt as a loss in this community. Fully sensible of this loss, we tender to you our best wishes for your success and sincerely hope, that in this country to which you are about to go, you may enjoy health, prosperity and extensive usefulness; and we accordingly beg your acceptance of this very inadequate expression of our feelings and of the accompanying testimonial, as a slight token of our regard for you.

Signed by 36 citizens: the County Court Judge, the County Crown Attorney, the Sheriff of the County of Essex, a number of barristers-at-law and attorneys-at-law, members of the medical profession, managers of banks, Clerk of the

Division Court, Town Clerk, railway agents, newspaper proprietors, clergymen, and other prominent citizens.

The 'very inadequate expression of our feelings' was a beautiful silver watch with a suitable inscription. Aleck held it in his hands, read the inscription, and then slowly looked up at the crowd, who were applauding noisily. He took his time in doing so because he was, uncharacteristically, tongue-tied by this surprising and thrilling occasion. He pulled himself together and stepped forward.

"Your Honour, distinguished friends...I." He had to pause, still choked with emotion. He swallowed hard.

"My friends, I am overcome by this message and this gift. I am honoured. I am...well, you have probably never seen a speechless lawyer before!" The crowd roared its approval.

"I thank you most sincerely for your kind message and your wishes for my future in the far-off colonies of the west. I leave Windsor with regret. This is a fine town, and it has been very good to me. It is here in Windsor that I started my legal profession, and I have many dear colleagues and friends to show that I have not been totally unsuccessful.

I must assure you that my reason for leaving has nothing to do with my feelings about Windsor. No, my reason for leaving is that I feel drawn to the western colonies, which are only just starting their lives as viable jurisdictions of Her Majesty. There is so much to be done to prepare them for the future. They have appealed to my sense of adventure, and I cannot resist the lure of them.

"So I leave voluntarily and happily, but also with regret – a most complicated condition I can assure you. But please rest assured that wherever I am, I shall always remember fondly the fine town of Windsor and its most hospitable citizens. Thank you and God bless you."

Macdonnell helped guide Aleck through the complex process of acquiring a passport for Canada. He also made sure that the city recorded its own farewell message.

Resolution of the Council of the Municipality of Windsor
March 16, 1864

Mr. Bloomfield begged leave to mention to the Council, that Mr. Alexander R. Robertson, Barrister at Law was about to leave Windsor for Vancouver's Island. He remarked upon the high esteem in which Mr. Robertson was held in the Community and thought it fitting that the Council should express the sentiment of the Public by a Resolution. Mr. Strong and the Mayor made observations to the same effect. Others concurred.

The following Resolution was then unanimously passed by the Council.

RESOLVED "That this Council learn with regret that Mr. A.R. Robertson is about to leave this place for Vancouver's Island. That the Council cannot allow a young Gentleman of such high character and promise, born and educated in this part of the Province, to depart for so distant a portion of the British Empire, without their appreciation of his excellence and worth, nor without expressing to him their wish for his success in a more extended and profitable field for the exercise of his abilities."

On March 17 Aleck said good-bye to his Windsor friends and took the train to Chatham, the first stage of his trip to real adventure.

7

A LONG VOYAGE INDEED!

Their trip started at the Chatham railway station, where there were at least 100 people gathered to say "good-bye and good luck" to the Waddell family and Aleck. Maggie was there with her parents and brothers Hermann and Melchior. While Mary Bell was watching her daughter to be sure she was bearing up, Maggie in turn was watching Bella Waddell make her rounds. John Waddell's oldest daughter, Bella was the same age as Maggie, and really quite lovely. She was attractively dressed for travel, and her smiles and excited chatter added to her lustre. At one point Maggie saw her in close conversation with Aleck, pointing occasionally at the Waddell team of children milling around, impatient to be on board and away.

For just a second Maggie's heart stopped. Were her worst fears to be realized? One of her oldest and dearest friends was about to launch forth on a long voyage with her Aleck. And not just a voyage, but going to live in the same far-off colony with him as well! Could she have designs on Aleck? Maggie could not believe that Aleck had any such thoughts in mind, but she could believe that Bella was attracted to Aleck, and might well be entertaining such an idea. There was no evidence, but Maggie was suddenly aware of an unwelcome tingling of doubt and jealousy.

After the train trip from Chatham and three nights rest at the comfortable La Farge House in New York, they went on April 4 to the harbour to board ship. They were a substantial party – Aunt Nancy Waddell, John's wife who was weak and feverish at the time; their oldest child Bella, 20 years old and delegated by John with full responsibility for the family; the other Waddell children – William 19, Anne 15, John 10, Fanny 8, Henry 5 and Hamilton 3; Aleck, who had volunteered to help as much as he could; and two family members who had come with them from Chatham to see them off – Ingram Taylor and Hermann Eberts.

The ship was the *Champion* of the Vanderbilt line, an iron-clad side-wheeler. It had an official capacity of 450 passengers, but as they filed on board Aleck had the distinct impression that far more than that were boarding. He had a tiny cabin to himself. The Waddells were squeezed into two larger cabins, stuffy in spite of the small windows, and cramped with their luggage stowed in every available space around them.

When they were all fully stowed and out on deck saying their goodbyes to Hermann and Ingram, Bella exclaimed on the crowded condition of the ship. "There seem to be people everywhere! Aleck, have you seen the salon? Even it has luggage stored at one end of it. I wonder how many people are on this ship."

Aleck accosted the Purser who was hurrying by, and received the discouraging news that the total passenger list numbered just under 900 people! "But you need have no concerns Sir. This is quite normal for us in these troubled times." Aleck sought to reassure Bella, with the others listening in, but when the whistle blew for "all ashore that's going ashore", Hermann and Ingram left with worried looks on their faces.

What an amazing sight it was! The towering thunderclouds on the horizon sent the northeast wind flying across the white-capped ocean, blowing the spume into a million sparkling droplets that fired like shotgun pellets into the waves ahead. The sky was a dramatic mixture of dazzling blue and scudding clouds ranging from dull grey to deepest black. Aleck stood at the rail near the bow of the ship, hatless and warmly dressed, breathing in the glorious air that was so welcome after the stuffiness of his tiny cabin and the fetid stench of the common rooms. There were a few other hardy souls nearby, but he knew that most of the passengers who had ventured out on deck in this rough weather were leaning over the stern railings, vomiting any vestiges of the food that had been served so far on this wretched ship.

They were two days out to sea and had still not turned south. Upon leaving New York they had been struck by a northeast gale so strong that the captain had been forced to turn into the wind to avoid foundering. And so they had bounced for two days, with just enough leeway to keep the ship into the wind.

The ship was an overloaded ark of crowded, spewing mankind. Nancy and all of her brood except Bella and the youngest child Hamilton were confined to their bunks, taking occasional sips of water and soup, but for the most part rolling and groaning in unison with the disgusting motion of the ship. Their cabins were a scene from Hades – stuffy, messy, smelly and rumpled.

Aleck turned from the horizon and saw Bella walking carefully toward him across the pitching deck, holding the hand of young Hamilton. The boy was as pleased as was Bella to have escaped the cabin, where he received nothing but growls in response to his requests for play. Bella also looked pleased. They had both been seriously ill at the start of the voyage, but were now almost recovered. Aleck had suffered a brief period of queasiness the first day out, but was now quite over it and able to attend meals.

He smiled as they approached, and bent down to welcome Hamilton. "Hello Hammy! What do you think of this weather today? Do you like the wind? Look at the big waves!"

Hamilton clutched with both hands at the lower rail, which was just over knee height to Aleck. "I love the waves Cousin Aleck! They are so huge!"

As he stared out to sea, Bella turned and took Aleck's arm, both of them hovering over the excited youngster. She breathed in deeply and smiled happily. "And how about you, Aleck, are you enjoying the waves?"

"Oh yes Cousin Bella. They are wonderful!" They both laughed. "And they certainly keep the deck nice and clear! It's so good of people to stay in their cabins, isn't it?" This he said with a straight face, in a voice very close to that of the officious Second Officer whose job it was to keep people as happy as possible in the circumstances. They laughed again, and listened to Hamilton exclaiming over the waves and an occasional seagull.

"Have you heard anything about our turning south?" she asked, turning to him. "Oh I do hope we can do so soon."

"Yes, I have in fact. Our friend Mr. Smale, the Steward, says that he expects us to turn south this evening, when this gale is supposed to subside somewhat. Heaven help us if it doesn't! We'll arrive in England in about one year's time on this course!"

They talked on about the weather and the very poor conditions on board, and about Nancy's fragile health. "We really should have postponed out departure until she improved" said Bella, "but with all the arrangements made, it seemed impossible to do anything except follow the plan."

"Of course" said Aleck, who then lifted Hamilton up into his arms to explain the lifeboats to him, not entirely dislodging Bella's hand as he did so.

April 15, 1864

My Darling M.

Already thousands of miles from my beloved. How tediously these weary – wearisome days pass, and yet each one as it softly sinks into the eternity of the past witnesses a wider separation between us. So far as space goes, how superior our hearts and minds are to our bodies. The latter are affected by distance, but our thoughts can in a moment's time seek the familiar presence of each other's spirit, linger over the words we have spoken or the caresses we have lovingly exchanged. Do you not think Darling 'tis sweet for me to abandon in thought this wearing, wearying sea voyage and seek my loved ones in dear Canada?

Tomorrow we will reach the Isthmus and cross to the Pacific. Oh how glad I shall be to get off this crowded, uncomfortable ship. We have in my opinion nearly 1,000 on board, though I understand the purser said there are only 875. He, I suppose, has made his estimate from the tickets, and then lost sight of the great number of little children on board. However, whatever be the number what it may, we are shamefully crowded – so crowded that exercise is almost impossible. Add to this the great discomforts arising from the heat of these latitudes, the miserable water we have on board, and you can imagine my Pet what an unpleasant predicament we are in.

The Pacific steamers I am told are larger and much more comfortable. I hope it is true. We had heavy weather very shortly after leaving NY, and were by reason thereof delayed something like 48 hours, i.e. the ship had to be brought up to the wind and that was from the NE, whereas our course was S. We bobbed about, pitched and rolled for I think about 2 days and nights and then the ship resumed her course which she has kept ever since. By today's reckoning the Captain has ascertained that we were at 12 o'clock 211 miles from Aspinwall, a distance which he expects to accomplish by tomorrow at two o'clock PM.

Our water becoming exhausted, we had to stop at an island called Magna (Inawgwa as they call it). A great number went ashore, I among their number. Although the day was exceedingly warm, I in company with 3 or 4 others strolled about the queer little village, looking at the pomegranates, figs, lemons, oranges, cocoanuts – the latter are about the only fruit ripe at this time. I got 4 cocoanuts and some green lemons and oranges. The lemons and oranges, although green, make a most agreeable drink. An old colored woman made some and it tasted very nice.

In a future letter I must tell you more about the island. My means of writing just now are so indifferent that I take little pleasure in scribbling. I have omitted to mention that aunt and the children, Bella included, suffered very much from the sickness. I had a touch of it the first day but have since stood the incessant pitch and roll first rate. Some of the passengers have suffered intensely, their misery being very much aggravated by the crowded state of the ship.

Now my Pet, I've given you a hurried, scrawling sketch of the ship so far. Let me forget it and think of you. It seems strange when I reflect upon it that we parted so philosophically. 'Twas right but strange. I could not scarcely yet feel that I am going so far away from you and all I love. Perhaps I'll have to experience it in greater intensity when I reach our destination. My own Darling you've felt it I know. But keep up a good heart little Darling, and God grant that I may return happily and safely in 2 or 3 years. Will you keep our love warm and earnest as it has always been? Will you love me still? I wish I could press you to my heart now. Could keep you – my Darling.

Saturday Morning

Land ho! We are now running along the Isthmus toward Aspinwall. We have passed the lights of Porto Bello, and will soon be offshore of an island covered with guano. The coast is rocky enough and very high. We expect to be landing by 12.

Adieu my Darling. My warmest love and impassioned kisses to you. I love you.

Your betrothed
Aleck

Having started in an unhealthy state, Nancy Waddell never recovered enough to feel truly well, or to walk the deck with Bella or Aleck. Throughout the voyage Bella kept a firm but soft controlling hand on the family, and Aleck helped out when she requested. The most pleasurable times were when he and Bella could meet and walk the crowded deck, and discuss the voyage and the family, and what lay ahead for all of them. He found her a most amiable companion – pretty, always well turned-out, thoughtful and eloquent.

They reached Aspinwall in Panama around noon on April 16. They were told that the town had about 6,000 inhabitants, but it didn't look like it. They also learned that most of the inhabitants were Negroes, probably brought from the West Indies to help build the Panama Railway. The place was oppressively warm, but even so the passengers were all delighted to disembark. There were few fond glances back at the ship that had caused them so much discomfort.

Aleck employed two porters, who shepherded them through the customs and into carriages. The whole process took just over an hour, and by the time they left the quay they were all thoroughly hot and damp, and tempers were high. At 2:30 pm they arrived at a comfortable looking inn called Howard House, where they rested and had a splendid meal before boarding the train to cross the Isthmus.

They arrived at Panama City station at just after 11:00 pm. Aleck organized porters for the transfer from train to carriages, and they proceeded immediately to the harbour where they boarded small vessels – tenders – and climbed on board their next ship at midnight.

And what a ship! The *Constitution* was like a wonderland after the awful *Champion*. It was just three years old and still shiny with new paint and gleaming decks. At 350 feet in length and 3,300 tons it was a substantial vessel, with a well-trained crew of 160, plus 20 soldiers to ensure the safety of the passengers as they sailed up the west coast of North America. The decks were clear and clean, the common rooms open, well-furnished and inviting, and the cabins spacious. The crew offered refreshments to any who wished them.

Captain Watkins cared for his passengers in a personal way, taking a direct interest in their welfare. As the Waddell party came aboard he saw that Nancy needed immediate attention. He ordered his medical officer to take charge, and within 20 minutes of boarding, Nancy was being bathed by a nurse in the ship's sick bay, after which she was put to bed with a sleeping draught.

The captain was A.G.W. Watkins, a former Commodore of the United States Navy, described later by Aleck as…*a real old bit of salt – erect, portly, dignified, gentlemanly, authoritative as an officer and skillful as a sailor…as fine a specimen of an ocean skipper as I could imagine.* It was clear to the weary travelers boarding the *Constitution* that Captain Watkins would not permit any overloading of his ship.

Several days of calm and smooth sailing in glorious sunshine brought the passengers on deck for exercise and vast doses of sparkling fresh air. Even Nancy appeared for breakfast on the second morning, announcing that she felt considerably better and would be moving to her cabin later that morning. She was full of praise for the staff of the sick bay.

As they approached Acapulco, the crew informed the passengers that at the present time France was intervening in Mexican affairs. It was blockading Mexican ports, permitting ships to stop there just to take on water and supplies, but evidently not permitting passengers to land. Two French officers from the blockading ships boarded the *Constitution* as it entered the harbour, and delivered this message in person to a clearly unimpressed Captain. He told them that some of his passengers might wish to stretch their legs on land, and that he would vouch for their safe return to the ship. The soldiers agreed unhappily, seeing no practical way to disagree with the impressive Capt. A.G.W. Watkins.

The younger Waddell children and Nancy preferred to stay on board during this brief stop in Mexico. Aleck and Bella, however, agreed that a stroll on land would do them good, and headed down the gangplank amidst a small group of other passengers. As they walked along the quay they waved at their family and other new acquaintances grouped along the rail of the towering ship. Then they were on dry land, and walked along the dusty road that led to an area of beaches and seaside shanties.

Bella took Aleck's arm, and they walked in companionable silence under the shade of the towering palm trees. When they reached the beach they stopped under a large tree of unknown species. Bella looked up at Aleck. "My dear Aleck, you have been wonderful with Mamma and the children. I really don't know how we could have made this trip without you. I am most grateful to you. We all are."

He looked down at her shining face and smiled. About to reply, he found himself virtually impaled by her blue eyes looking straight into his. There was something there that he had not seen before, and had not expected. Her gaze had an intensity that seemed to speak of more than just gratitude – more than a casual thank-you for helping out. The trials of the past weeks had formed a bond between them, and Bella was expressing her belief in that bond and its possibilities in the future. He knew it without asking, and it set within him mixed feelings – panic on the one side, as he was not interested in any such relationship except with Maggie, and yet excitement on the other hand. A beautiful woman, here in a tropical setting, asking for him. What man would not be excited?

These thoughts flashed through his mind in a second as he stood, reddening and tongue-tied. He finally managed to say "You are most welcome Bella. I have enjoyed it." He ran out of words, and found himself just looking into her eyes. Then it was panic again as she rose on her tip-toes and inclined her face, clearly seeking a kiss. Aleck could not submit to a romantic kiss, lips on lips and mouths parted. He simply could not do it. It would be treason. On the other hand he could not slough Bella off with a cheek-to-cheek formality. That would be unacceptably rude. So he settled for middle ground – a brush of the lips, a good smack on the cheek, and a quick hug. It appeared to be just enough to satisfy Bella.

They returned to the ship deep in their own thoughts. When they boarded the ship Bella smiled warmly at him and thanked him for the walk. He muttered some reply, turned and headed for his solitary cabin, there to sit and brood. One of the results of his brooding was that he decided that he would not ever mention to Maggie that he and Bella had left the ship at Acapulco. Nothing had really happened, of course, but on the other hand something had happened that he knew Maggie would not be happy about if she knew, and that gave him a bad feeling that was perilously close to a bad conscience. So he didn't, whereas Bella made it quite clear in her memoirs that they went ashore. She did not, however, elaborate.

Excerpt from the Memoirs of Bella Waddell Rogers

Aleck and I went on land and walked around but there was nothing much there but natives.

On April 30 the *Constitution* docked in the harbour of San Francisco at 2:30 pm. The Waddell family marched off with Nancy leading the way on Bella's arm, and with Aleck bringing up the rear, prodding the stragglers to keep up. The Waddells went to the Hotel Occidental where they had three spacious rooms reserved for them. Aleck went to the less costly Brooklyn House, which was very comfortable and within easy walking distance of the Occidental. He settled into his room with relief, being one step away from the demands of the family.

Their ride through the streets to their lodgings had left Aleck with the impression of a city gone mad with excitement. He enjoyed describing it to Maggie.

May 5, 1864

…With a mixed population of about 100,000, consisting of adventurers from almost every part of the world – mad with a thousand excitements – a perfect sea of life and activity – it presents in spectacle such as I never witnessed on ordinary occasions in any Canadian city. Almost every man is a specu-lator – a speculator in mining stock – and crowds of cunning,

anxious jobbers may be seen near the cluster of brokers' offices on Montgomery Street at almost any time during business hours. Thousands are made, thousands are lost daily. Never in any country, I suppose, have such colossal fortunes been made with such rapidity as here...

Several days after arriving in San Francisco, Aleck followed up on a letter that McLean had written for him back in Chatham, introducing him to Mr. Stephen Knight, a Canadian lawyer formerly from Chatham. Knight had arrived about four months ago, and was set up in legal practice in California. Aleck sent a note to him at his office, and Knight replied promptly by inviting him to lunch at his favorite dining establishment, a high-end tavern called The Star.

Knight was a large, outgoing man who smiled a lot, thought hard but quickly before speaking, and spoke eloquently. Aleck thought that he was probably in his mid-40s. They received their foaming mugs of beer in short order, and drank to the health of Her Majesty, and to the prosperity of dear old Chatham.

Under questioning from Aleck, Knight said that his practice had grown quickly and profitably from the start. "As you can see by looking out the window, this is a place of excitement and excess, which means that there are always lots of people getting into trouble and in need of legal help, or planning complicated business transactions that need our guidance. There are a lot of lawyers here, mind you, but as long as the gold fever continues there will be plenty of work to go around."

"Was it difficult to qualify?" asked Aleck.

"Not at all; surprisingly simple, in fact. The Bar Association wanted to see my credentials from Canada, and when they found them sufficient they had me take an oath of allegiance to the President of the United States, and that was about it. Needless to say the laws down here are a bit tricky because the place is changing so fast, but I have had little problem dealing with them."

"Do you go into court, Mr. Knight?"

"Oh yes, certainly. And I must say, that is the fun part of the practice down here…as it is in Canada as well, I suppose. Here they have a great flair for the dramatic gesture in court – wringing of hands, scenes of despair, beating of breasts – all for the benefit of the jurors, who seem to like that sort of thing. The more you maul the witnesses, the more they like it. They see the courtroom as a field of battle where every trick or stratagem is fair game, as long as you don't lie, of course."

Aleck then fielded questions from Knight as to his background and prospects, as he saw them, in the west. He spoke optimistically, hardly pausing to nibble at his roast beef. "The main issue that I will have to face, as I understand it, is that my qualifications from Upper Canada will not yet be accepted on Vancouver Island. So I shan't be permitted to practice there until some legislation is passed. It's under preparation now, but there's no firm date for its passage. I believe it may be easier for me to practice on the mainland in British Columbia. As you know BC is a separate colony, and quite competitive with Vancouver Island. So I will be applying in both jurisdictions, and hope I can get started in reasonable time."

Knight was smiling at this. "Ah yes, the wonderful cooperative spirit in the colonies! And of course, if it doesn't come from Mother England, it is not to be trusted. Correct? And I have heard that the Chief Justices of both colonies are prejudiced against lawyers trained in Canada. What a difference from this great country, wherein everything developed or trained or made right here is treasured, while things coming in from the outside are suspect. This is publicly, of course. In private anyone here will admire a well-trained barrister from England!"

Aleck snorted. "In our colonies it is still definitely a world of English rulers, with their appointees and rules and regulations, and of course their bureaucrats to slow things down. But really, I must not be so cynical. The west is new and changing fast. I would not be surprised to see the western colonies soon joined up with Canada to give us a country stretching from the Atlantic to the Pacific! We might even have a railroad across the country to bring us all together."

"Tell me Robertson – I should have asked you already, do excuse me

– are you married? Do you have a family?"

"No Sir, I am not, but I am engaged to a most lovely woman, and I hope to be able to marry her as soon as my practice is running profitably."

"Excellent" cried Knight, calling for two more beers. "Then you shall certainly want that railway to be built quickly. It takes so very long, now, for letters to pass between the two ends of this continent, as you will quickly find out. A letter from Chatham sent overland by carriage takes about three weeks. Then it is sorted here and sent on by steamer to Victoria, making a total time of 28 to 30 days. And that is if everything works perfectly, which it seldom does, and a fair amount of mail is lost for one reason or another. In fact, it is generally more reliable for mail to come on the same sea route that you have taken to here, and then on by steamer to Victoria. I say safer – more reliable if you will – but then it takes six weeks or more!"

"How about telegraph messages?"

"Oh yes, the telegraph is just becoming available here in San Francisco. That makes it possible to transmit urgent messages instantaneously, but it is very expensive, you know. I think that there are plans to extend the line to the British colonies soon, but I have no details."

Their conversation moved on to cases, and key points in the legal side of a gold rush economy. It was a thoroughly enjoyable lunch and discussion, and as they rose Aleck thanked his host for the pleasure, and said that he hoped they could remain in touch.

Aside from that lunch, Aleck spent most of his time with the Waddells. Nancy was now quite healthy and lively, but she continued to let her daughter run the family unit, ably assisted by "that delightful Aleck Robertson. My but he's a fine man!" On May 7 they boarded the steamship *Sierra Nevada* in great form, and sailed via Portland, Oregon to Victoria.

8

VICTORIA

Tiny Fort Victoria was built in 1843 by the Hudson's Bay Company (HBC) under its charismatic leader James Douglas. It was in a beautiful natural setting at the foot of Vancouver Island (VI), at the westernmost extremity of British North America. When the British Colonial Office declared Vancouver Island a crown colony in 1849, it granted to the HBC the right to oversee and encourage the populating of the area, island and mainland, to develop the economy, thereby discouraging any acquisitive ideas of the Americans. The non-native population of this western region at that time was around 450, of whom 300 were in Fort Victoria. The native population was estimated at 75,000, of whom 5,000 lived in and around Fort Victoria.

The populating of the west coast region proceeded slowly, and the company's control of the region became highly unpopular due to the strictly commercial approach it took to settlement, seeking profit out of every possible transaction. The Crown then appointed a Governor of Vancouver Island who was not an HBC man in order to calm the criticism. Unfortunately Governor Richard Blanshard, who arrived in 1850, was forced to resign by year-end due to the total lack of support he received from the company, which was still very influential.

The Crown finally appointed James Douglas as Governor of the colony of Vancouver Island in May 1851. Fort Victoria was now outdated, and Douglas oversaw the development of the town site of Victoria itself. While the HBC continued to operate with a heavy hand, and Douglas had an appointed Legislative Council, he did establish some of the institutions that would be required in the future – the VI Supreme Court of Civil Justice in 1853, and an elected Legislative Assembly in 1856.

Victoria was starting to look like a town, but was still small and growing slowly. Then, in early 1858, all Hell broke loose. The discovery of gold on the Fraser and Thompson Rivers on the mainland changed Victoria almost overnight. The gold fever that had gripped California in the previous decade moved north, where Victoria was the only ocean port and outfitting center for the new gold fields. Miners would come there by steamship, buy their tools and supplies, and perhaps team up with others. They would then take a coastal steamer across to the mainland, up the Fraser River to Yale or Hope and, later on, inland to the rough Cariboo region when it opened up.

The first miners landed in Victoria on April 25 on the *Commodore*, a wooden side-wheel American steamer. Between then and September of that year, as many as 30,000 people arrived in the region. Most flowed through to the mine fields, but the non-native population of Victoria rose from around 500 to more than 5,000. A large temporary tent village sprouted on the outskirts of the town.

Victoria was now thriving, but so was the mainland where most of the mining action was taking place. Britain knew that it had to have firmer control there, so it established another colony on the mainland, the crown colony of British Columbia. Governor Douglas and Judge Matthew Begbie proclaimed the formation of this colony on November 19, 1858 at its proposed capital Fort Langley, a small town on the Fraser River. This town had originated as a Hudson's Bay Company post, built in 1827. It was a lively place in 1858, a staging point for miners heading up the Fraser to the gold fields.

Douglas soon realized that the site of the colony's capital would be better situated farther away from the border with the United States, and on tidewater. Thus on February 14, 1859 he proclaimed the recently established town of Queensborough, at the mouth of the Fraser River, as the new capital of the colony. The government in London sent a large party of Royal Engineers to create this town out of the dense forests. The officials in London disliked the name Queensborough, so on the instructions of Queen Victoria it was renamed New Westminster. Its citizens took this recognition by Her Majesty seriously, and gave their town the nickname 'Royal City'.

Looking ahead, the British government also foresaw the combining of the two colonies into one, and let it be known that New Westminster would be the capital of the combined colony. That same year it finally revoked the unpopular charter of the HBC to run the colonies. Governor Douglas of Vancouver Island was given responsibility for the new colony as well, which he ruled by decree rather than with the help of a council.

The government's decision in favor of New Westminster was not well received in Victoria, where most of the important citizens of the region lived. They saw no reason to move themselves and their operations from well-established Victoria to that backwater on the Fraser, so they simply ignored the government decree. Douglas remained in Victoria, as did the new colony's Secretary and Attorney General, and most officials.

There was naturally considerable tension between Victoria and New Westminster, but Victoria was far and away the more established, and therefore able to control events. So confident were the Victorians, in fact, that while this was going on they were building government buildings in Victoria at James Bay that were christened 'The Birdcages'. There were now two Chief Justices in the region. Mathew B. Begbie was Chief Justice of BC, and Joseph Needham was Chief Justice of Vancouver Island. To deal with the large number of problems brought to Victoria by the gold rush, the government established a regular police force under the authority of Augustus Pemberton.

In 1860 Douglas established a Municipal Council in New Westminster. Although the five councilors in New Westminster were subject to Douglas' approval, they still raised a strong voice for more rights for the mainland.

These western colonies were tumultuous places, riven with tensions of which the competition between Victoria and New Westminster was but one cause. A major issue was the widespread dislike of Governor Douglas, and distaste for his regal style of rule over the colonies. The newspapers were strident in their calls for his resignation. On the coast there was continuous tension between the settlers and the indigenous peoples. In the interior tensions arose as the traditional economic base of the fur trade was replaced by one of competition for gold. Crime was now a serious problem. In the year 1860 alone, 755 charges were laid for misdemeanors such as assault, larceny, felony, desertion and selling liquor to the natives.

Victoria was incorporated as a city with its own Municipal Council on August 2, 1862. Mr. Thomas Harris was elected by acclamation as Victoria's first mayor on August 16.

In 1863 the Colonial Office permitted the appointment of a partially elected Legislative Council on the mainland. It was to have 15 members, with five each from colonial officials, magistrates and the citizenry. Douglas divided the mainland colony into five districts, and invited each to elect a citizen member. That same year he resigned as Governor of the colonies. Arthur Edward Kennedy was appointed to replace him on Vancouver Island, and Frederick Seymour on the mainland.

By the start of 1864, with the gold rush tailing off, the population of Victoria had settled at around 3,000, and New Westminster at 700.

The steamship *Sierra Nevada* entered Victoria harbour in the early afternoon of May 14, 1864. The Waddell party stood in a tight group among the many passengers lining the railing, exclaiming at the sights and searching the crowd below for their father. The first lines were being thrown from ship to wharf when William shouted "there he is! Over there!", and pointed at a man at the back of the crowd on the dock, who was waving his arms vigorously. And the cry went up – "there's father!" "There's Papa!" "Oh, look at him Mamma – he looks so fine doesn't he?"

Aunt Nancy was naturally happy and relieved to see her husband again, but the look of Victoria was not pleasing to her. After the refined buildings and streets of Chatham and other Upper Canada towns, this place of muddy streets and clapboard siding looked quite horrid, in spite of the few acceptable looking buildings along Wharf Street. Yet even Nancy was smiling when the group finally squeezed out of the busy customs hall into the bright sunshine and the arms of John Waddell. She claimed his first hug and kisses and clung to him briefly before the rest of the family fell on him like a swarm of bees, hugging and kissing and shouting stories about their trip. Bella was the last to hug him and receive in return a great bear hug and kiss. Then the noisy party started gathering their luggage while John came over to Aleck.

"Aleck my boy, welcome to Victoria, and thank you a thousand times for bringing my family here so safely and well!" They exchanged a warm handshake, smiling widely.

"Thank you Uncle John. I can assure you it's nice to be here. It's been a long trip, and we are all thoroughly tired of it."

John and Aleck herded the family and their luggage into three carriages. They rumbled off the dock onto Wharf Street, followed its curve to Fort Street, and jogged up Fort to Douglas Street. Here they turned right, and were soon stopping in front of an attractive cottage close to James Bay.

The Waddell house on Douglas Street was compact, but efficient. "It's certainly cozy" said Nancy, somewhat wryly, after John had shown them all through the house and given them their orders. "But I must say, John, it really is quite pretty. Ah well, we'll just have to move in and see what we shall see. It will be an adventure!"

"Yes dear" replied John, "but only a brief adventure, I think. I have my sights set on a considerably larger property over in the James Bay area. We may be able to have it later this summer. Indeed, I'm counting on it."

"Oh John, what splendid news indeed! You'll have to take us there once we are moved in and show it to us!" Nancy smiled broadly, and headed off to the fourth bedroom to help the young children unpack their belongings. With the family thus engaged, John took Aleck aside and suggested that they take a stroll down Douglas Street to stretch their legs.

After discussing the long trip out from Chatham, they turned to the subject of John's affairs here in Victoria. "How is it with you now, Uncle? Are things going well?"

"They are indeed, my boy. I did well with the steamships, but this position with the Macdonald Bank over on Yates Street is another story altogether." John went on to describe the remarkable rise of this first bank west of the Great Lakes. It started when Alexander Davidson Macdonald arrived in Victoria from Scotland in 1858 to establish a local branch of an American freight company. In his travels to the interior he became involved at the very start of the gold strikes, and used 50 ounces of coarse gold as the basis for starting a bank. The bank had flourished, establishing itself as a safe place for successful miners to sell their nuggets and dust, and to deposit their earnings. It also bought and sold all other manner of merchandise not normally associated with banking, including saddles, cognac and mining equipment. John Waddell, ever the entrepreneur, was in his element.

They walked across the waterfront, and then turned up Yates Street. John drew Aleck into a reasonably respectable tavern for a welcoming beer. "Come on Aleck, it's time to drink your health. Don't worry about the ladies. They'll still be sorting things out, and I have a woman coming in at six o'clock with a wonderful great dinner to make everyone happy."

Over their first beer the conversation turned to Aleck's prospects in the colony. John described the current political situation, and laughed over the decision of the British Colonial Office to designate New Westminster as the capital of the combined colonies. "I realize that there is some reasonable logic in their decision, but the fact is that Victoria has become really quite a pleasant place to live and work, whereas New Westminster is still a dirty village. So of course all the high mucky-mucks in the government service have decided to stay here no matter what the Colonial Office says. It's a very sore point on the mainland, I can tell you. It will be interesting to see how it works itself out."

"It will indeed, Uncle. But tell me, how do you see the prospects for me here in the colonies? I understand that I will not be permitted to practice here on Vancouver Island until a bill to that effect has received royal assent?"

"Quite so. I have asked my friends in government about this matter, and they say that the legislation is working its way along, but very slowly. One of the problems, as you might imagine, is that the Governors and judges all come from England, and they have little respect for lawyers trained in Canada. Of course, if you would like to work in beautiful New Westminster, you could practice there. Governor Douglas proclaimed it so last year. I don't think you would want to live there, but you could at least do some work in New Westminster and up in the gold fields."

Aleck sipped his beer, thoughtful. "Yes, that's just what I've heard. Well, I hope you will introduce me to any people who have something to say about the legislation. Perhaps I can add a few words of encouragement. And I will visit New Westminster very soon to see what I can do there. But in the meantime, Uncle, I have to earn a living. Any ideas?"

"My main idea is to introduce you around as broadly as I can. You're a bright fellow, and can speak as well as the devil himself, so meeting the influential people here and in New Westminster will be a good start. And speaking of contacts, I would like to introduce you to the Freemasons here. They're a splendid bunch of fellows – the best possible group for you to become involved with. I know that they would be delighted if you were to join them."

Their conversation drifted to the subject of living quarters in Victoria, and John said that Aleck would be more than welcome to stay with the Waddells as long as he pleased. "We'll be moving soon to a much larger place in the James Bay area, so there will always be room for one more!"

"You are most kind, Uncle. I do appreciate it. And the church – where do you recommend that I go?"

"I am very pleased with St. John's, over on the corner of Douglas and Fisgard Streets. I feel certain you will like it, and Robert Dundas is a fine Rector. You must come with us next Sunday and I will introduce you."

They rambled on through another beer, and then headed home to an uproarious home-coming dinner with the family.

Although he was extremely busy at the bank, John was as good as his word, and took every possible occasion to introduce Aleck to the influential people of Victoria. He started with his own President, Alexander Macdonald, who proved to be as forthright and charming as described by John. He welcomed the young lawyer to Victoria, stating that this was the place to be for bright young people like Aleck.

The meetings with other people were also informal and informative. Over the next three weeks they called on the Governor of Vancouver Island Arthur Kennedy (who had just arrived in March), Mayor of Victoria Thomas Harris, Vancouver Island's Chief Justice the Hon. Joseph Needham, and numerous senior officials and businessmen. These included Messrs McMillan and Higgins, the proprietors of the newspaper the *Daily Chronicle*, and a thoroughly intriguing man named Amor de Cosmos.

Born in Nova Scotia as William Smith, he made his fortune in California and changed his name to Amor de Cosmos, which translated into 'Lover of the Universe'. He then came to Victoria where he established the newspaper the *British Colonist*, and speculated in real estate. As an active and articulate man with an editor's platform to work from, he became one of the chief spokesmen in Victoria expressing opposition to colonial rule. In 1863 he was appointed to the Legislative Council of Vancouver Island, where he was a strong supporter of Confederation with Canada and critic of the Imperial connection. It was de Cosmos who had introduced a bill into the Legislative Council that would permit lawyers trained in Canada to join the Bar of the colony. Attorney General Carey had prevented its passage, and de Cosmos had re-introduced it in 1864. Carey was still blocking it.

Aleck liked de Cosmos instinctively for his energy, imagination, knowledge and strong views on matters of great importance, and he gave the man a most sympathetic ear. As with de Cosmos, all of the people he met encouraged him to hold on, that the legislation required to permit him to practice law would receive the Governor's assent soon, and that there was a great need for people like him in this exciting place.

His exploration of Victoria and its beautiful surroundings continued, as did a pleasant round of social occasions including picnics in the gorgeous summer weather. He liked St. John's Church, with its articulate Rector and delightful choir. It was a good place to meet people and make friends, and the level of service was, in his view, just right. It was flexible enough to accept outside speakers, and Rev. Dundas told him that should he wish to, he would be permitted to address the congregation as long as the subject matter was appropriate.

His residence at the Waddell home gave him little privacy, but he was fond of them all, and played an active role in their family life. There was no further sense of intimacy with Bella, but she was certainly very friendly with him at all times, and welcomed opportunities to do things with him – walks, picnics and even occasional adventures. Was she waiting for him to make a move, or had she come to her senses? He didn't know, but hoped for the latter.

On June 18 Aleck made his first visit to New Westminster, armed with a letter of introduction to the Hon. H.P.P. Crease, Attorney General of British Columbia. Henry Pering Pellew Crease was an impressive man, formal in style, intelligent and articulate in expression. Unfortunately he was well known for his disdain for Canadians, and especially for professionals, including lawyers, who had received their training anywhere but in England. He felt strongly that the Imperial connection was the mainstay of governance in the colonies, and was suspicious of those who favoured responsible government.

He was also, however, a gentleman, and honoured the letter of introduction that he had received from his friend John Waddell. He welcomed Aleck, reviewed his papers, and then assessed the young man through conversation over a cup of tea. He was grudgingly impressed with what he saw, and agreed to support Aleck's application for membership in the Bar of British Columbia.

Aleck left the meeting satisfied with his performance, but as he told Maggie upon his return to Victoria, not with the town itself. He described it as…*a wretched little village, dignified now however with the name of 'city'.*

He was now determined to go to the Cariboo as soon as he was allowed to practice there. But even with the more liberal legislation on the mainland, Aleck still had to wait until his application for admission to the Bar of British Columbia was received and accepted by the Chief Justice, Matthew Begbie.

Thus at this precarious point in his life, Aleck found himself thoroughly frustrated, and he questioned himself endlessly about the wisdom of his move.

July 2, 1864

...I am a little bit low spirited today. You know one cannot always be light-hearted and hopeful – I have now been four months idle. I little anticipated so much delay in getting into business, else I should certainly have paused longer before taking the important step I did. In so many of my letters I have dwelt upon the reasons of this unlooked for difficulty, that I feel scarcely inclined to touch upon them now... There is only one judge in British Columbia and he is now "up country" – that means up in the mining district, and will not return to N.W. before the middle of October. My notice will not expire before the 7 of next month. I have written to a lawyer who is with the court to try and get the judge's fiat for my admission...

At the heart of his concern was the decline in the business prospects in the western colonies. The gold rush had brought with it prosperity in almost every field, but now it was waning, property prices had dropped, business was stagnant, and there were numerous bankruptcies. He wrote Stephen Knight in San Francisco, describing his predicament and seeking advice on the possibility of relocating to 'Frisco' and pursuing his legal career there.

His letters described some of his social life, which frequently involved Bella and Bella's close friend Miss Jane (Jenny) Branks – a Californian lady and sister-in-law of Mr. Macdonald, the banker. He described her as...

small and not beautiful, but from her vivacious, agreeable manner, pretty. As Miss Branks was a friend of Bella's, he saw her quite often. She lived close to the Waddells, and he went riding with her several times. He explored a good deal of the country around Victoria, and enjoyed picnics out in the Langford Lake area with her and Bella and other friends.

Another new and extremely influential friend was Dr. Israel Wood Powell, a Canadian from Ontario described by Aleck as…*an exceedingly nice, handsome, clean young fellow.* Powell was 28 years old, and had been educated at McGill University in Montreal before heading west to seek his fortune. He had actually planned to keep going all the way to New Zealand, but found Victoria in the midst of a gold rush to his liking, and settled there. Powell had been elected as a member of the Legislative Assembly of Vancouver Island the previous year, and was now the head of the Canada Party which urged Confederation with Canada. He was an important member of the Victoria Lodge of the Freemasons, and enthusiastically supported Aleck's application for membership.

Aleck was particularly interested in Powell's views on education. The doctor was a strong and articulate supporter of the concept of government-supported, secular schools for all children. He had just been appointed Chairman of the colony's Committee of Education, and was now working on recommendations to the Legislative Assembly concerning 'An Act Respecting Common Schools'. In one of their meetings Powell brought along his friend John Jessop, a teacher who had operated his own school until he ran out of funding earlier that year. Jessop was a constant, loud voice promoting universal education. Aleck was strongly attracted to these two men and their ideas.

In addition to all this, Powell was reported to have the best medical practice in Victoria. He had also, it was obvious, taken a strong liking to Bella Waddell.

9

A HARD LESSON

As the Victoria summer progressed, Aleck brooded over the place he had come to, and his thoughts naturally turned to prospects in the United States, which he admired greatly for its energy and entrepreneurial spirit. Soon, however, he received a reply to his letter to Stephen Knight in San Francisco that put paid to that thought, for the moment at least. Knight said that the boom was over in California, and there was a surfeit of lawyers there with not enough to do.

He sat in his room at the Waddells' house, Knight's letter in hand, and gazed absently out the window. Aleck was now completely frustrated, and a sorry sight when John Waddell came into the room to show him an interesting article in the *Victoria Daily Chronicle*. "Look at this, my boy" cried John, his voice at its usual high pitch of enthusiasm. "It looks like gold has been found near here on the Island, over in the Sooke area. Now wouldn't that be something, indeed! Imagine having a gold rush right here on our home turf. That would give those buggers in New Westminster something to think about! Perhaps we should go and take a look!"

The paper said that one of the Vancouver Island exploration expeditions led by the botanist and seed-collector Robert Brown had discovered some gold on the Leech River near its confluence with the Sooke River that flowed into Sooke harbour, west of Victoria. The find had actually been made in mid-July by Brown's second-in-command Lt. Peter John Leech of the Royal Engineers, so it was Leech's name that was attached to the gold-containing river, and to the mining town that soon sprang up nearby.

Aleck the lawyer's initial inclination was to treat it as an unimportant, minor incident without any of the serious prospects of the mighty Cariboo. But Aleck the adventurer could not rest with this unsatisfactory conclusion. He longed for action. After all, some gold had been found. There was some chance of success, and this could present a good opportunity for him to gain a first-hand taste of gold prospecting, without having to pay the severe entry fee of travel to the Cariboo.

He left the room, and found John in the front yard with his son William. A rapid negotiation was concluded with the decision that Aleck and William would leave as soon as possible for Sooke on the steamship with enough mining equipment to give it a try in the Leech River area. John agreed to bankroll their expedition in return for a share of the profits.

The steamship *Golden Otter* left Victoria harbour at 10:00 am on Monday, August 14, loaded to the gunwales with miners, mining equipment, live-stock, food and liquor. They landed in Sooke just before 1 pm, and as the ship approached the dock the crowd of miners hefted their packs and moved to the rail, jostling for position. As soon as the gangplank was lowered into place, they streamed onto the dock and up to the start of the Sooke River trail. It was a sight to see – truly, a gold rush! The two beginners, Aleck and William, waited until the last before striding down onto the dock and following the crowd onto the trail.

They were both young men in good physical shape, but they were not miners, and soon realized it. They had never had such a walk before, climbing over great hills and rocks, and now and then crossing the river by stepping from one to another of the great boulders that were strewn in endless confusion in its bed. They halted frequently to rest and relieve their backs for a few minutes of the burdens that seemed to grow heavier as they proceeded.

Aleck and William were bone weary as the sun started to sink somewhere ahead of them, behind the forest fence that was their constant companion. Aleck had blisters on one of his shoulders, and on both hands from hanging onto the straps of his heavy pack and constantly shifting it to ease his aching shoulders. William was in better shape, with no such problems except the general sense of exhaustion that he shared with his older companion. Both of them were bemused by the fact that all of the miners from their steamer were so far ahead of them that there was no longer even the faint hint of the noise of their clambering and talk.

Aleck decided that it was time to stop, no matter how far they still had to go to reach the mining fields. They pitched their tent on a small beach beside the river, and prepared their supper of ham and beans over a small fire. After the dinner – perhaps the most delicious either had ever tasted – Aleck went for a stroll down the river until, finding a comfortable log, he sat and contemplated the wonderful beauty of the BC wilds.

His senses and good humor restored by the food and scenery, Aleck then returned to the campsite where he found William seated at the edge of the river, cooling his feet in the flowing water. It looked like a fine idea, and he sat beside him and did the same until, after some desultory conversation and much nodding of heads, they agreed that it was time to sleep.

Unfortunately their sleep in the tiny tent, on the hard ground, was more a nightmare than a rest, and the next morning they were up and away at sunrise. After another day of hard walking, they reached the confluence of the Leech and Sooke rivers, where the mines were located, at about six o'clock. Their dinner of dried fish, biscuits and peas tasted superb, and this time they had the good sense to remember one of the lessons of their youth, namely that it helps to create a mattress of evergreen boughs if you must sleep on the ground. This they did, it eased somewhat the rigours of the night, and they both slept deeply.

While washing at the edge of the stream next morning, Aleck was surprised to discover at a distance of twenty feet his old friend Thomas Gawley, formerly of Chatham. His camp turned out to be only sixty or seventy feet from theirs, and yet they had been quite unconscious of it the preceding evening. Gawley and his son Robert had taken up a claim, and were working it in the certainty that they would soon strike it rich. It was pleasant to have such neighbours for a few evenings.

Later that morning Aleck and William took out their shiny new pans and started in on the serious business of panning for gold. With a few instructions from Robert Gawley they learned how to pan, and soon were moving along the river, delving into the mud and gravel in search of the elusive treasure. After just one hour Aleck and William both started to learn that panning may look easy and even a bit glamorous, but it is, in fact, cold and hard work. Their feet and hands stung with cold, their backs ached with the continual bending and twisting, and their concentration wandered uncontrollably. They stuck with it, but had to take frequent breaks to rest and recover, mercifully out of sight of any real miners. It was not fun, and was miserably unsuccessful.

They stayed at it for almost five days. After three nights at their first camp on the Leech River, they moved upstream several miles to another spot that was clear of claims. They set up their camp with its badly diminished supply of food, and spent two more days working from there. But there was no question that they were failures as miners, and on the second evening of their stay in their new campsite, Aleck posed the idea that miners were really very admirable fellows, and it would be a good idea to leave the prospecting to them. They agreed that they would head downstream at first light.

The hike back down to Sooke harbour took just over two days, thanks to their lighter packs and a week of hard conditioning. They arrived at the dock just as the steamer came in with yet another crop of miners. By early afternoon they boarded and were on their way home to Victoria. As they cruised along the coastline they talked over what they had learned. As later reported by Aleck -

> ...The general aspect of the country as a mining region did not, I confess, impress me very favourably, and yet the reports that reach the city from day to day are generally of a very encouraging character. My inexperience in such matters leads

me to attach very little importance to my personal opinion, and on the other hand the absolute uncertainty that hangs over all mining operations makes me very distrustful of the judgment of others. We shall see what we shall see. Meantime the exploration of the Island is being carried on, and gold – in paying quantities as it has been said – has been discovered in other localities. I earnestly hope all this may exert a beneficial influence upon the rather depressed condition of affairs in the colony...

10

THE EDITOR

At the start of September, Aleck moved into a room in a private residence in Fort Street owned by Mr. John Little. Mr. Little charged him $12.50 per month, which was reasonable in that most rooming houses in town cost $10 per week for room and board. He went for his meals to the Colonial Restaurant.

Aleck could afford the luxury of his own place in that, as of Monday, September 5, he had employment. A week after his return from Sooke, his uncle told him that he should call upon the owners of the *Victoria Daily Chronicle*, James McMillan and David Higgins. They were looking for a new Editor, and would like to meet Aleck to discuss it. This was the first real prospect of paying work that Aleck had seen, so he was pleased to go along with the idea.

McMillan and Higgins welcomed Aleck warmly, and after Higgins had taken him on a brief tour of the facility, they settled comfortably over tea. McMillan, the older of the two at 39 years of age, opened the discussion by welcoming Aleck, and telling him what John Waddell had already said in fewer words.

"As you may know, Mr. Robertson, we have taken a more moderate stance than have our competitors both here and in New Westminster. We do not believe that a newspaper should be a platform for political posturing. No, our job is to inform the public, and to give a fair and balanced sense of the issues facing our community."

Aleck liked what he heard. "This is a fine approach, gentlemen" he said. "You strike the balanced tone that this colony needs. I'm not surprised that you have been successful." They went on to discuss some of the main issues of the day – union of the colonies, confederation, responsible government, education – and then turned to the business matter at hand.

McMillan said that, based on John Waddell's comments and what they had seen of Aleck so far today, they would be prepared to offer him the position of Editor, beginning at once. "The work will involve long hours from early afternoon to late at night when next morning's issue is finalized and sent to print" said Higgins. "This will not improve your social life [smiles all around], but you will I think find the work stimulating, and it will bring you into contact with many of the most important people in the colony. Indeed, some of them will seek you out, hoping to ensure friendly coverage of their activities."

"Gentlemen" said Aleck, "I am flattered to have your offer, and it appeals to me. But there is an important point to consider. As you have said, I am unemployed at the moment, and will be until the Governor approves the Barrister's Bill here on Vancouver Island, or at least until I am accepted by the Bar of British Columbia. But you must realize, as I am sure you already do, that when I am accepted at the Bar of either colony, I will be sorely tempted to leave any other employment and commence at once with my practice. I might of course change my mind after I have tasted the pleasures of editing your fine newspaper, but you should not bet on it."

"Of course, Mr. Robertson" replied McMillan. "We are fully aware of your situation. As we see it we will likely have at best a couple of months of your time, and by then we will surely come up with a candidate seeking a more permanent situation. We can offer you $25 per week for six days of work in the week, with Sundays off, and we would like you to start as soon as possible."

"That is fine. Thank you, and I am pleased to accept your very kind offer. May I suggest that I start on Monday?"

That he did, and the work was so onerous that it was seven weeks before he could take the time to write his next letter to Maggie.

October 20, 1864

> *…After idling away several months I was at last happy enough to get into the editorial chair of the "Daily Chronicle" which I have occupied since 5 Sept. Sunday is now my only day of rest and I hail its weekly advent with sincere delight. The duties incident to my new position being so perfectly novel, and my knowledge of local affairs – particularly – so limited, you may easily imagine they were arduous enough at first. Though I am less diffident now after wearing the harness nearly seven weeks, I still find my daily task laborious…*

The new insights that he gained in his editorial work gave him a mixed impression of the future of the colony as it related to his prospects there. The decline in the gold business made it a pretty dull place. On the other hand there were still opportunities for lawyers.

As Aleck started his newspaper career there was, unbeknownst to him, great sadness in Chatham. On Sunday, September 11 his father Alexander Rocke Robertson, MD, Chatham's beloved physician, died quietly in his bed, just two months short of his 63rd birthday. The doctor had been unwell for some time, his condition aggravated by the financial pressures that weighed upon him since he had closed his practice. They were still living in the family home 'Heatherdale', and had sufficient savings to carry on with perhaps a little help from grown family, but it would continue to be meager times for them all.

Maggie was terribly saddened because the doctor had been her wonderful 'Uncle Rocke'. He had always had a kind word for her – a comment on her pretty dress or a word of praise for her singing in the choir. His gifts at Christmas were thoughtful and welcome, and of course Uncle Rocke had been at their house many times to take care of sick Eberts children, Maggie included. She was also distraught that Aleck did not know what had happened, and would not know for some time to come. How terrible it would be when he found out!

On Vancouver Island, late September was a time of tumultuous happenings. On the night of September 22, John Waddell's bank was robbed. The vault was wrenched open, and all valuables stolen. The bank was ruined.

Alexander Macdonald himself was away at one of his branches in the Cariboo, so John was in charge of all activities in Victoria. He was, naturally, a suspect in the crime. There was no direct evidence linking him to the robbery, but as the public grew aware of the disaster which would bankrupt many of them, he became a useful target for the press and the more aggressive members of the community. A clerk named Barnett was arrested on the basis of a seemingly lame alibi, but was then released.

To everyone's surprise Macdonald did not return until the end of November. He kept to his house, refused to meet the press, and spoke to the police, John Waddell, and everyone else as little as possible. The rumour circulated that he was bankrupt because he had not bothered to insure the bank.

A meeting of creditors was called for December 26, but Macdonald left town before it took place. In a letter he said that he had gone to California until the dust settled because he was afraid of violence. This angered the creditors, but they confirmed their trust in John Waddell by appointing him as manager to wind up the bank. Macdonald never returned. His house and property were sold in January to cover part of the huge financial obligations he left behind. Public pressure, especially from those who lost their investments, goaded the police into action, and a $3,000 reward was offered for information that would lead to an arrest and a conviction. But never a word was heard from anyone.

II

AT LAST!

The British Columbian
New Westminster
November 5, 1864

Seeking Admission: Alexander Rocke Robertson, Esq., a young and talented Upper Canada Barrister, came up by the Enterprise yesterday for the purpose of being present at the assizes to seek admission to practice in the Supreme Court of this colony.

The courthouse in New Westminster was a small, one-room wooden building with a canvas ceiling and no means of ventilation or heating. Lawyers, witnesses, jurors, journalists and all other interested parties would gather in an adjoining building that had several rooms, and wait there to be summoned by the clerk of the court. In the hallway of that building Aleck met once again the Hon. H.P.P. Crease, the Attorney General, and Crease introduced him to another lawyer named George Walkem, who was also making his first appearance in the court.

Of Irish decent, George Anthony 'Boomer' Walkem had grown up in Upper Canada and come to British Columbia in 1862 at the age of 28. He was a member of the Bar of BC, but had not appeared in court until that day, due in part to his duties as a member of the colony's Legislative Council. They exchanged friendly small talk until Aleck was called by the clerk to come to the courtroom, accompanied by the Attorney General.

Judge Begbie was an imposing figure with an impressive reputation. Now 45 years old, he had left his law practice in England in 1858 to take up the challenge of bringing British law to the soon-to-be-declared colony of British Columbia. Begbie was an adventurer, and was reported to have taken several very long walks around the province, walks measured in hundreds of miles, to familiarize himself with the land and the people. When trails and then roads became more established, he took to horseback to cover the territory. He would set up court wherever it was needed, and was known for his strict but fair judgments. He knew that in this rough place populated by hard, sometimes desperate men, it was important that his judgments be clearly understood and considered to be the right ones. Thanks in large part to him, the gold fields were remarkably free of serious crime.

His regular pattern of work was to spend the spring and summer months in the upper Fraser River and Cariboo regions, and the fall and winter months in New Westminster. So that is where Aleck first appeared before him on the morning of Monday, November 7, 1864.

Aleck stood before the judge as the Attorney General presented him. Begbie glanced quickly through the papers before him, and then raised his head and looked Aleck straight in the eyes. "Welcome to British Columbia, Mr. Robertson. Your application is most welcome, as there is much to be done in administering the law in this colony. But tell me, do you intend to come here often, or is Victoria your preferred location?"

"Thank you your Honour. I am pleased to be here to serve your court. It is my intention to open an office in New Westminster, and to practice the law wherever in this colony I shall be needed."

Begbie smiled. "Carefully put, Sir. You clearly understand the gist of my question! However, I am not here to discuss your living arrangements. You are here, and this colony is in need of your services. Your credentials are acceptable. You have in fact done well in your short career. May it so continue! Thus it only remains for me to accept you as a member of the Bar of the colony of British Columbia, and I do so now, in the hope that the Bar will have no occasion to regret the step. Mr. Barnaby, please be so kind as to enter the name of Mr. Robertson on the roll of practicing Barristers of British Columbia."

"Thank you your Honour" said Aleck, "I shall try not to disappoint you."

The judge looked at him with a half-smile. "I should hope so. Now then Mr. Robertson, if you have nothing better to do, may I ask you to step outside and wait in the rooms next door? There are some cases coming up that appear not to have representation. Perhaps we shall be able to start your career in BC off with a rush!"

"Of course, your Honour. Thank you Sir" said Aleck, but the clerk was already calling the participants in the first case, and the judge was bending over his papers and did not hear him, so he left quietly. He went over to the second building, took out of his satchel the gown and wig that he had brought all the way from Toronto via Windsor, donned them, and then sat down on a bench and waited expectantly, chatting quietly with George Walkem.

After 10 minutes the clerk approached Aleck. "Mr. Robertson" said Barnaby, "we have several cases today that require representation, and you are requested to take three of them. The first two are criminal cases, where your fees will be paid by the court if the accused cannot do so. Is that acceptable to you?"

"It is Mr. Barnaby."

Barnaby led Aleck into a small side room where there were three men already seated in front of the bare desk. "Here is your first client" said Barnaby, asking Aleck to sit behind the desk, and placing on it a file labeled 'Queen vs Chacotomakah'. "Stand up Jim". The accused, a short, relatively young and very unhappy native man rose under the careful eye of the constable, and nodded to Aleck. "This is Chacotomakah of the Bella Bella tribe. Fortunately he answers to the alias of 'Jim'. The man next to him is our translator 'Jackson.'" Jackson smiled and nodded as Barnaby proceeded. "Jim is accused of murdering a man named Jack Holmes in October of 1862. He has pleaded 'not guilty' to the judge, and his Honour has asked that you take up his case. You will be called in 30 minutes or so. Constable McNair will stay with the prisoner at all times."

Aleck nodded, shook hands with the scowling Jim, and then opened the file as Jim sat down again and Barnaby left the room. The file consisted of a few brief reports, including statements from several witnesses to the effect that Jack Holmes had been a tough, vicious man who hated the Indians, and took every opportunity to taunt and annoy. He had headed south from mining country in late September of 1862, deciding to go out to the coast at Bella Bella and cadge a trip by sea to New Westminster, where he would seek a job in the shipyard in the winter months. A drunken session in a tavern on the evening of October 1 had led to a fight with several Indians. They had tried to boot him out of the saloon, but could not. Jim had killed him with his hunting knife, and then rushed out and disappeared into the woods.

For almost two years Jim had been a hunted man, protected by his people who felt that the murder had been justified. He was finally brought to justice when recognized in Bella Bella by an adventuresome constable.

Aleck was not hopeful. Many people had seen Jim murder Holmes, and had testified as much to the authorities. He stated the facts of the case briefly and succinctly to Jim, and asked him if there was any doubt that he had committed the murder. Jim replied through the interpreter simply "no. I am sorry, but he was a bad man and he deserved it." Aleck knew that the only possible defense would be justifiable homicide.

Five minutes later Barnaby opened the door and called them out. Aleck stood and led the small group out of the room and across to the courtroom. He proceeded, hopefully with dignity, to the counsel tables, shook hands with the prosecuting attorney Mr. Jonathan Blaze, and then sat down at his own place. Meanwhile the constable led Jim to his chair, with the interpreter seated nearby. There was a brief hush, the clerk read the charge, and then Judge Begbie looked up and said "Mr. Blaze, please proceed."

Blaze stated the facts of the case briefly and succinctly. There was no question that Jim had committed murder, so there was no doubt that the jury should find him guilty as charged. The prosecutor sat down with a look of supreme confidence on his face. Jim slouched in his chair as Begbie called "Mr. Robertson, may we please hear from the defense?"

Aleck rose and turned toward the jury. There was complete silence in the room, a sense of expectation as this new, young lawyer launched his career against seemingly impossible odds. "Gentlemen of the jury, we are here this morning to ensure that justice is carried out in this most unfortunate case. The accused, Chacotomakah, also known as Jim, of the Bella Bella nation, stands accused of murdering Jack Holmes. My esteemed colleague has pointed out that there are sufficient statements by witnesses to the crime to prove that there is no question that Jim did in fact kill Mr. Holmes. The question we must address today is – why did he kill Jack Holmes?"

Aleck sensed in the corner of his eye a movement on the judge's bench, and turning slightly he saw that Judge Begbie was now gazing out the window at the side of the room. He knew that he was skating on thin ice, as Begbie was known to have little patience with the concept of 'justifiable crime'. Either a man committed a crime or he did not. If the court started trying to judge the merits of justification, there would be no end to the trials, and the verdicts themselves could always be considered justified or unjustified, turning the court into a sort of high level debating society. Aleck knew that he had little time to make the case, and little hope of succeeding, but it was the only avenue open to his client, so he must at least give it a try.

He quoted passages from the case file that spoke of the character of Jack Holmes. He cited the conditions on the evening of the murder, when Holmes had been drunk and particularly nasty and aggressive, and had already hurt several Indians and smashed glasses and two chairs. He said that had Jim not done what he had done, Holmes would in all likelihood have caused even more trouble, including bodily harm to more Indians and property damage to the saloon. Jim was sorry that he had killed Holmes, but he had felt at the time, and still did now, that it was necessary to do so.

"Gentlemen of the jury, there are times when an action, however regrettable and even illegal, must be taken to save lives and property. On October

1, 1862, in that saloon in Bella Bella, Jim took that action. Killing a man is a grievous offence, but in this case the action was justifiable by whatever form of measurement or judgment you may wish to place upon it, and on those grounds I urge you to find Jim 'not guilty.'"

Aleck sat down and watched the judge, knowing what he would say and regretting it greatly. "Thank you Mr. Robertson. Thank you, Mr. Blaze. I take it there are no witnesses to be called, and that you have both said what you have to say?" They both nodded. Begbie turned to the jury.

"Gentlemen, I ask you now to withdraw and consider your verdict. In doing so, kindly remember that while Mr. Robertson has argued most persuasively that the murder of Jack Holmes by Jim was justifiable in human terms, the concept of justifiable homicide is not accepted by this court. Either murder was committed, or not. If it was, then the accused is guilty. Thank you, gentlemen. Please proceed."

Aleck looked sadly at his file of papers. He knew that he had lost – indeed, that there had never been any other possibility – but he still felt downcast at losing his first case in BC. The jury filed out, and Jim was led away to a cell. Barnaby asked Aleck to return to the small room next door, where another client awaited him. As he left the courtroom a new defendant was being led in to make his plea, accompanied by his lawyer George Walkem.

Aleck's next client was an Indian named Squasmitz, alias Tasok-mack, accused of murdering the Chinaman Poningkoo between Harrison mouth and a point six miles below Hope some time last winter. As with the previous case, Aleck had the accused, an interpreter and a constable in the room with him, and a slim file before him on the desk.

This was, however, a different situation altogether. There was substantial circumstantial evidence linking the accused to the victim at the approximate time and place of the murder, but the only concrete proof of this connection was that the Indian was reported to having been found to have in his possession Poningkoo's boots and a poke of gold dust that several of the victim's friends identified as being his. Aleck asked the interpreter to go into the courtroom and request that Barnaby come to see him. When the clerk arrived, annoyed at having been summoned away from the court by this junior lawyer, Aleck told him that he wished to see the boots and the poke of gold dust that were the only material pieces of evidence for this case. Barnaby paused for a moment before telling Aleck that "well Sir, that evidence seems to have disappeared. Anyway it ain't here today, that I know."

Aleck smiled and thanked Barnaby. A quick second scan of the file confirmed to him another key point, namely that no murder weapon had been found. He spent the remainder of the time available to him asking Squasmitz what he had to say about the case, and receiving little in reply.

Aleck was summoned back to the courtroom to hear the verdict in Jim's case. Instructed by the judge, Jim stood up, Aleck stood up, and the foreman of the jury announced the verdict of 'guilty'. Jim was led away by the attending policeman, and before Aleck could leave he saw that Squasmitz alias Tasok-mack was being led to the accused's chair, and Mr. Blaze was scanning the file on the case of his next victim.

Blaze said that Squasmitz was known to be a hard man with a bad temper, occasionally violent. He had been hired to sweep and clean the saloon where Poningkoo worked as a cook, and on several occasions witnesses had seen them arguing in angry tones. According to the dishwasher at the saloon, just before Poningkoo had disappeared on that fateful day, he had a particularly noisy exchange with the accused, and the accused had stormed out of the saloon swearing in his native language. After Poningkoo's body had been found, the constables had learned of this event, and had seen fit to search the accused's 'modest residence'. There they had found the boots and the poke of dust that were known to have belonged to the deceased. Thus while there had been no witnesses to the murder, it was clear what had happened. Squasmitz had murdered Poningkoo, and it was incumbent upon the jury to find him guilty.

Aleck started by saying that while there were no witnesses before the court today, it was clear from sworn statements by people who knew the protagonists that there had been bad blood between them, and that the accused had in fact stormed out of the saloon after a particularly violent argument with the victim. He said that while no murder weapon had been found, it was alleged that two articles purported to belong to the victim had been found in the possession of the accused. He asked the judge if the two pieces of evidence might be presented to the court for its consideration. The judge ordered the clerk to produce the evidence. There was a hush in the room, and then Barnaby rose and announced that the evidence had not been submitted to the court.

A babble of whispering arose from the jury benches, quickly silenced by an angry Judge Begbie, who turned to the prosecution's desk and thundered "Mr. Blaze, is this true? There is no evidence? Where has it gone, Sir?"

"I don't know, your Honour. It, ah, it seems to have been lost or mislaid somehow." Blaze was clearly angry and embarrassed, his face a wretched shade of red. Begbie glared at him for a second before turning back to Aleck and nodding for him to continue.

Aleck took little time to take advantage of this opening. He described to the court the amazing scenario wherein, based solely on the reported disagreements between two men over a period of time – the sorts of dis-agreements that unfortunately arise far too often in a racially mixed society – one is accused of murdering the other. There had been no witnesses to the crime, and no weapon had been produced. The only evidence was sup-posed to be a pair of boots and a small sack of gold dust, but even that had not been seen by the court!

"Gentlemen of the jury, you have been asked to find a man guilty of a crime when there is no evidence that he has committed it! This surely must lead to your finding him 'not guilty.'"

As Aleck sat down the judge turned to the prosecutor. "Mr. Blaze, do you have anything more to say?"

"No, your Honour."

Judge Begbie was clearly angry as he charged the jury. He spent little time reviewing the facts of the case, but stated in no uncertain terms that the absence of the physical evidence that had weighed so heavily in the case presented by the prosecution must be considered most seriously in their deliberations.

Twenty minutes later Aleck was called back into the courtroom to witness the 'not guilty' plea announced by the jury foreman. His client grinned sheepishly at him, and then walked away to the waiting arms of his family members. The judge thanked the jury, and then turned back to face the courtroom, calling for silence and looking directly at Aleck.

"Mr. Robertson, in the course of a few hours you have appeared before me twice. In both cases the decisions have been the correct ones. This court has done its duty as it should, and I feel compelled to state that you, Sir, have comported yourself in a most admirable manner. You are young and will, I am sure, learn much over the next year, but you have already shown me that you have a fine knowledge of the law, and of the propriety of the proceedings of this court. You are, Sir, a most welcome addition to the legal community of this colony."

Aleck was stunned, and could only smile and nod his head in thanks. As he left the courtroom Barnaby approached him, now considerably more polite and even deferential than before, and suggested that he take some lunch at a nearby restaurant, and then return because there was one more case for him that day.

He returned at 2 pm to find George Walkem awaiting him. He would be assisting Walkem in defending the Antler Bed-rock Flume Co. against the suit brought by Mr. Garfield for engineering services rendered for upwards of $1,800. After the excitement of the criminal cases, it was difficult for him to focus on this civil case, which was familiar to him as he had dealt with a number of such cases in Windsor. Fortunately Walkem needed little help. There was no hope of winning – the company should clearly pay its bill.

The judge agreed. He was tired, and it didn't take him long to dismiss the pleadings of the company, award Garfield the money, and head home for his dinner.

The British Columbian
New Westminster
November 12, 1864

The Bench and the Bar...
...The admission of two young and talented members of the colonial Bar to

practice in this colony is of itself a circumstance demanding more than a passing notice. The monopoly of the profession in Victoria by a few persons of mediocre caliber has realized in our experience the truth of the homely proverb: "It's an ill wind that blows nobody good.", inasmuch as we are doubtless in some measure indebted to that circumstance for the advent of two Upper Canada Barristers amongst us.

One of them, Mr. Walkem, has been in this colony for some years; and although he made his first appearance in this community as a practicing Barrister on Monday, yet he is by no means unknown in the colony, where his professional talents are rapidly making him felt. Mr. Robertson's debut Monday, as counsel for the two Indians indicted for murder, although made under somewhat trying circumstance, was a decided success. He not only drew encomiums from the Bench and from his brother barristers, but we can congratulate him on having made a favourable impression upon all who were present, whether in the capacity of jurors, suitors or spectators.

We are glad to see the infusion of such an element into the Bar of British Columbia, not because they are colonists like ourselves, but because we think they are young men of talent and liberal views; and the presence of such is needed both in judicial and political circles.

12

WINTERTIME

For the rest of November Aleck lived at a rooming house in New Westminster and attended the British Columbia assizes. One morning his newspaper brought the welcome news that the Governor of Vancouver Island had finally signed the Barristers Bill into law, so he would now be able to practice in both colonies, and in the combined colony when they were put together in the future.

On December 1 Aleck returned to Victoria for a quick visit to settle his affairs at the *Chronicle* and seek admission to the Bar of Vancouver Island. He moved back into his room at Mr. Little's house, and that evening he walked over to the James Bay area to pay his respects to the Waddells and tell them of his adventures in BC. This visit brought him two pieces of very bad news – his father's death, and the decision by the Waddell family to move back to Canada.

That same week he was welcomed into the second level of membership in the Freemasons. He was now a Fellow Craft, and with some further study of the order and its activities he would soon be invited into the third degree of membership as a Master Mason. The Craft had been a good idea. He found the members stimulating, and he liked the culture that espoused good citizenship and service to the community. He knew that the network of members would, over time, be important to him in his business.

The next day Aleck returned to New Westminster and to work. By then he had received Maggie's letter offering her condolences. He had calmed down, written to his mother, and was sufficiently tranquil to write to Maggie.

December 6, 1864

My M

...I thank you my little one for your words of love and sympathy. I know they come from your heart. You tell me how I must view an event that could not have taken place but for God. I know this Darling, and I wish to accept it as a part of my education for eternity...

He returned to Victoria for Christmas week, where he enjoyed his visits with friends, the church services at St. John's, and the traditional dinner with the Waddells. He was surprised to see that Bella was not present for the dinner, and learned that she had gone by steamer to San Francisco for a brief visit with some friends there during the holiday season. He also learned some other interesting things about Bella and her Victoria friends, which he described in a letter to Maggie that he wrote soon after he returned to New Westminster on December 28.

January 4, 1865

...I have not seen Bella for upwards of a month. There is no engagement between her and Dr. Powell. They were very intimate, but a very decided reaction seems to have taken place. The doctor is a most decided flirt. At the present time he is doing the amiable to my little friend Miss Branks, but with what success I don't know. She is one of the good and noble, and by far too good for him...

Maggie would always remember the winter of 1864/65 as a thoroughly mixed up affair. It started with the sadness of Dr. Robertson's death, a sadness that, until early 1865, hovered over Chatham and affected every event in one way or another. For Maggie there was the added problem of having her lover so far away that even regular letters sometimes became lost or delayed in transit. She was always following his life and his thoughts at least six weeks behind the fact. Mind you, she had settled down considerably from those cruel early months after his departure, when she had been almost unable to bear the loneliness, the sheer desolation caused by his absence. She had a good life in Chatham. It just could have been a whole lot better.

Maggie's greatest pleasure was always to retire to her room with a new letter from Aleck. His words of love buoyed her. His stories and descriptions interested her. His ruminations about the future of the colonies, and of their role in them, frustrated her. The young couple had two interlinked levels of uncertainty to deal with. One was the question of where they would live when they were married. In one letter Aleck would be excited about living in the west. In the next he would be thoroughly depressed about the prospects out there, siding with a return to Canada. The other question was when? When would he feel that he was sufficiently secure financially that they could be married? Maggie wished that they would just be married and face the world together and wherever, but her man was not so decisive, and it was his decision to make.

That letter of January 4 was particularly welcome to her as it seemed to clear away any concerns she had about her Aleck forming a liaison with Bella or the mysterious Miss Branks. From his letter in early December she knew that the Waddells would be returning to Chatham in the spring, so that would bring Bella back, well away from Aleck. Now Miss Branks, whom Aleck had seemed to like very much, was being courted by Dr. Powell.

Aleck's letter of January 30, written from New Westminster, completed the story to her entire satisfaction.

January 30, 1865

I heard yesterday of Dr. Powell's marriage at Victoria to Miss Branks. So you see my M., Uncle's conclusion has turned out to be far more correct. Powell has got a most excellent wife, and though she may have at some former period given the first place in her heart to another, I doubt not she will do her part well...

...I am hoping to get all the particulars in a letter from Bella tonight, but I must say she is a very uncertain correspondent... Just fancy – it will be two months tomorrow since I left Victoria and she has not written to me once...

On the evening of March 21, William and Mary Bell Eberts had one of their rare visits to the Shades Saloon for a quiet dinner. Light snow was falling on Chatham's streets as they left the carriage and walked into the warm, friendly atmosphere of the restaurant. They waved at several friends, and settled in comfortably at a table close to the fireplace. After they had survived the usual greetings and flapping of napkins by the waiter, and William had ordered a bottle of claret to get them started, he looked around the room reflectively.

"By Jove, my dear, I do still miss the good doctor when I come here. We used to have such splendid lunches, sitting over there by the window watching the pretty girls walk by."

"Oh William, really! What a thing to say!" But Mary Bell also felt, once again, a pang at the thought of the departed doctor, so she let William have his little joke, and smiled at him.

Their quiet evening progressed through wine and good soup, and an excellent cut of beef. They talked about business and the war down south that surely was just about to end, and then about family and friends. Finally the time was perfect for Mary Bell to raise the subject that was foremost on her mind. "And speaking of Maggie, dear, I think we should talk about her relationship with Aleck Robertson."

William's easy, relaxed smile turned instantly into a frown. He put down his knife and fork, and took up his glass to fortify himself for the onslaught that he knew must be coming. "Yes my love, I suppose we should, although I wish we didn't have to. I must admit the whole thing worries me. What do you think?"

"I think, as I know you do, that it is unfortunate that they are first cousins, for all the obvious reasons. If they marry it will be a sin in the eyes of some people, and may cause them some unpleasantness. On the other hand it is not really a sin, and I am sure that time will heal that wound very nicely. I also think that this waiting for Aleck to come back to Chatham is very difficult for Maggie. It breaks my heart to see her so down at times. She should be out enjoying herself and romancing. Heaven knows there are enough nice eligible men out there to keep her happy. But if that is what she chooses, then I think that we should live with it and support her."

William looked away from his wife, staring into the fire. "I do support her Mary Bell. You know I do. But you're right, I don't like it, and I suppose I show it at times. That is, I don't like the situation for the reasons you have mentioned. I must say I do like Aleck. He's a brilliant young man, and delightful as well. It would be marvelous to have him as part of our family, but..."

"You know, dear, it may end up quite differently than we think. After all, Aleck is far away, and he might well not return for some time, and Maggie is having some social life and may meet someone else. You never know. But my heart – my intuition – tells me that it will happen. They are absolutely smitten with each other. You know, he has told her many times that as soon as he establishes himself in his profession and can afford it, he will seek her hand."

"Oh yes, I am sure of it" said William sadly. "And that is another cause for concern. If they do get married, they will likely end up in Victoria or some other God forsaken place, far away from us. We shall never see them again, or their children! What a damned sadness that will be!"

For once in her life Mary Bell ignored William's swearing. "William, dear..."

"Well, what? What do you want? What do you want me to do?"

Softly Mary Bell, softly. "Well, Maggie means the world to us both. We simply must see her happy. If we don't then we will have failed as her parents. So what I am saying – all I am saying – is that we both accept the situation as it is, and love and support her as it moves along. If we try to discourage her, it will hurt her badly. I know it will. And of course, I suppose she could even move out on her own if we were against it. So what I want is – well, that's what I want."

William sat silently for some minutes, gazing at the fire. Then, with a confident gesture he turned to stare directly at Mary Bell. She was amazed to see that he had tears in his eyes.

"You are right of course, my dear. Yes, of course. If we can't have our precious Maggie happy, then what on earth are we doing?" He paused. "But I cannot simply put my concerns behind me, for they are real. You know that, and Maggie is certainly aware of the problems, although she naturally overlooks them." He paused. Mary Bell held her breath. "Let me say this. I will not tell Maggie that I support her affair with Aleck, but I promise you that I will not provoke her in any way, and will not work against her. If it happens, if they marry, I will accept it and that will be the end of it. I hope that will satisfy you?"

They sat in silence for several minutes, both staring into the fire and dabbing their eyes with their napkins, before Mary Bell could speak. "Yes dear, that is fine."

13

SEARCHING FOR GOLD

April 1865 was an historic month in that the civil war in the United States came to an end on April 9. Then on April 14 President Abraham Lincoln was assassinated. Aleck reported to Maggie that this tragedy was recorded in New Westminster in an exciting way.

April 15, 1865

> *…The first telegraphic message was received at this city this morning, and that, the unwelcome announcement that President Lincoln was shot on the 14th inst. We are now in communication with the east via San Francisco…*

This amazing communications feat made a great change to the sense of isolation felt by the citizens of British Columbia. True, telegraphic messaging was expensive, and certainly not made for everyday communications or messages of any length. The fact was, however, that if a person in BC had an urgent message for a person in New York or Canada, he could send it knowing that it would be received the same day! Without telegraph, the postal system delivered in four to six weeks, so this was a dramatic improvement.

The first of April found the Waddell family, except for John, on a steamer headed for San Francisco en route to Chatham. John stayed in Victoria with the idea of once again trying his luck in the gold fields, this time in the Kootenay district.

For Aleck, April marked the start of his work in the gold fields of the Cariboo. He had to wait until April 25, because on that day he was admitted to Third Degree Membership of the Victoria Lodge No. 783 of the Freemasons. The ceremony was quiet and dignified, and he felt honoured to have been accepted so soon at the third degree. He then went immediately to New Westminster, where he purchased clothes and supplies for the rough life in the interior. He left New Westminster by steamer on April 28, heading up the Fraser River.

They arrived at the tiny settlement of Yale late next morning. Aleck proceeded with a number of other passengers to the office of the Barnard Express, and booked his passage to Richfield on the coach scheduled to leave the following morning at 8 am.

The trip was rough and extremely tiring in spite of the surprisingly good quality of the Cariboo road that had been completed the previous year. It was an amazing feat of engineering and a tribute to hard labor, having been built entirely by hand, pick and shovel. It had numerous bridges and passages cut along steep canyon walls, giving the passengers spectacular views that were often terrifying as well. All of the passengers were going to either Barkerville or Richfield, and they got to know each other well during the long days on the road, the occasional stops for refreshment of horses and passengers, two short detours around washouts, and five nights in wayside inns. Their last night was at an inn in Quesnellemouth, the northern tip of their journey.

The next day they turned due east, and by mid-afternoon Aleck found himself standing on the board sidewalk on the main street of Richfield. It was a sparkling, clear day, but even so the street was muddy from recent rains. The town was in a valley between long slopes that had been partially cleared of timber. It had the same frontier look that Aleck had observed in every town they had visited on the trip up from Yale: rugged wooden and log houses; raised board sidewalks to keep citizens above the mud and occasional floods; and an intermittent but noisy stream of horse-drawn conveyances churning up the streets.

He left his luggage at the Express office and walked around the town to get his bearings and seek out accommodation. The place was primitive in appearance, but it did have a reasonable array of establishments and services. There were several stores supplying everything from foodstuffs to clothing to mining gear. There were large stables, four saloons, branch offices of the Bank of British Columbia and the Bank of British North America, a combined hotel and restaurant called the 'Paris & London Restaurant', and a Chinese restaurant. Aside from the Express office, the service facilities were mainly government – the courthouse, the jail, government offices and a post office. The most impressive structure was St. Patrick's Roman Catholic Church. The most important private residence was the log cabin of Judge Begbie.

Aleck found that all of the rooming houses in the town were full, but thanks to a helpful introduction by a friendly government clerk named Michael Watson, he managed to secure two rooms in the back of the general store owned by Jonathan McCracken, a jovial Scot. They were the smallest of the four storage rooms, and had very little inventory in them. They both had windows, and the larger one had a table and three chairs in it, and opened through a door in the side of the store. Aleck thought that it would be possible to make the larger room into his office, and sleep in the smaller room. There was a privy outside the back of the store and a water pump in the store itself, so it would be livable.

After some discussion and negotiation with McCracken, they agreed to try it out for a month at least, with Aleck paying $30 for the month and having access to the pump and privy, and use of the table and chairs and a book case that was sitting idle in the largest store room. McCracken also offered to bring two blankets and a towel for Aleck to use until he could purchase his own supplies. Aleck moved his luggage in that afternoon, and bought a bale of hay from the nearby stables to use as his mattress. With the blankets over the hay and a row of nails on the wall to hang his clothes, he felt almost at home.

The next day he ordered a small sign saying 'Law Office, Alexander Rocke Robertson, Esq., Barrister', to be nailed outside the door of his office, braced at an angle so that it could be seen from the street. He set up his books on the shelves, laid out his writing materials on the table that was now his desk, and then headed out in search of business.

The courthouse of Richfield was a tiny one-room building set back in a clearing above the main road. It was one of several buildings in the clearing that constituted the heart of the legal system in the area. They were the courthouse itself, a second slightly larger building for the judge's chambers and offices and a waiting room, a cabin that was the residence of the local magistrate, and another cabin farther up the slope that was Judge Begbie's local residence.

Aleck opened the door of the courtroom, which was empty at the moment. The room had the usual facilities of a small courtroom, with one row of benches for spectators. A door in the back led to the other building that held the judge's chambers and the clerk's office. As Aleck stood at the entrance of the courtroom, gazing around at its crude appointments, the back door opened and a tall, strong looking man entered. When he saw Aleck he stopped, looked Aleck up and down, and asked him what his business was here in the courtroom.

"Good day, Sir. My name is Alexander Robertson. I am a Barrister and member of the Bar of British Columbia. I have just arrived in Richfield where I intend to practice, and have come here to present my compliments to the officers of the court."

"Are you indeed" replied the other, smiling and striding forward to shake Aleck's hand. "I am Edwy Stewart, clerk of this court, and you are most welcome. I trust you have found a place to stay?"

"I have Sir, and have established an office at the side of McCracken's store. Here are my credentials."

"Thank you Mr. Robertson." Stewart sat down on a bench and took his time to go through Aleck's papers. "Well done! Well done indeed! Ah, I see you've appeared before Judge Begbie on several occasions. Good. His Honour is here in Richfield these days, and will be pleased to learn of your arrival. Your timing is excellent, you know, for we'll be commencing sessions tomorrow, and we have a full docket of prisoners to see to. As I am sure you are aware, we have some violent crime in the area – it is only natural – but remarkably little given the hard nature of the local industry. You will likely find yourself more involved with commercial crimes and disputes, and of course the usual battles with the Indians. In this regard you may also know, perhaps, that Judge Begbie has great respect for the Indians. You will want to keep this in mind.

"As far as your prospects for work are concerned, we have few Barristers here in Richfield at the moment, so I am certain that you will be quite busy. If I might make a suggestion, you will want to pay a call on our Assistant Gold Commissioner, Mr. Ball, as he is often seeking assistance with troublesome claims."

"Thank you, Mr. Stewart. I will do so. Concerning this court, I am at your service. What would you like me to do?"

"I will be attending upon Judge Begbie this afternoon to give him papers for the upcoming trials. I will tell him of your arrival. May I suggest that you present yourself here tomorrow morning at nine o'clock sharp?

Aleck arrived at the courthouse at 8:45 am next morning, gowned and wigged. There were already several people in the waiting room, including one other lawyer with clients, and one massive member of the local constabulary who introduced himself as "Peterson, Sir, at your service". The lawyer was John G. Barnston, who like Aleck had recently come to Richfield to take advantage of the Cariboo gold trade. He welcomed Aleck to Richfield, and in their brief exchange Aleck learned that several more lawyers could be expected to arrive as the season progressed.

Just before 9 am the clerk poked his head in and looked around. Seeing Aleck, he called to him and motioned him to follow. "His Honour would like to have a word with you" he whispered, and led the way to the judge's chambers. Judge Begbie sat behind the desk, deep in his papers. As they entered he looked up and, seeing Aleck, cried "Ah Robertson, there you are!

Do come and sit for a moment."

Aleck sat down on the lone chair in front of the desk as His Honour finished the last line of the paper he was reading and then closed the file with a flourish. "Thank you Mr. Stewart" he said to the clerk, who was hovering in the doorway. "You may take these in to the bench. We will begin shortly." Stewart followed these instructions, and the judge turned to Aleck.

"So Mr. Robertson, Stewart told me that you were here. I am very pleased. You are most welcome."

"Thank you Sir."

"Does this place please you? Are you settled in?"

"Yes it does Sir. Very much so. And yes, I have an office and a place to stay, and I am ready to serve the court."

"Good. We will need you. As you know the gold fever seems to be cooling somewhat, but there is still plenty of activity. It is to be expected, I suppose, that as the prospect of finding gold diminishes, so do many of the miners become more desperate. And that, of course, leads them to our courts. As you will see, there is an amazing variety of things that people can do to each other in this sort of place."

"I am sure of it, Sir."

"Right," said Begbie, starting to collect himself for the court. "As in New Westminster, so I will assign you to cases as we proceed. Stewart is very efficient, so keep your eyes on him. Incidentally, I understand that your colleague George Walkem will be coming up here at some point this summer. He can be a tricky fellow at times but, like you, he will be welcome. He may be doing some work as a member of the Legislative Council, but I'm sure that we will be able to claim at least some of his time. Do keep in mind that we have assizes in several places hereabouts, including Barkerville and Quesnellemouth, so we need enough lawyers to go around! And of course, you will also find things to do in the Gold Commissioner's court. I am sure you will not be idle. Well, it's time. Good luck, Robertson."

Aleck rose, thanked the judge, and leaving his office almost walked straight into Stewart. The clerk handed him a file, and instructed him to go immediately to the side room off the entrance hallway, there to meet his first client.

Aleck's life in Richfield was surprisingly pleasant. Most importantly, he was busy at his profession. He had a steady stream of cases, generally concerning commercial disputes, but some involving violent crimes. He was busy at the court in Richfield, before the Assistant Gold Commissioner, in his own office, as well as with several trips to the courts and gold offices in Barkerville and Quesnellemouth.

His social life improved as he met an increasing number of friendly people. Michael Watson was a frequent table companion at the Richfield Saloon, as was George Walkem when he came to Richfield in late May. Jonathan McCracken, his landlord, always enjoyed good conversation, and he and his wife made Aleck welcome whenever he was available for a meal and a lively discussion. Rev. Andrew Garrett, the minister of the Anglican Church, became a good friend, and Aleck particularly looked forward to his evenings at the Garrett home.

George Walkem, who stayed at the Paris & London Restaurant, shared with Aleck the more demanding cases before the courts in the region. Aleck found Walkem somewhat stiff, but an interesting and welcome professional colleague and friend. As a member of the colony's Legislative Council, he had a clear picture of the state of the western colonies and the politics involved. He described the fiscal state of affairs as serious, and saw no alternative to uniting the two colonies, the sooner the better.

Aleck's office was just sufficient for the task at hand, although it did draw some puzzled looks from his more affluent clients. It was there that he wrote his letters to Maggie, and where he read hers. They arrived at the post office like nuggets of pure gold. He would take them to his office and read them over several times, savouring them, but generally ending up feeling lonely and dispirited in spite of the words of love they always contained.

She put her feelings, her strong emotions, so beautifully that he almost felt intimidated. She loved him so much, and she knew that they lived under the hand of God, and that was a comfort to her just as it was to him. Her letters were constantly urging him to return to Chatham, if only for a visit.

He would have liked to have written to her every day, even just a few lines to express his thoughts and his love, but that would not be practical with the lengthy and unreliable mail service. He was busy, so wrote less frequently than he should have. As a result he carried a load of guilt with him, albeit tempered by the harsh realities of the area.

June 26, 1865

My Beloved M.

...Well, Darling, I am in far famed Cariboo, the land of gold so much written about, so much talked about, but really very little understood or appreciated except by those whose wandering feet have brought them hither. How widely different the scene, as my eye arrow daily rests upon it, from what my excited imagination in days now past was wont to picture it. Fancy then, in its riotous, capricious mood – gave it many glowing, vivid colors of which it is now entirely divested.

It is not a place where labour always brings a golden reward, where all are happy and prosperous, where the sky is ever bright, but the same circumstances which characterize life at home – exist in one form or other here. Some have waged long, and are waging still, war with fortune. Adversity, with its chilling enfeebling influence has been the steadfast companion of others, while others, and they are few, have been prospered abundantly...

Aleck was pleased that he was succeeding in his quest to make money so that he could marry Maggie as soon as possible and support her in the manner to which she was accustomed. He was not there yet, however, so he could not respond positively to her appeals that he come home for a visit.

From receiving $25 a week at the *Chronicle*, he had improved to $200 per month in New Westminster. Now his situation had improved yet again. It was expensive to travel to and from the Cariboo and to stay there in his lodgings, but he nevertheless hoped that on his return to New Westminster he would have saved about $2,000 cash. It was a far better result than had he stayed in Windsor, but must not be squandered.

August 10, 1865

...You expect and wish me to return to Canada in the fall. How delighted I'd be if the necessity for returning here did not exist. My means however are yet so limited – I want to make the best of present opportunities, and though I may not acquire any very large sum, I trust I may be favoured with what will answer as a nice little capital at home...

On September 4 Aleck called upon Judge Begbie to pay his respects, closed his affairs at the bank, and enjoyed his last dinner for the season at the Richfield Saloon, matching Watson and McCracken toast for toast through three bottles of wine. The next day he closed his rooms and took the morning Express coach for the weary return trip to New Westminster.

14

PARALLEL LIVES

The lovers had been apart for over a year as the summer of 1865 came, shone, and then passed into fall. Aleck had his summer in Richfield and Maggie faced the usual summer of heat and humidity, helping with the family, music and reading, and her visit to Owen Sound to enjoy the lake and the parties on its beaches. The Waddell family arrived back in Chatham, just over a year after their brave departure with Aleck to join father John in Victoria. Maggie was happy to see them back, and she saw a lot of her old friend Bella. She still suspected that Bella had entertained hopes for Aleck out west, but clearly either she had been wrong or it had not worked, and she welcomed her, along with the whole family.

In August Aleck's mother Effie decided that it would be best if she and the remaining children move up to Owen Sound. She was not comfortable about her finances, and she had received an invitation from her oldest son James to come and share his large house. With some help from lawyer McLean they rented out Heatherdale to a promising couple, and in early August moved to the Sound. Maggie assisted the Robertson family, and stayed with them until early September to help them settle in.

⋖⋗

Upon his return in September from the Cariboo to New Westminster, Aleck decided that he had better open some sort of office there. Notwithstanding that he intended to return to Victoria for the winter since he could now practice there, he had told Judge Begbie that he would be establishing himself in New Westminster, and he wished to honour that commitment. He took a small and inexpensive room in a recently completed commercial building, put his name on the door, and made arrangements with the office next door to tend to his mail when he was absent. He furnished it sparsely with desk and chairs and one bookshelf, and within the first three days had the pleasure of receiving two clients there.

The Pioneer Saloon in Front Street was an agreeable place to have dinner on a chilly New Westminster night in September. There was a modest but palatable selection of wines, the beer was fresh, and the food coming out of J.T. Scott's kitchen was often referred to as "better than expected". On the evening of Monday, September 18 the saloon was reasonably quiet, so the three men could have a good conversation at their corner table.

George Walkem, like Aleck, had recently returned from the Cariboo, and this evening he was introducing Aleck to one of the town's most prominent citizens, John Robson. A Canadian from Upper Canada, Robson was, at 40 years old, the outspoken editor of the *British Columbian* newspaper, and since 1863 had been a member of the New Westminster Municipal Council. As a reader of the *British Columbian* Aleck felt that he knew the man, as Robson took full advantage of his editorial position to express his strongly-held views on almost every subject.

Like many citizens of BC, he was not in favor of union of their colony with Vancouver Island. He disliked the governing institutions on the Island, convinced that if the two colonies were joined, Victoria would do everything in its power to take over the running of the whole show, leaving the mainland out in the cold. He much preferred the idea of Confederation with Canada, wherein a railway linking the disparate parts of the huge country together would be of great benefit to BC and to New Westminster.

He supported the ideas of responsible government for BC and of free, universal and non-denominational education for all.

"I'm pleased to meet you, Robertson. Walkem here says that you've done well in our courts, such as they are. How have you found it?"

"I've found it most interesting and at times challenging" replied Aleck. "I just wish that the economy was still running at top speed as it was a few years ago. I've done acceptably so far, but the prospects for business in the coming years are cloudy."

"Oh yes, I am sure of it" replied Robson. "And if this is the way it is with gold fever, then we must diversify ourselves away from it as quickly as possible. I don't think those slugs in Victoria have thought of that. All they think of is taxing us as much as they can. But enough of that. Robertson, you're new to these colonies. We're in the midst of an economic crisis, and the two colonies are at each other's throats. Everyone out here is a politician. What do you think of all this?"

"Shall I make a speech, Sir?" asked Aleck, grinning across the table. Walkem and Robson both laughed, but made no reply.

"Oh very well then, I will confine myself to a few thoughts. Let me start by saying that I can now practice law in both colonies, so I refuse to state a preference for either. They are both large territories, with fine prospects for the future if we care to make it so. It's true that Victoria is farther ahead than is New Westminster, but I don't see that as a major issue. Indeed, I don't consider the location of the capital to be particularly important at all.

"Wait" he said, raising his hand to fend off Robson's startled rejoinder. "Let me elaborate.

"As I see it, Britain will grant responsible government to dominions that prove they are capable of it, but there will always be close ties at the highest levels, especially in areas such as military and commerce. And so it will be with the British possessions here on this continent. Canada and the Atlantic colonies are, as I understand it, close to forming a Confederation. The next step will be to join the rest of the British possessions north of the United States into a Confederation stretching from sea to sea."

"Absolutely!" cried Robson. "Why, that's the only way that we can keep ourselves out of the clutches of the Americans."

"Precisely. However, there's still much work to be done before then. Britain must rescue the prairie lands from the Hudson's Bay Company, and establish proper governance there. Then it will be our turn to join in."

Walkem was smiling happily. "And Vancouver Island will be part of this paradise?"

"Of course" said Aleck, "First we must have a union of our two colonies. There's no way around it. It makes no sense to have two separate governments and court systems in a space that is geographically a combined unit. So the colonies will be joined, the railway will come out to link us to the eastern areas of the country, and we'll be part of a very large and powerful unit."

Robson and Walkem, both politicians, could no longer leave the floor to their inexperienced colleague. They intervened to support his thinking, raised issues of timing and taxation, and then came back to the sticky question of the location of the capital.

Robson said that he believed that London favoured New Westminster, due to the simple logic of its being the capital of the larger piece of the pie. It was on the mainland, with more immediate access to the railway and the many huge economic activities that must spring up in its vast expanses. He knew that the officials in Victoria would fight the idea tooth and nail, preferring the comforts of Victoria to the ruder living in New Westminster. But this would change over time.

Walkem said that he was not so certain that it would change over time. It is very difficult to move an entrenched bureaucracy, and that was a precise description of Victoria.

Aleck took a different approach. "I said earlier that I did not consider this question to be very important. Let me now explain. Drawing on some current examples – would you consider Ottawa more important than Toronto or Montreal? The government is there, true. But the commerce, the entrepreneurship, the energy – these are in the other cities, and that makes them every bit as important as Ottawa. Look also at the United States. Would you prefer to live in Washington or New York? Or even San Francisco?

"Oh, it's nice to have all the perks and ceremonies of a capital, but it's also very nice to have solid business and flourishing financial markets. So I believe the real question for us is – where will that be? My view is that it will be more on the mainland than on Vancouver Island. The railway, when it finally arrives, must naturally end on the mainland, at the water's edge. Even if there is an extension built on the island, the major traffic will come to a stop and the freight and passengers distributed from this side of the water. Where? Perhaps New Westminster, or perhaps even right on tidewater, out where Gastown [later Granville and then Vancouver] is located. When that happens, you here on the mainland will not care where those government people are located. Indeed, it will probably be more convenient and economic to leave them tucked out of the way on the island."

Several days after that dinner, Aleck moved back to Victoria, planning to spend the winter establishing himself there. As he worked at developing his business, he participated actively in the discussions on the subject that was on everyone's lips – the question of the union of the two colonies. On Vancouver Island, Governor Sir Arthur Edward Kennedy was strongly in favor of union, and was pleased when the VI Legislative Assembly passed a resolution proposed by Amor de Cosmos in favor of union. On the mainland, opinion was divided. Cariboo residents wanted union, while people in New Westminster generally favored the *status quo*, and Governor Frederick Seymour held to this position.

The Colonial Office in London summoned Seymour to London, and he departed in September. The rumour on the street was that London wished to see union, the sooner the better, and that Seymour would get his marching orders.

In the many conversations that he had on this subject, Aleck stuck faithfully to the position that he had laid out to Robson and Walkem. He was particularly insistent that the legal systems of the two colonies be combined into one.

Aleck attended St. John's Church regularly. He was getting to know the minister, the Rev. Samuel Gilson, who had replaced Robert Dundas in mid-year. Gilson had to deal with the serious financial problems facing the church, but he still had time to meet and get to know parishioners like Aleck who attended regularly, paid their fees and showed a keen interest in church affairs. On one occasion in late November he invited Aleck to address the congregation on the subject of union, and Aleck had a chance to make his views known publicly. His remarks were well received, and a number of influential people saw in him that day the makings of a useful politician.

Aleck also attended meetings and events at the Masonic Lodge in Victoria. He found it a priceless source of contacts, rubbing shoulders on a collegial basis with many important men. His social life in Victoria was increasingly dominated by official or business-related events and activities.

A business relationship of considerable interest to Aleck was with the distinguished lawyer John Foster McCreight. Thirteen years Aleck's senior, the Irishman had arrived in Victoria in 1860 after a seven-year stint practicing law in Australia. He was a learned, disciplined type of lawyer who believed totally in the rule of the law, strictly applied, to the affairs of men. He was respected in the courts, but not generally known in Victoria's social circles. His life outside work revolved around the Masons and Christ Church Cathedral, both appealing to his sense of contact with important persons, and the latter to his strong religious bent. As time went by, Aleck dealt with McCreight more and more in court, in cases outside the court, and in the Masons. They developed a mutual respect and liking, fortified by the occasional lunch during breaks in court proceedings.

His friendship with Dr. Powell was particularly important in bridging the gap between personal and business affairs. The doctor was a rising star in the community – a successful and popular physician, and also active politically. He was a member of the VI Legislative Assembly, strongly and volubly in support of union with BC, and then Confederation with Canada. In addition to all of that he was a delightful fellow, and he and his new wife Jenny offered Aleck the most friendly and relaxed hospitality in their home. The Powells were the only people in Victoria who knew of Aleck's secret engagement. He had told them of it during one visit when, in the deepest mood of depression, he had sought the comfort of their support. This fact alone made them truly special to him.

Aleck continued with his serious indecision about future plans with Maggie. It was a case of indecision based on a foundation of uncertainty.

December 14, 1865

...I know one question we'd try and settle tonight: were we together would we – shall we delay our union longer? I believe I have pondered more over this point latterly that at any previous period. Almost two of the three years to which I purposed to limit myself out here have expired, and I begin to consider with more than usual earnestness whether, should I be spared, it is probable I shall be enabled to accomplish my object here and return to my loved ones, in that time – or on the other hand find it expedient – perhaps necessary – to prolong my absence for a longer period.

I trust God will graciously direct me in this and all things...

(Continues on December 15)

... I feel so undecided, and am so desirous of returning home. But should it so happen that I must delay that return two or three years longer, may we not, and indeed should we not be united in the meantime? ...

The year 1866 passed in much the same way. Aleck and Maggie lived their separate lives, with Aleck prospering but lonely, and Maggie longing for her man to make up his mind and come for her.

She had an enjoyable three-week visit with relatives in Detroit in March. It was always nice to get away in winter, breaking the monotony of the endless dark days of the Chatham winter. On return, she received a letter that Aleck had written on January 20. He started by protesting that he had not been a good correspondent over the past months. Then he moved on to some very interesting things. First was a passage that showed that he was enjoying the adventure of the west, and that this might foretell a life for her in the west, with many long absences on his part.

January 20, 1866

> *...I propose to immigrate to some of the mining fields in a few months. My life here, Darling, seems to be of rather a nomadic character. Spending the winter on the coast and in the summer going far into the interior – say 500 or 600 miles. I confess to you, notwithstanding its discomforts, such a life has charms for me. As the Indians strike their tents and go off for the annual buffalo hunt, so I like to break up my winter encampment and go off to the mines for a few months. I have sometimes wondered how I should manage if you were to come out to me. How would you like, Darling, to remain in Victoria during the summer in my absence? A great many ladies have to submit to this.*

She thought hard about this idea. Her own preference, and certainly that of her family, was for them to marry and settle down in Chatham, or at least in Ontario. But while this was obviously an option for Aleck, he was still drawn to the excitement of life in the west. She consoled herself with the fact that life with Aleck anywhere would be wonderful.

He then made a typically vague comment about the possibility of his returning that year, and finally he made a comment that shocked and amused her at the same time.

> *The Canadians and Americans are really the best adapted to the work of opening up and developing a new territory. Englishmen, with their nonsensical and fossilized ideas, are mere obstructionists in a colony. Had this colony been under American rule it would have had today three or four times*

its present population. Retrenchment is the great cry here now. The staff of officials quartered upon this feeble colony has been an incubus always hard to bear, but under the present depressed state of affairs – insupportable. Hence the Legislative Assembly have recently immortalized themselves by extinguishing several offices, reducing the salaries pertaining to others, and amalgamating others, so that one man might do the work formerly and unnecessarily distributed among several. It is not known yet what course the executive will take, but in all probability he'll dissolve the house, in which event we may get a worse one next time…

She spent that summer in Chatham, unable to escape to Owen Sound due to a rash of visits from family and friends, many of them from Owen Sound. In fact, Maggie had time for only two picnics at the lakeshore all summer, one accompanied by the jolly Mr. Jonathan Wylde, the other by the attentive Mr. Richard Harris. Harris continued his attentions to her in the fall, calling on her and attending upon her at social occasions. With his bushy moustache, thick, tousled hair and charming smile he was an attractive man, and she knew that were it not for Aleck she would be fully accepting of his attentions. But of course she was not accepting, and as usual was forced to content herself with Aleck's letters.

June 26, 1866

My beloved M.

The first month of the summer's business is over and I begin to have some leisure. The first is, so far as my experience goes, the busiest and most profitable. In it appeal cases from the previous season are tried, the assizes held, and ordinarily a little "rush" in the "Mining Court" held by the gold companies disposed of. Often too there is a call to attend the

*assizes in Quesnellemouth, (a place about 54 miles distant)
and the journey thither and back and the delay there generally
consume a week or more.*

*…I must now tell you my beloved how I am situated here this
season. Last year I certainly was not comfortable. I slept as I
may have told you in a little room behind my office – unpleasant and unhealthy. This year I am lodging as well as boarding
at the "Paris & London Restaurant". What think you of such
a dignified name for a public house in the wild mountains of
Cariboo?…*

Interesting to be sure, but his next letters then returned to the old theme
of uncertainty and indecision.

On November 16, when she still had hopes of him arriving in Chatham
before Christmas, she wrote a letter to him that would, in the end, be the
spark that would cause Aleck to advance his plans for their marriage. She
did not know it at the time, but by next spring the memory of it would
make her laugh.

November 16, 1866

*…I must tell you something of my life during the past summer
and fall. In the way of general amusements I had very little,
two picnics at the Lake Shore being the only things in a
general way which I attended. To the first I went as I wrote
you before with Mr. Harris, to the second with Mr. Wylde, a
young gentleman about Melchior's age, and a great friend of
his. Both of them I enjoyed immensely…*

ALECK ROBERTSON, LAWYER TO THE GOLDFIELDS, 1867

DOWNTOWN VICTORIA CIRCA 1863
COURTESY OF THE ROYAL BC MUSEUM CORPORATION, (A-03023)

NEW WESTMINSTER CIRCA 1863
COURTESY OF THE ROYAL BC MUSEUM CORPORATION, (A-01670)

DR. ISRAEL WOOD POWELL
COURTESY OF THE ROYAL BC MUSEUM CORPORATION, (A-02410)

JOHN ROBSON, PUBLISHER
COURTESY OF THE ROYAL BC MUSEUM CORPORATION, (A-08953)

JUDGE MATTHEW BAILLIE BEGBIE

COURTESY OF THE ROYAL BC MUSEUM CORPORATION, (A-08953)

15

PROGRESS

On Christmas day of 1866, Aleck was sitting in his room, reminiscing over the past year. The fire was warming and gave some comfort, and he had a pleasant Christmas dinner party at the Powells' to look forward to, but his loneliness and longing for Maggie and his family back at Chatham were painfully strong. He felt certain that he was doing the right thing staying out in Victoria and pursuing his course with respect to Maggie, but at times like this he could easily just give it up and take the next steamer back to her side.

This had been a dramatic year in the west, and there could well be better times ahead. He remembered with pleasure the day back in November – November 19 in fact – when Governor Seymour of British Columbia had issued simultaneously in New Westminster and Victoria the proclamation of the union of the two colonies. The mainland colony had won the day, a fact that did not please the Victorians. Governor Kennedy of Vancouver Island had gone, and Seymour now ruled the entire colony. New Westminster was the capital of the combined colony of British Columbia, and BC's constitution and tariff laws were the model for the combined colony. The Vancouver Island Legislative Assembly was disbanded, and the BC Legislative Council was expanded to 23 members, with the mainland having five districts and the island four.

Aleck had been at work in Victoria when the official declaration was made, and had seen and felt the anger of the Victorians in the streets. In several conversations with officials he had found, in fact, that there was a general feeling that they would simply not make the move to New Westminster, no matter what London said. In New Westminster he had found the opposite, albeit laced with a realistic sense of the future. Robson told him that the capital would grow and prosper if given half a chance, but that "...those sluggards and bureau-hats will not be pleased, and I wouldn't be surprised if they refused to come." He proved to be correct.

For himself, Aleck was perfectly happy with this state of affairs. There was finally one colony rather than the inefficient two. Business would continue to be in both places, and he enjoyed his life in the comforts and sophistication of Victoria shared with the crudeness and adventure of the mainland.

The provision in the Act of Union concerning the senior courts was a tribute to two very intelligent and powerful men. Before union Mr. Justice Matthew Begbie was Chief Justice and the only judge for the mainland, and Mr. Justice Joseph Needham was Chief Justice and the only judge for Vancouver Island. Needless to say neither wished to resign in favour of the other, and the Colonial Office was leery of forcing out properly functioning Chief Justices. Thus the Act provided that upon the death or resignation of either of the two judges, the other was to be Chief Justice of BC, and another judge was to be appointed to the colony's Supreme Court to share the workload. It might take some time, but the court systems would finally be combined, to the benefit of all.

Aleck had enjoyed his work in the Cariboo over the summer of 1866, and since returning to Victoria in the fall he had done well professionally and financially. His growing list of clients included many of the leading citizens of the colony. He also had found himself often called upon to attend and participate in gatherings where political issues were raised and discussed. In spite of his neutral feelings on the capital question, Aleck believed that less damage would be done if the capital were in Victoria. A move to New Westminster would be hugely disruptive and expensive, a serious problem at this delicate stage in the colony's life. Thus at those meetings he had spoken in favor of Victoria.

On the issue of Confederation he had left no room for doubt, saying that without Confederation the colony would slide irresistibly into the hands of the United States. His speeches had been appreciated and applauded.

Now, on this chilly Christmas day of 1866, he had every reason to be satisfied with himself. Except of course, for the most important question of all – Maggie.

On January 10, 1867 Aleck received Maggie's letter of November 16. As always he devoured it, and smiled when he read her brief description of her social life in the summer of 1866 – the picnics with Mr. Harris and Mr. Wylde. He was pleased that she was enjoying herself in society, keeping herself busy while waiting for him to return. But oh! how he missed her, and the letter he wrote to her that same evening showed his increasing determination to end this isolation, along with a sense of satisfaction with his growing reputation and recognition in Victoria.

On February 17 he received a packet of letters from back home. As he read them in his room that evening two of them, taken together, kicked him into action with respect to Maggie. One was from Maggie herself, dated December 25, 1866. Its loving words were, as always, a joy to him, but it had a sad, lonely tone that struck him deeply.

He passed on to the other letter, which was from Melchior Eberts, Maggie's younger brother. Melchior was a favorite of his, an intelligent, amusing young man, full of life and plans, always wanting to travel and see new things. He was a great admirer of Aleck, and they corresponded occasionally. Melchior was aware of Maggie's love for Aleck, having learned of it by osmosis through simply living at home and hearing things. In this letter, in a playful mood, he was describing the social life in Chatham the previous summer and fall, and he mentioned that Maggie had attracted the attentions of Richard Harris, and they had attended several functions together. In a good natured way he chided Aleck for being away so long, and leaving them all to seek their own ways in life.

This mention of Harris brought Aleck to a halt. Harris? His old friend Harris? He went to his desk and found her previous letter in the drawer. There it was, in black and white. She mentioned just a picnic with Harris – now Melchior spoke of 'attentions' and attending functions. He doubted that there was really anything to this, but his mind would not leave it alone. She had seen this man several times aside from that picnic, but hadn't bothered to mention that to him.

Images flashed though his mind: of her loving face and warm caresses; of her loneliness and tears in his absence; of her attending functions with Harris, warming to his attentions. It was a crazy mixture of things bouncing around in the air, but when it all finally settled, Aleck knew that it was possible that she was slipping away from him. It was time for him to make his move. It took him several days to craft his letters, but in the end he was satisfied with them. He mailed them with a great sense of relief, already impatient to have a reply.

On April 15 Maggie received Aleck's letter of February 23. She fled to her room (she wished she would stop rushing upstairs with Aleck's letters, but she could not), closed her door, sat at her desk and tore open the envelope. Alongside the letter she found, to her surprise, a smaller envelope addressed to her parents.

Her heart was beating so hard that she had to get up and walk around her room to calm it down. The letter to her parents, in unsealed envelope, lay there on her desk, looking up at her. She was certain that she knew what it was about, but was still terrified to read it – just in case! Perhaps he was apologizing to them for causing them so much concern, and promising to cease and desist? Oh, that was impossible! Well…she sat down and read his letter to her.

February 23, 1867

…By the way Pet, I must tell you that brother Melchior

informs me that an old friend of mine Mr. Harris has been very assiduous in his attentions to you – for six months. Is this so? Should he win your affections I am willing that you should be his, but I am persuaded my Darling that you love me as solely and earnestly as in the days of yore. But shall I tell you, the singular thought that Melchior's remark originated in my mind? I began to think of our love and of the obstacle that our friends always placed between us and its consummation, and then wondered – if it could be or might be – that having thought much over what had been said against us, you had begun to feel it your duty to gently let me go my way in life – alone.

So confident am I in the constancy and sincerity of your love that I believe nothing but a solemn sense of duty in the sight of God would induce you to undo the bonds of love and sympathy that have held us to each other for nearly ten years...

With this letter I enclose one to your Mother and Father. Read it before delivering it. I think it best to have our relation understood and confirmed by them. If you are unwilling that the matter should be laid before them now, destroy the letter...

In about two months - i.e. 1st May – I expect to leave for Cariboo. From what I can learn the prospects for the coming season are good. I am doing but little here, from the fact that there is very little to do. Business is almost stagnated...

Then she opened and read Aleck's letter to her parents.

February 26, 1867

My dear Uncle and Aunt

I have been in constant correspondence with Maggie since I left Canada – and that fact I trust you have always regarded as a sufficient excuse for my not writing to you. Such parts of my letters as she may have deemed would be interesting to you I doubt not she has from time to time made known.

Today I address you for the purpose of bringing directly to your notice that which I am sure you have been conscious of for a long time. I mean the mutual attachment between Maggie and myself, and I do so because I am strongly desirous of getting some definite expression of opinion from you – relative thereto.

I shall not affect to be ignorant of the disapprobation you have commonly expressed with respect to our attachment. Neither shall I say that you were unkind in so regarding it because I know your opposition resulted not from any ill feeling toward me personally – but rather from a desire to do what you were persuaded would be the best for her, and therefore in asking you now to sanction what you have so long censured, I know I am taxing your parental feelings – much –

Years have rolled on rapidly – my boyhood is gone, and manhood finds me grappling with the realities of life – in this far off land. Maggie too has passed from girlhood to womanhood, but the only change in our affection that I am conscious of is that having lost perhaps some of the impulsiveness of childhood – it has gained the maturity and strength of a profounder sentiment, based as I believe upon a deeper feeling of mutual respect.

This being the case I wish to make her my wife should Providence restore us to each other – and your consent to this plan I now ask –

I abstain intentionally from any extravagant expressions of love for her. I prefer to leave you to measure the strength of my attachment by its duration.

The mail steamer will leave tomorrow morning.

May I expect a reply to this at an early date?

With kind love to all, yourselves included.

> *Believe me*
> *Most affably yours*
> *A.R. Robertson*

She sat dazed for a moment, unable to move or even think. All of the years they had loved each other and pined for each other, all of them brought together in this one lovely (somewhat lawyerly) letter. *"I wish to make her my wife..."*

She leapt up and danced around the room, holding the fluttering letter in her hand, kissing it, singing to it. Oh, her stern, careful, lovely man had finally taken the daring step! Oh yes! He had! But why all of a sudden, like this? It didn't matter, of course, but what triggered his decision? She paused. Wait...I wonder if...she picked up his letter to her and scanned it quickly, and there it was. Harris! Richard Harris, for heaven's sake! Aleck had heard of his attentions, and had become jealous! Now he must claim her for his own, or risk losing her. Oh yes, his letter definitely said that, in so many words at least.

She laughed, and then whooped for joy and, predictably, the door swung open and her mother strode in to see what was happening. Maggie stopped and handed her the letter. Mary Bell read it, smiled and took her delirious daughter into her arms. They both burst into tears and cried for a good ten minutes.

Aleck's personal concerns were strong and important to him, but by no means did they dominate his time or his thoughts in the early months of 1867. Aside from his lively practice in Victoria, the two major political issues of the day had seized his attention and taken up a lot of his time. He spoke at several public meetings on the subject of the location of the capital. The newly expanded BC Legislative Council had taken up the question, and on March 29 it passed a resolution recommending to Governor Seymour that he recommend to the Colonial Office that the capital be moved from New Westminster to Victoria. The Governor forwarded the proposal to the Colonial Office for its decision.

The question of Confederation was also now the subject of great debate. At a public meeting in Victoria on March 19, Aleck proposed, seconded by Dr. Powell, that BC would be benefited by its admission into Confederation on equitable terms. His speech was well received, and he was accorded the loud applause to which he was now growing accustomed at such events. In the Legislative Council Amor de Cosmos proposed and had passed a motion calling for Governor Seymour to send a telegram to the Colonial Office asking for a provision in the forthcoming British North America Act that would allow for the eventual entry of BC into Confederation.

Governor Seymour delayed sending this message until September 24, long after de Cosmos had travelled to Ottawa to press the case there.

Working hard in the Cariboo starting early in May, Aleck was in personal turmoil as the weeks went by without a reply from Maggie's parents. He felt some anger, in fact, for surely they must say "yes", and why did it have to take so long? After all, he and Maggie were plenty old enough to go and get married without the permission of the parents, but that would be most unpleasant.

June 4, 1867

> *...By every mail I am expecting to receive an answer from your parents to my first and most important letter to them. You see I take it for granted that you delivered the letter referred to. I am also expecting a letter from my dear mother on the same subject...*

In the last week of June he received a note from Maggie saying that as far as she knew her parents had not as yet replied to his letter. This disappointing news arrived just before he was involved in a sensational case [so much so that reports of it lived on for a century in literature, and even on television].

Aleck was called upon to defend a man named James Barry, a drifter in the Cariboo who carried a six-shooter and mooched money for his liquor and pleasure with the girls in the saloons. He was accused of killing a man named Charles Morgan Blessing at a place called Beaver Pass, stealing his $50 cash and a gold nugget. They were travelling together on foot from Quesnellemouth to Williams Creek. Various circumstances and witnesses had placed Barry on that trip with Blessing, and Blessing had died from a revolver shot in the back of the head. The story of the murder spread quickly in the community, and there was public outrage that the man could have done such a thing.

Aleck was brought into the case three days before it opened in court, and it worried him from the outset. He was concerned that the case was so much in the public eye that it would be difficult to find a fair jury. He had little time to work with his client, who swore that he was innocent, but who was a silent man who was slow to divulge information. In the end Aleck felt that the only defense he had was that of lack of hard evidence. Thus in court he focused on the circumstantial nature of the evidence brought against Barry, but to no avail. The jury found him guilty, and Judge Begbie clearly approved of the decision.

Aleck returned to his quarters for dinner, and then retired to his room and wrote Maggie. He mentioned the trial, but his letter showed his preoccupation with personal matters and, of course, his indecision.

July 1, 1867

My little Maggie

Today I was engaged in the arduous and responsible labour of defending an unfortunate man accused of murder. My efforts however were unsuccessful. A strong chain of circumstantial evidence brought the guilt home to him, and he now lies in the little prison here awaiting sentence, which I presume will be passed tomorrow...

(Referring to her letter)...The most important thing you mention my M is the final inaction of your parents to our engagement. As yet I have received no communication from them on the subject, but I suppose it will come in due time. My own dear Mother writes to me herself that I have her "fond blessing" – upon anything that will make me happy in this world. This is so characteristic of my Mother.

Legal business is not so flourishing as in '66...I am sure there are more chances of attaining influence and position in Canada than here. Offices here such as would suit a lawyer are few in number, and are generally filled with men from England. The Colony in point of population is so ridiculously small, and so unlikely to improve in this respect for some time to come, that I am in doubt sometimes whether it is well to remain here where, from the nature of my surroundings, I am not improving as rapidly as I think I should in Canada. The best place for a young lawyer is at a good bar where there are many clever, sharp and eloquent men.

What think you of all this, my wife?...

The following morning Judge Begbie sentenced Barry to death. But the case was not over yet for Aleck. As he was leaving the courthouse following the sentencing, he received a note from the jailor saying that Barry was asking to see him. He found the man sitting slumped forward on his bed in his cell, a haggard expression on his face. Aleck sat opposite him on a tiny stool, notebook in hand, and waited. Barry finally looked up at him and started to speak in a low monotone.

"I am innocent, Sir. I have told you so before, and I say so again. Damn their eyes those buggers in the jury, they heard no real evidence. No Sir. No real evidence." His voice trailed off in a sigh, but not for long. With urging from Aleck he started to talk about his life and his friends, and the events surrounding the case. He gave Aleck facts and background information that could have had a bearing on the case had he revealed them sooner.

By the time Barry stopped talking, Aleck was extremely upset. He had known that he had not had time to prepare himself thoroughly for such an important case, and that his client had been short on facts in their interviews prior to the court session. This was a common circumstance in his work in the interior. But in this case the man's reticence to speak out sooner would probably cost him his life. After a further brief exchange of questions and answers, Aleck told him that he would do what he could to have the case reopened, but that Barry should not be optimistic.

Aleck returned to his office and wrote to the Governor, through the Colonial Secretary, asking for a retrial. The reply came back, remarkably quickly, that there was nothing that could be done for the unfortunate man.

Aleck's loneliness and uncertainty as he awaited a reply from Maggie's parents were nothing compared to the consternation that raged in Maggie. Aleck's proposal had led her to believe that their time had finally come. But now – this! Her normally decisive father, William the businessman, was faltering! He seemed to have come to an impasse within his own head, and could not put pen to paper and welcome Aleck's request.

Spring turned to summer, and Maggie took the month of July and some of August at Owen Sound. She hardly noticed the celebrations that occurred on July 1, 1867 when the Confederation of the provinces of Canada was declared. Upper Canada was now officially 'Ontario'. It was important, no doubt, but she had more important things on her mind. She prayed that William would reply to Aleck in her absence, but unfortunately he took her absence as a reprieve from the pressure of having to do so. Maggie felt a hint of panic, for she was certain that Aleck would come to Chatham that fall no matter what, and then they would do what had to be done. It would hurt the family terribly if William had not done his duty.

She told her mother about these feelings and uncertainties when she returned to Chatham in mid-August. Mary Bell promised Maggie that she would have a serious discussion with William in an attempt to get him to act. She engaged him in several discussions, spread out over several weeks. At the end of the first week of September Mary Bell finally lost patience. She could not stand the thought of Aleck arriving back in Chatham without the issue being settled, so she decided that it was time to push her husband into action.

Her weapon of choice was stony silence. She told him that the issue was absolutely clear, and he should sit down at his desk and write poor Aleck, who must be distracted with worry. She would resume conversation with him when he had done so.

This unhappy, ridiculous state of affairs lasted for five days, wherein the household waited in silence and trembling for the siege to end. It was William who finally capitulated. He went to her room one afternoon and, standing next to her at her desk, cleared his throat and said "Bell my darling, this cannot go on. I will not tolerate it...or rather, I cannot stand it. Aleck Robertson is a fine young man. I have found it very hard to accept the idea of losing our Maggie, so I have delayed replying. And I know...we must reply. But my dear, I am a poor correspondent. Will you write him, with my blessing?"

Mary Bell rose, put her arms around his neck and kissed him firmly on the lips, tears streaming down her face.

September 18, 1867

Dear Aleck

We received yours some time (ago) and should have answered it before, but I have been waiting for your Uncle to do so. I asked him to write to you, but he says he cannot write any more but for me to write myself, a task that I am neither good at, nor yet fond of, and tell you to do as you pleased, is that consent in law.

Now dear Aleck you know our only objection to your union is the tie that now exists between you and Maggie, but after years of faithful waiting on both sides you still think the same, we can offer no objections to your marriage, And when you take her I hope you may fully realize all your expectation.

I know that I shall feel her loss more than I can tell, as she has been for years almost my sole companion and confidant, but such is the way of Providence, and dear Aleck I feel that in giving my child to you that she will have a kind heart and a strong arm to guide her through life.

May you long live to be a blessing to each other, and may your journey through life be happy and prosperous. I shall not give you any news as Maggie is going to write tomorrow.

Now dear Aleck may God bless you both and spare you to meet again in the sincere wish of your loving Aunt.

Mary B. Eberts

She handed the sealed letter to Maggie to put in the mail. When she did so she smiled sadly at her daughter, but then winked as she turned away. Maggie wrote her own letter, reflecting upon Aleck's latest letter where he had seemed to side with the idea of staying in Canada to practice.

September 18, 1867

…I am more than delighted that you are not going back to BC. I may as well just make the confession here that my heart almost failed me when it seemed possible that I was going so far away from all I loved, though for your sake I would have tried to be brave…

(Mamma) wrote to you today. I sent it off immediately. I hope you'll let me see what she says when you come home, for she seemed much affected…

At the end of October Aleck finally received Mary Bell's letter and Maggie's letter. Her conviction that they would not be returning to BC surprised him, as he did not believe that he had expressed himself of that opinion with any degree of certainty. He did not feel that the matter was closed, and a letter he received on the same day from an old friend in Windsor, Albert Perrin, showed him that further thought on the matter was definitely called for.

September 20, 1867

Dear Robertson

Yours of 20th July reached me only two or three days ago and from it I was glad to hear that you were well and comparatively well to do. I say comparatively because you used to tell me that your business in Windsor was but small, and if it was small then I can assure you it would be almost imperceptible now; there is nothing whatever doing...in fine at no time since I have been in practice (19 years now) have I seen business so stagnant as now – there's my answer to all your business inquiries...

This sense of caution was echoed in the occasional letters that he was receiving each month from family members and other friends. In the middle of November, as he was preparing to leave for Canada, he received Maggie's final letter to Victoria, in which he saw that she was firmly committed to their remaining in Ontario. There would clearly be some important discussions in Chatham!

October 3, 1867

...I have spoken to Papa about Chatham as a place of business. He thinks by all means, your best chance is here. There is no one here capable of pleading. Even Atkinson employs

someone from a distance to plead in the higher courts...

Hermann thinks this the place for you. However, my darling, when you come home we'll settle all this. I have quite made up my mind that you are not going back to BC. You know you couldn't go unless I said you might!...

With an active practice that covered both Vancouver Island and the mainland, Aleck had to arrange his affairs so that all open files would be covered while he was away, and in a manner that they would be completed even if he and Maggie decided to remain and settle in Ontario. In this he was fortunate to have become friends with George Pearkes, a Victoria lawyer with whom he had worked on several cases. Pearkes was a superb lawyer, a Mason wonderfully connected into the establishment in BC, and he was pleased to help out.

On December 3 Aleck boarded the steamer for San Francisco, the start of his return to Maggie. He finally arrived in Chatham on February 4, 1868, delayed due to illness while he was stopping over in Owen Sound to visit his mother. He had been away for just under four years.

The next two weeks were hectic, with preparations for the wedding to be seen to and many friends to be greeted. It was a truly joyful time for the young couple, who even managed to meet briefly in their old place by the river for some merry laughter and a frozen kiss.

16

THE WEDDING

Tuesday, March 3 dawned cold and blustery, with light snow falling – a perfect day for a Canadian wedding.

Mamma and Maggie's sister Anne had offered to help her dress, but Maggie had begged them to let her be alone in this most private of moments. Her old, familiar room seemed now like a sanctuary, hiding her from the real world that awaited her. After bathing in the warm water brought in by their ageless Negro maid Miss Nanny, she put on her bathrobe and sat for a while at her writing desk. What a happy, sad, lonely, hopeful, dull and yet passionate place it was! This one small space, desk and chair, had been the core of her emotional world for what seemed like an eternity, and she blessed it and thanked it.

She removed her bathrobe and glanced briefly at her naked figure in the full length mirror beside her dresser. She had certainly put on some weight and gained some curves since she had last seen Aleck, but as she had told him in her letter not long ago, it had improved her looks. She was no longer a skinny little girl; she was definitely a woman, rounded and sleek. She knew by intuition, and by the delight he had already shown in her looks, that Aleck would be pleased when he finally saw her as God had made her. Oh my! She blushed and reached for her lovely new silk undergarments.

With lipstick, powder, slip and stockings on, she drew her wedding dress over her head and settled it in place. It was so lovely! The capped veil was not long, but adequate and really very pretty, and with her pointed white shoes and pink and red roses she would be a fine bride indeed.

She opened the bedroom door, and called to Mary Bell and her sister Anne to come in from the hall. They stopped their quiet conversation, turned to her, smiled admiringly and in unison exclaimed "oh Maggie". They each took a hand and walked her around the room, admiring her with their looks and comments. Maggie drank in their admiration like a thirsty child, rejoicing in the joy that every kind word brought to her. They helped her with her shoes, and then Mary Bell placed her cap and veil on her head in a quiet, motherly ceremony that she followed up with a tearful kiss. Anne kissed her other cheek, and then they opened the door and Maggie walked out of her old room and into her new life.

For Aleck, dressing for his wedding was less emotional and dramatic. Somewhat the worse for wear after the previous evening's 'socializing' with family members and several old friends, he swore off port wine forever as he washed in the warm water brought to his room at Hermann and Sarah's new home. He donned his best suit, starched shirt and collar and tie, fine new wool stockings and polished shoes. After brushing his hair and beard, he left the room and came downstairs to greet his ushers who, according to them, were there to ensure that he went to the church and didn't duck out at the last moment. His brother James and Maggie's brothers Hermann and Melchior escorted him firmly down the stairs, into his overcoat and out into the waiting sleigh.

St. Paul's Anglican Church was filled with crisp winter light glowing through tinted glass, and the dazzling colors of flower bouquets. Maggie and Mary Bell had invited a carefully selected list of 65 guests to the wedding, but at least 120 smiling faces greeted Aleck as he came out of the side door accompanied by his ushers, and took his stand in front of Reverend Sandys. He recognized many of them, but many others were strangers to him. He turned and stared for a second at James, who grinned and winked at him.

Hermann had warned Aleck that there would likely be quite a few uninvited but interested spectators at the church, but this was truly amazing. The many reports in the newspaper concerning his homecoming, welcome parties and plans for the wedding had done their magic. The issue of their being cousins had been discussed discretely, accepted and put to rest. If the church accepted their union, then there could be no disputing it. Aleck and Maggie now enjoyed a certain celebrity status, and people were not going to miss this event, invited or not!

Aleck smiled at the sea of faces, and received 120 smiles in return, and a few waves as well. Then, right on time, Mary Bell entered the church accompanied by Melchior, and took her place in the front row. The organ piped up, they rose en masse, and down the aisle came the bridesmaids, stepping carefully in their shiny blue brocade dresses, with flowers held before them like shields. First came Aleck's younger sister Elizabeth Robertson. Frail and clearly delicate of constitution, Lizzie was a favorite of both Aleck and Maggie. Then came Maggie's sister Anne, lively and smiling widely, almost prancing, like a second Maggie. Finally came Maggie's dearest and closest friend Katie Woods – tall, blonde, lovely and confident. They settled into place and then, after a breathless pause, Maggie appeared at the front entrance on the arm of her father William Eberts.

Every person in the church turned to look at them, and they returned cautious smiles as they started down the aisle. Aleck feasted on Maggie's shining face. He was transfixed. She found his eyes, and as they approached the minister she held them, relying on William to steer. She held them as Aleck stepped forth to join her in front of Dr. Sandys, and they finally turned away only when the minister cleared his throat, calling their attention.

From then on the service floated on a wave of images and sounds, chanted prayers and hymns, responses and lessons. Maggie was strong as a rock. Her spirits were soaring. This was her day, finally! Finally! Her Aleck was there beside her, so handsome and wonderful, and the whole world was witnessing their love and devotion to one another. She spoke her responses firmly and distinctly.

Aleck was a different story. He, the lion of the criminal courts of the Cariboo, who could lecture judges and cajole juries with charm and tact and firmness, who spoke to large crowds on the benefits of freedom and many other subjects, found to his horror that he was like a lovesick swain, nervous and blushing, with damp palms and a throat that demanded that he swallow just when he should be speaking out boldly. His responses were forced and quavering, and it was only the loving look in Maggie's eyes and the strong pressure of her hand holding his that pulled him through. He didn't know why. He felt no sense whatsoever of hesitation in this marriage, and the setting was totally friendly and supportive. He didn't even try to figure it out.

Then it was over, and they were walking joyously up the aisle, smiling at friends who called to them, some reaching out to press their hands or just touch their shoulders. Of course, nobody had noticed Aleck's problems at the altar, and he quickly forgot them as their friends crowded around outside the church to shake hands and kiss them and hand them into their sleigh. They bundled in with William and Mary Bell, and dashed off to the reception in a jingle of sleigh bells.

Riverside was beautifully decorated for the reception, with flowers and ribbons and evergreen boughs on every side. The punch bowl and wine, with a sea of glasses, awaited the guests on the side table in the drawing room, presided over by Jason Brewster, William's favorite waiter from the Shades Saloon. He sported an enormous moustache, and knew his instructions well: full glasses of wine for the gentlemen; punch as a rule for the ladies and always for the children; white wine for ladies who asked for it; and white wine in the punch for ladies who winked for it.

Miss Nanny was standing proudly at the front door as the wedding party arrived and a hired servant took their coats. She gave Maggie a hug and kiss of such magnitude that Aleck almost felt that he should leap to his bride's defense. "Maggie darling, you are the loveliest bride in the world. Bless your soul!" she cried, and then, turning to Aleck, gave him his own bear hug, which he returned with gusto and a hoot of laughter and joy.

For the happy couple it was a dream – a reverie in which they floated from one smiling friend or relative to another, accepting their congratulations and talking and laughing and carrying on with increasing volume as Jason Brewster plied his trade. Miss Nanny saw that the dining room table was kept well stocked, and soon the guests were tucking in with gusto. Aleck and Maggie had no time to eat, but they did enjoy their wine, which added nicely to their reveries. Every once in a while they would pass each other in the press of bodies. They would stop and kiss, to the delight of those nearby, and then move on to the next welcoming faces.

At precisely 1:30 pm William called for order, and the party settled down for the speeches. He welcomed the guests on this happy occasion, and then called for Aleck's brother James to propose the toast to the bride. Hermann Eberts then called for a toast to the groom, and finally William himself, concerned about the time, toasted the bridesmaids who were, in his estimation, as lovely a set of women as could ever be imagined with the exception, of course, of his wife Mary Bell. She blushed, everyone laughed and toasted, and then William asked Aleck if he had anything to say.

"I do Sir, and thank you for asking. (pause, laughter) I am as you know a man of few words (guffaws and loud laughter), but there is much to be said on this happy day. I am, without a doubt, the happiest man in the world today – in Canada, in the whole British Empire. As Hermann said so politely, Maggie has today married the love of her life, and I am glad to hear it, because I have done the same thing! Perhaps we should compare notes! (huge laughter) No, it won't be necessary. We are together and married at last, and have a fine life to look forward to. We shall see what we can do about grandchildren, Sir (glancing at William), but I shall give you no legal guarantees! (laughter)

"To you Sir, and to Mrs. Eberts, I say thank you for your welcome, your support, your love and your understanding. You have taken care of my

Maggie through these long years of our separation. We have relied upon you, and you have done your duty with such care and love that we are both unscathed by our ordeal. Thank you. From us both…thank you."

Aleck stumbled to a halt, his eyes tearing up, and after a very brief pause the guests burst out in loud applause. The party carried on while Maggie escaped upstairs and changed into her travel suit. The only one in her room to assist her was Miss Nanny, who was undecided whether to laugh or cry, so did both in great volume throughout the process. Maggie came down the stairs to a sea of smiling faces, and tossed her bouquet straight at Katie Woods, who caught it easily. Then the happy couple was led through a throng of kissing, backslapping well-wishers to their sleigh, which was packed with their luggage.

At 3:30 pm precisely they were bundled aboard the Great Western train to Detroit. They settled into their first class compartment (courtesy of Eberts & Eberts), and at 3:41 pm the honeymoon train left the station.

17

KALAMAZOO

The honeymoon plan was to spend four nights at the Tremont House Hotel in Detroit to see friends and relatives, and then continue on the same railway line to the pleasant town of Kalamazoo, near Lake Michigan, for their real honeymoon.

They held hands and chatted happily about the wedding until they arrived in Detroit, where a small delegation of relatives and friends met them at the station. There were great hugs and kisses all around, and then they were bundled into a carriage and sent on their way to the hotel. The relatives had done some planning at the hotel, so that when the carriage pulled up in front it was greeted with quite extraordinary ceremony. The doorman handed them down and into the warm lobby, while porters spirited their luggage away. Inside the door the manager greeted them with great aplomb, and an assistant handed Maggie a bouquet of flowers.

The manager's "A warm welcome to the Tremont House Hotel Mr. and Mrs. Robertson" thrilled Maggie. "Mrs. Robertson" – oh my, yes. Aleck signed a registration form presented to him on a silver tray, and then the manager escorted them to the bridal suite. Beside the glowing fireplace were an iced bottle of champagne and a collation of hot and cold foods, all nicely set out with the best silverware and candles. Within minutes the manager was on his way out the door, promising them all possible assistance should they need anything.

They stood looking at each other, and around the room. It was all so wonderful, and after all those years – so sudden! Here they were – alone together – it was true! They removed their coats and moved together for a long, soft kiss. Then Maggie, being romantic but also practical, said "my darling, I am famished. Why don't we warm ourselves by the fire and try some of these delicious looking dishes." And so the first hour at their honeymoon hotel was spent sitting before the fire, sipping champagne and devouring the food. They laughed and chatted gaily about their friends and relatives in Chatham and Detroit, and how nice they all were, and what a splendid plan they had made for this evening. They discussed the snowy weather and the state of the roads in Detroit.

But there was no question where the evening was heading. The huge bed, nicely turned down and bathed in candlelight, stood invitingly nearby, calling to them. As their conversation sputtered with occasional silences, it was clearly time to move on. It was also clear to Maggie that her beloved man was unsure how to take the next step. Well, she knew what to do. She told Aleck to relax by the fire while she "settled in". She rose and disappeared behind the screen that gave privacy to the washstand and the exit to the privy. Aleck sat quietly, gazing into the fire and nervously sipping his champagne.

Before long he felt a presence beside his chair. He turned to see Maggie standing there in a lovely fawn-colored negligee, a soft smile on her face. The negligee was tied at the neck, sheer and light, giving him a tantalizing look at her body. Before he could stand up she came to him and stood before him, taking his hands in hers so that he could gaze at her. He had fondled her breasts in the past, but had never really seen them, or the rest of her body. He reached for her and pulled her to him, still sitting so that his face was buried in her bosom.

"Oh Aleck, my darling Aleck" she whispered as he held her firmly, drinking in her scent and the luxury of her body. Then he stood up and folded her in his arms and kissed her soundly on the mouth. The move to the bed was swift.

The next three days in Detroit swept by on a tide of friends and relatives, lunches and teas, and brief walks through the chilly streets. Through it all their room at the hotel was their home, their secret place, their love nest. The manager had, true to his word, made certain that they always had a warm fire in the grate and refreshments on the side table. They found it all but impossible to keep their hands off each other in the room, and also outside it. When in the room they were either in bed, or sitting hand-in-hand beside the fire planning to go to bed, or recovering from recent exertions in bed. When away from the room they were always touching, arm in arm, hand in hand, or just standing close to each other while talking with friends.

On the fourth morning a delegation of relatives took them to the railway station and sent them on their way to Kalamazoo. They had selected Kalamazoo as their honeymoon spot because it was rumored to be a pleasant town, and was also at the end of the railway, so usefully far away from Chatham. They had reservations at the Burdick House Hotel, just two blocks from the station, and the hotel had sent its carriage to meet them at the station. At the Burdick House there was a fire in the hearth and a bottle of champagne to sip, but they had to go to the dining room for their dinner. This they did after enjoying the champagne in front of the fire, and then each other in the bed after the champagne.

The ten days in Kalamazoo floated by on a wave of dreams, love and enjoyment. Their hunger for each other continued from Detroit in the most passionate way, growing from exploration and deep desire to obsession until finally, in the last few days, they settled into a more manageable level of attraction and lust. All those years of separation, with their hundreds of letters and endless periods of loneliness and longing, were demanding retribution through fulfillment.

Two days before the end of their honeymoon they finally had the conversation that they both had been dreading. The subject of where they were to settle down had arisen back in Chatham before the wedding, and he had visited McLean and other lawyers and some officials to see what the prospects might be for him in that town. The subject had been left open, and somehow they had managed to avoid it during their honeymoon trip until then. But they both knew that it had to come, and the occasion presented itself naturally. They were sipping tea in front of their fire late in the afternoon, talking about the weather that was blowing cold and snowy outside their window. Aleck said that Victoria had very little of this sort of weather, and from there the conversation moved naturally into that most important of subjects.

Maggie put the question directly to him, asking him where his thoughts were with respect to their residence in the coming years. Aleck assumed his lawyer face, thinking carefully and organizing his thoughts before replying. "My darling, we have spoken so much on this subject through our letters, and I admit that I have been woefully indecisive. The trouble is, there is much to be indecisive about. I know how much you would like to stay in Chatham, or at least in Ontario, but we simply must consider where we can best settle from a financial point of view. The options are somewhere in Ontario – Chatham, Toronto, Ottawa or even Windsor – in British Columbia, or even in San Francisco. I don't see Frisco as a real alternative however, as I know that we would both prefer to remain in the Dominions.

"It's unfortunate that the economies of Ontario and British Columbia are both in recession at the moment. If one were significantly better than the other, it would make the choice much easier. What I have seen so far in Ontario is not promising. There's virtually no real business in the smaller places like Chatham and Windsor, and in Toronto and Ottawa things are not much better, and the profession is full of very competent people, so is fiercely competitive. A young newcomer such as me, no matter how good, would have to fight hard for a place in the market, and it could take years. I would also have to become involved in politics to build my clientele.

"In BC, I'm already well placed in the market. I'm sought after by the courts, and also have a good list of private clients who rely upon me for their legal advice. I'm even well-connected politically. BC is of course still very small, so you do tend to meet a good proportion of the important people if you keep your head up. I've done so, and am on a friendly basis with many of the top politicians and officials, not to mention the business people. I have in fact been encouraged by several of them to become involved directly in politics, and my speeches seem to be well received. All in all, Maggie, if I had to make a decision today, I would say that we should move out to BC."

They sat in silence for several minutes, gazing into the fire. He awaited her response, and when it came it was not unexpected.

"Yes darling, I know. I have watched your views shift one way and then the other, and this is where they rest. And you know, you haven't even mentioned another aspect of life out there that I think you enjoy, namely the adventure. I know you love being in the wilderness, riding and fishing and the like. You are a fine lawyer, but you are also an adventurer at heart, and I believe that BC offers you an opportunity to combine the two into one very satisfying life. You can of course have your adventure in Ontario, but in BC it seems to be combined directly with your work. But then, what about me? What about our children? Can we have a good life out there, or will we always be a source of concern to you?"

"Of course that is a worry for me, that and the fact that we would be so far away from family and friends in Chatham and elsewhere in Ontario. What are my views on these questions? Well, I do find Victoria very livable now. There are enough educated people there to give us a prospect of a pleasant circle of friends. The school system is inadequate, but is developing. There are fine churches and some reasonable restaurants. And the scenery and climate are a real benefit. Victoria is very pretty and nicely situated with parks and beaches and streams. We could have a lovely garden. I truly believe that we could have a good life there.

"As to the matter of being far from friends and relatives, I have no real answer. The one consolation would be that travel to and from BC will be greatly facilitated by the completion of the railway across the United States, which should happen quite soon now. And eventually, of course, we should have a railway from BC to Ontario. So at least we'll be able to visit back and forth frequently, and at reasonable cost."

There was silence again until Maggie spoke up, her eyes brimming with tears. "So that's it, then?"

Aleck could not leave it there, so coldly. He rose from his chair to kneel in front of her. "Not quite darling. I may well be painting far too bleak a picture of my prospects here in Ontario. After our return to Chatham I will continue my inquiries. You never know. Something may come up. Let's wait and see before making a final decision. But if we do find that we must go to BC, I shall make it my highest priority to give you a happy life there."

PART 2
1868-1880

Triumph

18

BACK TO WORK

The happy couple spent several months in Ontario following their honeymoon, visiting family and friends in Chatham and Owen Sound. Aleck's investigations into prospects in Canada proved fruitless, so they lingered for as long as they could, knowing that once they set out for BC they would not be back for a long time. Finally, in August, they endured a tearful farewell at the Chatham railway station, and then left on their trip to BC along the same route travelled by Aleck over four years previously.

Except for a total of three days of mild seasickness, Maggie enjoyed the trip immensely – far more than she had expected. She had been sure that she would be missing her family terribly, and would spend the whole trip dealing with homesickness. As it turned out she had a roaring good time with her man, in-cabin and out.

And then there was the matter of her wonderful secret. On her last visit to her Chatham physician he had confirmed that she was pregnant. She was not yet showing enough to rouse suspicions, and had decided not to tell anyone until the time was right, whatever that meant. With Aleck it meant a glorious afternoon on the Pacific Ocean as they sat sipping tea on the deck of the *Constitution*. He had been talking about the conditions in San Francisco, and how he looked forward to showing her the city. For some reason, out of the blue, that seemed like the right time.

"If I may change the subject, my darling, I have some rather special news for you." He turned to her and waited, eyebrows raised. "It's…well…Aleck, I'm pregnant! We shall have our first child in Victoria this winter!" She looked steadily into his eyes, he into hers. He was struck dumb – he simply stared. Then a smile started creeping across his face, came to full glory, and exploded into tears of joy. He leapt up and knelt before her, pulled her to him and hugged her. He was ecstatic. He gabbled his joy, paced around the deck waving his arms and whistling, and then came back, sat beside her and took her hand.

His speech was still almost incoherent, but what she gathered from it was that this was a total surprise to him, but it was wonderful news and he was very, very happy. With her delicate condition it was vital that they be very careful about things. She had become for him someone who must be coddled and cosseted.

"Aleck, I am not a delicate little flower. I am a strong woman and I feel wonderful. I will tell you when I should slow down. Until then, consider me unchanged except for a slowly expanding waistline and a glorious happiness in my soul."

They arrived in Victoria harbour on a beautiful sunny day in early September. Maggie had seen pictures of Victoria, so she was not put off by the dowdy nature of the town itself. Rather, she reveled in the glorious natural setting – the ocean, mountains, forests and beaches vying for her hungry eyes. She smiled up at Aleck as he hugged her to his side, standing with her at the rail and scanning the assembled crowd. He had sent a telegram from San Francisco to Dr. Powell saying when they would be arriving, and taking him up on his kind offer to put them up until they could find suitable accommodation.

There they were – Israel Powell and his wife Jenny holding their year-old daughter on her hip. They waved and smiled, and this warm welcome raised Maggie's spirits even more. They greeted her formally when she and

Aleck came down the gangplank. "Welcome to Victoria Mrs. Robertson", and handed her a bouquet of flowers. For Aleck there was a strong handshake from the Doctor and a kiss from Jenny. They chatted happily while they moved past the customs tables, and while the luggage was being loaded into the carriage. Then they were on their way to the Powells' comfortable residence at the corner of Douglas and Broughton streets. By 5 pm they were enjoying tea in the Powells' garden. The roses and the lawns were well cared for, and the birds and bees played in the sunlight. With one of Jenny's broad-brimmed hats protecting her from the warm sun, Maggie was thoroughly entranced, and felt right at home.

Two days later the morning newspaper reported that the town of Barkerville in the Cariboo had burned to the ground. Aleck was shocked by this turn of events in one of his prime areas of business, but his only substantive comment was "knowing those people, they'll have the whole place rebuilt by next spring."

In spite of his best intentions, Aleck could not spend much time showing Maggie around Victoria. As soon as he arrived, Pearkes brought him into several cases at his office. His call on the Attorney General H.P.P. Crease resulted in an immediate invitation to go to Yale as acting prosecutor at the assizes to be held there the second week of October. The pay would be $100 per case, which was certainly acceptable. This work, together with renewing acquaintances around Victoria in the business and political circles and at the Masonic Lodge, kept him on the go through very full days.

Jenny Powell took it upon herself to welcome Maggie to Victoria, and to help the couple to find lodgings. She showed Maggie around the town, introducing her to the shops and the hotels, and the best places for tea. She had several functions at her home to present Maggie to her woman friends, and accompanied Maggie on return calls.

With the assistance and advice of the property agent Mr. Pratt, they went around the town looking at houses for sale. Victoria had been nicely laid out on a grid, starting at the harbour with Wharf and Store Streets, then Government, the main shopping street, and then another eight blocks. Pandora Avenue was the main street on the other axis, heading away from the harbour. On one side, heading north, the roads rolled out through the countryside towards the Saanich peninsula. On the other side, past James Bay over the Government Street Bridge, was the James Bay area, the government buildings known as the 'Bird Cages', and the Beacon Hill Public Park with its race course. Esquimalt district was on the tongue of land that jutted into the heart of Victoria Harbour, turning it into a long, well-protected waterway.

The grid was well planned, but by no means filled with buildings at that time. Beyond Blanshard Street the houses started to thin out, leaving many vacant properties, and two blocks beyond that the town was a checker board of roads going through fields, with only occasional houses showing, many on very large lots. Property values had sky-rocketed during the gold rush, but they had declined sharply in the following recession, and Mr. Pratt was able to show Maggie a number of suitable places with reasonable prices.

While Maggie was house-hunting, Aleck was preparing for the assizes at Yale, and developing three promising cases in Victoria. After the depressing stories he had heard in Ontario, it was a relief to find himself immersed in very substantial legal work back here in British Columbia. The gold rush might be less vibrant, but other industry was starting to develop, along with the real estate and infrastructure developments that accompanied it. The word went around quickly that Aleck Robertson was back in town – the man who could get you out of trouble or even, better still, keep you out of it.

Powell filled him in on the political issues of the day. The capital had moved from New Westminster to Victoria, so that issue was settled, but not without considerable bitterness on the mainland. The big issue now was Confederation – to join or not to join Canada.

Powell said that Amor de Cosmos, in his determination to have British Columbia join Canada, had formed a 'Confederation League' back in May after the Legislative Council of British Columbia had refused to vote in favour of prompt union with Canada. He and other influential members such as John Robson and the businessman Robert Beaven gave it considerable driving force. It was almost a political party, albeit with a single agenda. It had staged events all summer designed to involve the public in the concept of Confederation. At the present time the League was having a conference at Yale, where they would undoubtedly bring in resolutions in support of Confederation, and also responsible government as well. In other words, they supported having BC part of the Dominion of Canada, but with its own Legislature to run most of its own affairs.

"But as you well know, Robertson, the sentiment in favor of Confederation is by no means unanimous. It's very strong on the mainland, where they would like to have some way to balance the power of Victoria. John Robson has, of course, made a few mild comments on the subject."

They both laughed. "But here on the Island there is still much opposition. Most of the appointed officials are naturally against it, as they would lose their authority to a higher level of bureaucracy here in North America. Poor chaps! Joseph Trutch is a good example. Here he is, a powerful man as Chief Commissioner of Lands and Works and a member of the Legislative Council, but what would happen to him with Confederation? Would there even be a Chief Commissioner? Would there be an Executive Council? I can assure you that he, and others like him, will oppose Confederation until it is clear that their personal interests are taken into account."

Aleck had to agree. "Of course they will. It's only human. And when you think of it, the arguments against Confederation do make some sense. We are, after all, a very long way away from Canada, with no direct means of communication except the stagecoach. The railway across to the Pacific in the United States will be completed next year and that will help, but that also helps those in favor of our annexation to that country. With the Alaska territory now in American hands, I'm sure Washington would be delighted to add BC to its portfolio, so that it would own the entire Pacific coast. And there are certainly a lot of people here who would prefer to live in the United States rather than in a British colony, or even an isolated part of the Dominion of Canada. Indeed, many would be happy if we were to simply go our own way, independent of any higher power."

"Robertson" Powell interjected, "I think you are about to deliver another of your long speeches about the need for a railway across Canada. Am I correct?"

"Absolutely" replied Aleck, laughing in spite of himself. "How can we confederate, if that is a word, with a country with which we have no real direct communication? As some people are saying, why not join up with Australia – just a voyage away!"

"Alright, alright" said Powell holding up his hand, impatient as always to gain new ground rather than rehash old arguments. "What can we ourselves do about it?"

Aleck thought for a moment. "You mean in addition to making supportive speeches whenever possible, of course. Well, there must be political action to move things forward. We have the elections for the Legislative Council coming up in November. Let's see if de Cosmos can make any more headway there. And how about you, Doctor. Do you plan to run again? It would certainly be good to have you there to support Confederation."

"Yes, I do plan to run. We shall see. In the meantime we must support de Cosmos in any way that we can, so dust off your speaking notes and start attacking the lecterns!"

It was hard for Aleck to leave Victoria so soon after arriving back, but the Yale assizes were important to him. For Maggie, too, it was a hardship. She was comfortable at the Powells' place, but Aleck was her key to the city, and now here he was heading off again on another adventure, albeit a business one. He would also be going to the assizes in New Westminster in November. Was this, then, to be life here in Victoria? Would she be on her own so often, awaiting his return and then preparing for his next departure?

It was too early to tell, so she faced up to it bravely, and on October 9 Aleck was back on the familiar steamer headed for New Westminster. The next day they left there late in the day, in the midst of a heavy fog, and arrived at Yale on October 11.

The assizes went efficiently and well. Aleck did not feel totally comfortable being on the prosecution side of the cases, but he certainly understood the role, and played it well. He arrived back in Victoria on October 21 after a brief visit to New Westminster to call on his friends and colleagues there. He was greeted at the dock in Victoria by his wife sitting happily in Powell's carriage, glowing with health and looking delightfully pregnant.

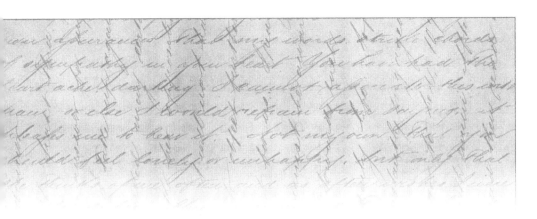

19

THE HOUSE

With the help of Mr. Pratt, Maggie soon found the house that would suit them perfectly. It was a square, quite simple one-storey house well away from the downtown area, at the corner of Vancouver and Johnson streets. The place had a quiet elegance, with a verandah and a picket fence across the front. It was effectively in the countryside, which would appeal to Aleck, with a few neighbors and a lot of fields and copses and woods in view, but still within reasonable walking distance of downtown. It was five years old and in excellent condition.

The house faced Johnson Street, but the property ran farther along Vancouver Street, covering just over two acres. It had three bedrooms, a parlour and small library, dining room and kitchen, and a washroom. It was surrounded by a promising garden with an orchard behind it, and the lot ended with a barn which served as the stable. Beside the house were the privy and a substantial work shed, with a wash stand and tubs attached. It was a very nice package, and they instructed Mr. Pratt to take whatever steps were required to secure it.

With Aleck off at New Westminster to assist at the annual assizes, Maggie was left alone to complete the transaction for the house, and to start the process of furnishing it. This she did with the help of Pratt, and with Pearkes acting for them in Aleck's absence. Sitting with Pearkes in his office, Maggie thought how appropriate this was. They were making by far the largest purchase of their lives, and where was Aleck? Why, far away, of course!

As they sat back following perusal of the documents, Pearkes made a passing reference to Aleck not being there, and what a shame it was that he was missing a transaction of such importance to them. It was a casual comment, but Maggie took it seriously.

"You are right Mr. Pearkes. It is indeed a shame that he could not be here when we are in the process of spending all of our money! But as you know, we have had a lot of time apart, writing endless letters to each other. So this is not unexpected." This last was said with a smile, but now Pearkes picked up the subject.

"I am sure it is not, and I do admire the way you have handled this affair so efficiently. If I may say so, this sort of thing is likely to happen frequently to you here in Victoria. Your husband has become rather well known during his time here – well known here in Victoria, but also elsewhere around the colony. He is Judge Begbie's favorite at his assizes on the mainland, and they take place not just in New Westminster but Yale, of course, and also in the interior. Aleck Robertson is the lion of Richfield, a favorite in Barkerville and admired in Quesnellemouth and Kamloops. Here on the Island he is recognized for his work in Nanaimo as well as Victoria. I must admit I am proud to have him as a colleague and friend.

"The point I am trying to make, rather slowly I'm afraid, is that BC is not like Toronto, where a competent lawyer can make his income by sitting in his office and having the big clients come to him. In this colony the business is spread out, and the clients want to see their lawyer on their home turf if at all possible. The judges know this and insist on holding their courts all over the colony. So if you wish to appear before them, you must be prepared to travel to them. This, as I am sure you know, is the hallmark of Begbie's success. He takes justice to the people wherever they need it, and he likes and supports lawyers who do the same."

Maggie nodded in appreciation of this candid remark. "Thank you, Mr. Pearkes for this realistic assessment of our situation."

"You are most welcome Madame" said Pearkes. "And of course, I say this because your husband is really quite brilliant, and is at the top of the profession in the colony – quite unusual for such a young man. I should add that in my view the political arena will inevitably insert itself into his career at some point. It already has informally, but I know from private discussions that some of our major figures are looking to him for direct involvement in the affairs of the colony as it develops."

"Now there, Mr. Pearkes, is a point to be discussed at greater length, but not today. I know that he speaks well and has firm ideas about the direction of our government, but whether or not that will translate into the cut and thrust of political life is a very open question."

"Oh certainly, Mrs. Robertson" said Pearkes, rising from his desk. "Now then, shall we take tea, and then complete these documents?"

With or without her husband, Maggie enjoyed the process of taking on their new home. The previous owners had left the house in good order, such that it needed no repairs or painting. She engaged a cleaning lady named Mrs. Hilda Brett, wife of a farmer from the Cadboro Bay area, and on the first day of occupancy they went to work. Maggie was now quite large with child, so had to be careful to minimize the bending and fatigue, but she directed the campaign like a sergeant-major, and helped wherever she could.

At noon Jenny Powell came to take her home for lunch. Maggie appreciated this prearranged kindness, for she was fatigued from the morning's activities. After lunch and a brief nap, Jenny took her back to the house, and Maggie took her new friend on a stroll around the property. "Oh Maggie, what a delightful place you have" exclaimed Jenny after they had completed their tour, and were standing on the verandah watching a carriage clop by on Vancouver Street. "It's so bright and refreshing out here away from the town, and yet you're close enough that Aleck could easily walk to his office if he wished."

"Which he will, I can assure you," replied Maggie. "As long as there's time, of course. But we will have to have a carriage, for I don't plan to stay at home all day, and I do not like having mud on my skirts!"

"Oh yes of course, my dear. A carriage and a driver I would say. You can see how useful our Dodson is for us. He drives, keeps the horses, tends the dogs and cleans and sweeps all around the house. He's learning a bit about gardening too. We really couldn't do without him."

"Well then, my dear Jenny, perhaps you would let us have Dodson, and you can find someone to replace him?" Maggie grinned.

Jenny burst out laughing. "Good heavens Maggie, what a thought! Oh no, I'm afraid not. But you should have no trouble finding someone good. You might start by asking Mrs. Brett for ideas. I understand that she has a large family, and I'm sure she'll have a well-trained, hardworking son who would like to take on the job."

Sure enough, Mrs. Brett did just happen to have a nineteen year-old son who could do gardening and outdoor work very well, and was good with horses, and would be delighted to meet Mrs. Robertson at her convenience.

James Brett was a tall, gangly youth, shy in manner but intelligent and polite. His mother had trained him well, as the income that came from work outside the farm was a valuable supplement to the fluctuating fortunes of the Brett farm. Thanks to his work on the farm, James was surprisingly strong, and clearly knowledgeable about gardens, and stables and horses. He loved to drive carriages, and assured Maggie that he had proper dress for when he did so. Maggie liked him, and engaged him on a part time basis.

By the time Aleck arrived back from the New Westminster assizes in the first week of November, Maggie had the house cleaned inside and out, and had scouted out the few furniture stores in the town. They had some prom-ising pieces on offer, but their main trade was in smaller items – lamps, small tables, tableware and so on. It was therefore a great stroke of luck that the day before his return she saw in the newspaper a notice of an estate sale to take place three days hence.

Thus two days after his arrival back from New Westminster, flushed with his recent success at the assizes, with a desk piled high with active cases to work on and two speaking engagements planned, Aleck found himself seated next to Maggie in a small crowd in the parlour of an elegant house in Douglas Street, bidding for furniture, lamps and household goods. Jenny was there with them, and there were several other familiar faces in the room.

The results were gratifying. Two days hence Aleck went to the offices of the auctioneers and had a pleasant word with one of the owners, the former Mayor of Victoria, Lumley Franklin. He was an important figure in the Masons, and Aleck knew him well through that connection. Aleck settled his account, and they arranged for delivery the following day.

Unfortunately, the following day found Aleck totally committed to a case that involved lengthy meetings at a bank office, and then the afternoon in court. So it was Maggie who was at the house to greet the auctioneers' wagons, thoroughly displeased that the weather had taken a turn for the worse, and a chilly drizzle made standing outside uncomfortable. She was the head of a substantial team of people, all either hired to help out, or simply determined to do so. The volunteers were Jenny Powell, Mary Finlayson and Cecelia Powers. Mary Finlayson was one of the 11 children of Roderick Finlayson, one of Victoria's most eminent citizens, and his wife Sarah. Finlayson was Chief Factor of the Hudson's Bay Company in BC, an important investor, and active in community affairs. Maggie had met two of his daughters at one of Jenny's teas, and had immediately struck up a friendship with the lively and witty Mary.

Cecelia Powers had no such high level connections, but was a friendly neighbor who lived nearby along Vancouver Street. Her husband worked at one of the hotels, and she supplemented their income by taking in the occasional boarder, and providing various household services. A very direct, practical woman, Mrs. Powers had appeared at the front door, introduced herself, and offered to help in any way she could. Maggie found it all quite charming, a far cry from the more formal situation in Chatham, where such casual self-introductions would be rare, and even frowned upon. The hired help were the Bretts: Mrs. Brett armed with cleaning things to fix up after "those damned (pardon me Ma'am) messy delivery buggers (pardon me Ma'am) who never seem to mind if they spread filth all over your floors", and her son James there to help with the heavy lifting and placing, and the 'outside things'.

The two auctioneers' wagons arrived at the front door at 10 am sharp. The work went quickly, if somewhat messily due to the rain. The black walnut motif that Aleck had admired so much at the auction was evident in all of the main rooms, including the master bedroom. Mrs. Brett seemed to be everywhere at once, working her wonders. Mrs. Powers, ever the practical one, disappeared at noon and returned an hour later with a large bowl of steaming hot vegetable soup and a big loaf of bread. Maggie and her volunteers sat down happily in the still chaotic parlour and had their lunch.

Then it was back to work, and by 5 pm, when they once again sagged into chairs in the parlour, this time to enjoy Mrs. Powers' tea and biscuits, the house was in good order. Maggie stretched in her chair and looked around the room at her friends. "My dears" she croaked, "you are wonderful. What a day we have had! And oh, what a fine house it is! I am so happy, and I owe you all a debt of gratitude. Mrs. Powers, you have saved us from starvation and exhaustion. I am exceedingly grateful to you. Mary, Jenny, my thanks to you for your very hard work. You have made me feel so welcome in Victoria. I cannot tell you how happy you have made me!"

They smiled and uttered their best wishes, and then Maggie put an end to the day. "Jenny, if you don't take me home immediately and put me into a hot bath, I shall expire!"

The furniture was, of course, only the start of it. The Robertsons had arrived in Victoria with their cases of clothes and one of books, but nothing else for their house. They had to buy everything – all of the decorations and curtains and knick-knacks that make a house a home, and then there was the important question of the kitchen and its supplies. With the ongoing help of her volunteers it all came together, and by the second week of December the house was ready for the Robertsons to move in except for two important details. They needed a cook, and they needed some sort of conveyance to take them around town.

The cook question was easily dealt with. Jenny had a word with her own cook, the Chinaman known as 'He', and two days later a Chinaman describing himself as 'Chin' appeared at the house in Johnson Street for his interview, accompanied by his wife and one son. He presented Maggie with a letter of commendation from a previous employer, who had left Victoria in July, and Maggie spoke with him briefly, struggling to understand his Pidgin English. She liked him, and told him that she would be in touch when they were moved in and ready for his services.

The conveyance issue was a bit more complicated, as their budget could not yet be extended to cover a horse and buggy. Aleck could walk to his office, or to where he could hail a taxi if he had a more distant destination, but this was not suitable for Maggie. For her it was a question of communication – ways that she could call for a conveyance when required. There was a taxi stand 20 minutes away by foot for Maggie, or eight minutes away for Brett if he was there. She could also call on the help of Mrs. Powers, who had a small but serviceable horse and buggy which she drove herself. Brett liked this option, as Mrs. Powers would sometimes let him drive it for Maggie.

On Tuesday, December 8, 1868 Aleck and Maggie moved into their home in Johnson Street. Aleck had a broad smile on his face as, hand in hand, he and Maggie visited every room, and he was effusive in his praise of the job that she had done.

20

A FINE SEASON

The office of *The Standard* was a gloomy place the morning after the November 1868 elections to the BC Legislative Council. The newspaper's owner and incumbent member of the Council Amor de Cosmos had been defeated in Victoria by Dr. John Sebastian Helmcken, a man with well-known concerns about the idea of Confederation. The pro-Confederation forces led by de Cosmos had in fact suffered a rout in this election of seats on the Island, with most of the members elected declared to be in opposition to Confederation with Canada, or at least highly skeptical of the idea. Some even discussed openly the inevitability of annexation to the United States.

So when Aleck called on de Cosmos in his office for a pre-arranged appointment to discuss tactics for further support of Confederation, he found the man in a foul mood. "Those damned idiots! Those fools! You know, Robertson, I've moved heaven and earth to convince the people of this colony that our future lies with Canada, and look what they've done! My God! The Confederation League at Yale – I wish you'd been there – was a huge success, and very convincing. Or at least it seemed to be. You and I and Powell and Robson and of course, Walkem, have spoken out convincingly, I thought. We seemed to be well received on the streets, but those bloody officials and stodgy old Brits that we have in the Council are so determined to preserve their little empire out here that this Council will never support it. And Seymour is a complete loss. Hell, the Colonial Office had to bash him on the head just to get him to support union!"

He ranted on, pacing around his office, scouring the recalcitrant Council members with harsh words. Aleck had to wait some time before he could finally get a word in. He held up his hand to bring de Cosmos to a halt. Smiling, he said "May I say something Sir?"

De Cosmos had to smile back. "Of course you can. What is it then? Don't tell me you're abandoning ship!"

"Certainly not. You may rest assured that I share your concern over this turn of events, but I do not feel dismayed. We know that the British Government is in negotiations with the HBC for the acquisition of Rupert's Land. Once that great expanse is in the hands of the Crown, you can bet that the next move will be to bring this colony into the Confederation. It will then be British territory under full British control from the Atlantic to the Pacific, safe from the Americans. Needless to say, London will have its way in this matter."

"Oh, of course. Of course." De Cosmos stood in silence, gazing out the window for a full minute while Aleck sipped his coffee. Then he turned back to Aleck with a twisted smile on his face. "It's ironic isn't it? We hope that the Imperial Government, by buying Rupert's Land and encouraging Confederation, will give us here in BC a chance for responsible government, free from daily rulings and orders from London. I believe that is called a 'virtuous circle'?"

"More or less, I suppose. Now mind you, there are many complicated issues to be sorted out before all this happens, but I truly have no doubt that it will. I feel that we should push on regardless, and that our focus should be on the Terms of Confederation. What really does 'responsible government' mean for us? I think that if we strive for full responsible government, which is called 'independence', we won't win, and we might end up with even more direct controls from London than we have today. So we should fight for the greatest possible degree of freedom of action from London and Ottawa, while at the same time insisting that they pay our debts and for a railway. You've been saying this for some time, and you continue to be correct."

"Quite right, Robertson." De Cosmos returned to his desk and sat staring at Aleck. "Indeed. Quite right."

As the Christmas season approached, Aleck was satisfied that, with Maggie finally by his side, he was now firmly and confidently established as a senior member of the business community in British Columbia. What he wanted more than anything was to have a successful legal career, to be recognized as an important member of the Bar of British Columbia. This objective was well on the way to being achieved in that he had a steady flow of remunerative and often high level legal work, was called regularly by the courts to deal with the most complex cases, and was treated well by BC's normally acrimonious press. He was also on the small committee established by Attorney General Crease to develop a Law Society of British Columbia.

In the context of his legal career, politics, whether practiced formally or informally, was a distraction. On the other hand, it was clear that a lively voice in the political arena was good for his reputation, and therefore for business. He also found that he enjoyed the discussion of the major issues such as the union of the colonies and Confederation. In his mind the issues were clear, and he was happy to take the side of the supporters, and make speeches on the subject whenever requested.

With just two weeks to go until Christmas, the first Christmas ever that she had been away from Chatham, Maggie was uncomfortably large with child, so they did not attend any large functions of the season. Aleck made brief appearances at a few of the more auspicious ones, but was quick to make his excuses and hurry home. Always the attentive husband, he was now almost comically careful with her, treating her like the delicate flower that she definitely was not. She was large in girth but strong and healthy, as she kept reminding him.

The weather had turned miserable – cold and windy, with frequent showers that occasionally firmed up to sleet, and even threatened snow. Maggie avoided going out unless absolutely necessary. She found to her delight that her new women friends rallied around to make her as comfortable and happy as possible. Cecelia Powers also made a point of dropping in some mornings, always with a cake or some new buns that she had baked. They would have their tea at the kitchen table, and discuss menus and new food items, and Mrs. Powers would help Maggie plan meals and prepare lists of groceries.

In the third week of December Maggie sent for Chin, the cook. She asked him to start coming in afternoons to prepare the evening meal, and perhaps set aside some prepared dishes for the following day. She wanted to be able to serve Aleck good meals, but was not yet very good at cooking, and was also quite tired out by the early evening. Chin would prepare the meal, and leave it for them to serve whenever ready. The timing of dinners was tricky as Aleck was often delayed at his work, so he might appear at home anywhere between 5:00 pm and 7:00 pm, or later if there was a reception to attend.

The doctor was also an occasional visitor, coming by every week or so to see how she was progressing. Dr. James Trimble was a distinguished, friendly man who was a leader in the community. He and his wife had arrived in Victoria in 1858, and he had been instrumental in the development of the Royal Hospital, and the medical profession in general. A colleague of Aleck's in the Masons, he was currently Mayor of Victoria, having served for several years in the Vancouver Island House of Assembly. His visits were always brief and efficient, with just enough time for conversation to be friendly and give her confidence. In early December he brought with him the midwife Mrs. Murchison, whom he recommended to Maggie for service when her time came. Mrs. Murchison put Maggie at ease with her chatter and obvious capability, demonstrated by her thorough inspection of the house, and list of instructions as preparations for the birth.

Maggie's days were quietly busy, and the highlight of her day was always when Aleck arrived home, storming in the front door shouting out his greetings, demanding to know where she was and how she was. He would wrap his arms gently around her and give her an enormous, soft kiss, gaze into her eyes, and then stand back and observe her large tummy. "What a fine sight you are my darling" he would cry, smiling from ear to ear and walking her gently around the room in a sort of lazy, careful dance.

They would move to the study, and he would hand her the letters that he had picked up that day from the post office, knowing as he did how she longed for news from home. She would read them and exclaim over items of interest. She heard quite regularly from her mother Mary Bell, and occasionally from her siblings. They all claimed to miss her terribly, and she believed them because she missed them in equal measure. Aleck would also place the day's newspaper on the table, and they would discuss the news as the evening progressed.

Then they would sit at the dinner table, and she would serve the dinner that Chin had left for them. On occasion Aleck would take on the role of server, but she preferred it the other way around. After all, it was her responsibility. After dinner they would sit by the fire in the parlour, sipping their coffee and talking about the news from back home and locally in BC, about family and friends, and about his work. Sometimes they would discuss the child who would arrive in January – would it be a boy or girl, and what would be the name? They drew up lists.

Christmas of 1868 passed quietly at the Robertson home, with warm fires to ward off the winter chill, and discomfort for Maggie in her advanced pregnancy.

Thursday, January 21, 1869 broke cold and windy, with a light, frigid rain washing the streets of Victoria. Aleck and Maggie had their breakfast as usual, and Aleck left the house at 8:30 am, heading for a demanding day in court. Maggie's time had now come. She was due to give birth at any time, and Aleck hated to leave her at home in this state. When Brett arrived early, as instructed, Aleck asked him to stay for the day to carry out his usual duties, and to be available to take instruction at any time.

The first instruction came 15 minutes after Aleck departed. Maggie, still sitting at the breakfast table, felt a strong pain, almost a convulsion, in her lower abdomen. She knew at once what this was as Mrs. Murchison had described to her in detail the signs of birthing. She went to the front door and called to Brett, who arrived on the run, calm and ready for action. She told him to go and ask Mrs. Powers if she might come and sit with her. After Mrs. Powers, Brett was to take a note to Mrs. Murchison, telling her that the contractions had begun. Brett ran off, and 20 minutes later Cecelia Powers arrived, bringing with her comfort and confidence where there had developed the first small edge of fear.

"So my dear Maggie, the time has come. How exciting! And you look so wonderful, so strong – I am certain that we will have a fine day, and you will have a nice present for Mr. Robertson when he arrives home this evening."

Maggie smiled, and then grimaced as the next contraction gripped her. Mrs. Powers held her hand until it eased, then went to the kitchen to prepare tea. They had a light lunch seated at the kitchen table, but a contraction put paid to any thoughts of dessert. Maggie went to her bedroom to rest, and just before 2 pm her waters broke. She called to Mrs. Powers, who helped her clean up, and then sent Brett off to fetch the midwife.

By 4 pm the contractions were coming at very short intervals. They helped Maggie to the third bedroom, and made her as comfortable as they could. The hot water was on the stove, in the way of Chin who was preparing an Irish stew for dinner.

The court had adjourned at 4 pm, when a problem arose with lack of documentation. Aleck had to accompany his client back to the company's offices, and then they had to go together to the bank. He finally left the bank at 6:15 pm, proceeding to his own office to deposit some papers and prepare a declaration for the court next day. As he approached his office he was surprised to see Brett sitting in Mrs. Powers' buggy, waiting for him. "What is it Brett? What's happened? Is Mrs. Robertson alright?"

"She's having your baby, Sir" replied Brett, grinning broadly. "Mrs. Powers sent me to fetch you, but I didn't know where to find you".

"Good heavens, man" cried Aleck, leaping into the buggy as it started to move down the street. "Has it happened? Is she alright? Tell me…"

"I don't know Sir. Mrs. Powers just said that it would happen soon, and that I should bring you."

They raced through the darkened streets – up Pandora Street and across Vancouver Street. Brett brought the buggy to a skidding halt in front of the house, and Aleck was off and running up the path and the steps. The front door was opened by a smiling Cecelia Powers. She beckoned him in, saying "this way please, Sir", and he followed her, hat in hand, down the hall and into the third bedroom.

The room was lit by candles. At the side was a large woman bent over the table – Mrs. Murchison was cleaning up her things. Ahead of him, lying propped up in the bed, was his Maggie. Her hair had been brushed and she had a soft, tired smile on her face. She held in her arms a bundle that moved and made clucking noises. She reached out her free hand and beckoned him to come to her.

"Come Aleck, my darling. Come and meet your son. Come and say hello to Alexander William Rocke Robertson."

Their friends had told them that the arrival of their first child would cause chaos in the house, but would compensate by also bringing joy and fulfillment. The advice proved to be absolutely correct. Indeed, if Mrs. Powers had not agreed to live in for a week or so to help out, they would have been at a loss as to how to deal with the situation. Maggie was happy but exhausted, Aleck was thrilled but distracted by his work, and the baby was noisy and demanding. Mrs. Powers knew how to deal with babies, and understood what Maggie was going through, and she played the role of mother hen with love and enthusiasm. She even helped them decide what to actually call the baby. They had decided to call him 'Rocke'; she talked them into the gentler 'Rockie'.

21

POLITICS BECKON

As 1869 opened into an early and lovely springtime, the politics of Confederation swirled around Victoria. It was the talk of the taverns and the drawing rooms, and the preoccupation of the colony's Legislative Council. Governor Seymour continued to waver on the subject, supported by many people who put no trust in the prospect of joining Canada, so far away. A surprising number preferred annexation by the United States. Aleck continued to feel strongly in favor of Confederation, and to express this view whenever and wherever he could. But he had little time for direct involvement in politics. His legal career was proceeding apace, and the new baby in the house had him rushing home whenever he could get away early enough.

Early in May he received notice from the desk of H.P.P. Crease, the Attorney General, that he had once again been appointed prosecutor at the Yale assizes, scheduled to begin on May 10. Thus on May 8 he boarded the steamer *Enterprise* headed for New Westminster, with onward reservations to Yale. His travelling companions included Judge Begbie and his fellow lawyer George Walkem, coming to defend the poor souls Aleck had been engaged to prosecute.

As the assizes proceeded there was a particularly important news item in the press. The last spike had been driven on the first transcontinental rail system across North America. The joint project of the Central Pacific Railroad and the Union Pacific Railroad, called 'The Pacific Railroad' or 'The First Transcontinental Railroad', linked Oakland, California, across the bay from San Francisco, with Omaha, Nebraska. There were railway connections from there to other locations in the eastern United States, including Chicago. Canadians could board the Great Western Railway at Chicago and travel in comfort to Canada via Detroit. This huge technological feat meant, for Victorians, that they could travel or send their mail from BC to Canada in ten days rather than the four to six weeks it took by ship via Panama.

To Aleck and Maggie this was very significant personally. Suddenly, with this one report, they felt closer to and more in touch with their families in Chatham and Owen Sound. Their sense of isolation was relieved, to an extent at least.

While Aleck was away at Yale and then New Westminster, there was a by-election for the Legislative Council to replace Dr. John Davie, who had died. It was no surprise that Amor de Cosmos put his name up for election, and won his way back into the Council. Aleck visited him soon after return from New Westminster, and found him in an expansive mood.

"You see, Robertson, we're starting to win this Confederation war we're involved in. I'm back in the Council, and I can assure you that they will be hearing a lot from me on the subject in the coming days. Oh yes. Those damn laggards will be hearing from me, I can assure you, and they had better listen and learn!"

"I have no doubt that they will" replied Aleck quietly, sipping his coffee. "But of course, the issue is not really you fellows in the Legislative Council, it's the Governor. I take it poor old Seymour is still waffling on the issue, and as long as he does, it's going to be difficult to move it along."

De Cosmos frowned. "Absolutely right. Well, all we can do is keep the heat turned up on him, and hope that he gets a move on. He's not well, you know, so I'm not holding my breath. However I'm convinced that London would like to see Confederation for us, as does Ottawa, so the pressure must be on the poor fellow."

De Cosmos made some further comments on the issue and the people involved. Then he changed the subject. "Tell me, Robertson, are you interested in becoming involved directly in politics? You seem to give plenty of speeches, and very fine ones too. How about jumping right in?"

Aleck was surprised at the directness of the question, but this was, after all, Amor de Cosmos. You would expect nothing less from him.

"At the moment I would have to say 'no'. I have certainly thought of it, and I do realize the importance of us all pitching in to develop this colony the way it should be developed. But I feel that I'm playing a reasonable part in the legal system, and even, in a way, in its development. And I must admit, I'm not naturally inclined as a politician. I'm repelled by the arguing and insulting that seems to pass as debate in political arenas. I see too much passion and defensive polemics, and not enough sensible argumentation being exchanged. I don't know, perhaps I'm just afraid of it. I would certainly dislike having some chap shout me down with what seems like an inane argument, and then find out that he is correct, and it's me who is the crazy one."

De Cosmos howled with laughter. "Not very likely, my dear friend. Oh no, I don't think so. However, you have answered my question, for now at least. But I can tell you, if I had to place a wager on it, I would bet that you will be in the political arena, in one way or another, within a couple of years."

The Confederation train, as Aleck liked to put it, moved ahead very rapidly after June 10, when Governor Seymour died up the coast at Bella Coola while on a trip to deal with Indian issues. He had been accompanied by the colony's Chief Commissioner of Lands and Works, Joseph W. Trutch. Prime Minister Macdonald's choice for Seymour's replacement, blessed by London, was the experienced and decisive Anthony Musgrave, Governor of Newfoundland. Musgrave arrived in Victoria on August 23, and very quickly published an important dispatch dated August 14 from Lord Granville, British Secretary of State for the Colonies. He had received this dispatch in reply to his request to London for instructions concerning the Confederation issue.

It started by noting that the territory east of the Rockies would be incorporated into the Dominion of Canada, and then posed the rhetorical question of whether British Columbia should hold itself aloof. Though the colony did not seem unanimous, Lord Granville said that Her Majesty's Government was unhesitatingly in favour of union with Canada. After giving the arguments, he then bluntly announced that as British Columbia was a Crown Colony, the Home Government felt bound

...to give for the consideration of the community and the guidance of Her Majesty's servants a more unreserved expression of their wishes and judgment than might be, elsewhere, fitting.

Musgrave had been instructed to take such steps as he properly and constitutionally could to promote favourable consideration of the question. Aleck read of these clear instructions while on his brief summer visit to Richfield. It came as no surprise, and gave him much to think about. The colony was finally to become a province of an enormous country called Canada. What was his role to be?

Aleck's work and political ruminations that year took place against the backdrop of a home life of idyllic happiness. He had a loving wife, an adorable baby son and a wonderful house. Victoria's early spring brought with it glorious blossoms and early flowers, which he would admire as he strode happily to and from his work, often whistling or singing quietly. Their garden had a fine display of buds, tended carefully by Maggie with Brett assisting. The baby was strong and healthy, with active lungs, but also a ready smile. Aleck marveled at the volume of diapers that he used. "He's certainly a productive fellow" he said to Maggie once, as he helped Maggie remove a large supply from the clothesline.

Later that week he came home with a dog, a young boxer with the imaginative name of 'Boxer'. Maggie fell in love with him instantly.

By the end of March Maggie was in excellent form. She was still nursing

Rockie, but had taken to strenuous walks and gardening, always with Boxer at her side, and had regained her attractive figure and all of her energy. She was visiting friends and enjoying the shops once again, and soon decided that it was time to liven up the house. She thought that Aleck should get out his violin and tune it up. They could use some music in the house, and she knew that it relaxed him to play it. She was also ready to start entertaining in their home.

Shortly after Aleck's return from the assizes at Yale, and not long before his departure for the Cariboo, they gave their first dinner party. Maggie had engaged Mrs. Powers for the evening to supervise Chin, serve, and make everything run smoothly. Aleck was his own bartender and, for the first time in Victoria, the entertainment for the evening. After the dinner there were the usual cigars and port for the men. Then, when the men had joined the ladies in the parlour, Maggie asked if anyone would like to hear her husband play his violin. They agreed immediately, and Aleck was only too happy to oblige.

He confined himself to well-known old country airs, and the guests joined in happily. This, as it turned out, set the tone for future evenings at their home. Aleck became well known for his playing and singing, and Maggie for her table, and invitations to the Robertsons' home in Johnson Street were coveted.

Aleck planned his trip to the Cariboo to be brief, from mid-August to mid-September. He assisted at the assizes in Richfield and in the Magistrate's Court, but his heart wasn't in it. He missed his wife and child terribly, and in any event his business in Victoria and occasionally in Yale and New Westminster left him little time to seek more cases in the far-away Cariboo.

Not long after his return to Victoria, on September 30, 1869, Victoria's Christ Church Cathedral burned to the ground. It was a terrible tragedy for the Rector, the Rev. Edward Cridge and his congregation, which included many of the luminaries of the city. They moved their services to an abandoned Presbyterian church while their church was being rebuilt. This was a major event in the religious life of the city, of which Aleck and Maggie were very much a part. They attended St. John's regularly, and Aleck was on the Pewholders' Committee, and the board of the Sunday school. He had also joined the church's choir, and enjoyed the singing on Sundays as well as other occasions. He and Maggie had a pleasant, growing personal friendship with the new Minister at St. John's, the Rev. Jenns, and his wife Emma.

On October 29 Aleck departed once again, this time for the New Westminster assizes. As with his previous trip, he and Maggie did not exchange letters as the trips were too short. Three days later there came the news that Governor Musgrave had broken his leg very badly in a riding accident. Aside from the pity that everyone had for the man in his pain, this raised the question of whether the accident would affect progress on Confederation.

When Aleck returned to Victoria, the fall season was in full swing, Musgrave's leg notwithstanding. There were several balls to attend, and numerous dinner parties, one of which the Robertsons hosted. At one of the dinners, in this case at the splendid home of Joseph William Trutch and his wife Julia, Aleck had a brief, interesting discussion with his host. They had met on numerous occasions and exchanged correspondence on business matters, but this was the first time that Aleck had been able to have a personal discussion with him. Aleck was surprised that Trutch neglected his hosting duties to take him aside, whisky in hand, for a chat. He felt honoured that the man seemed to want to get to know him better.

At 43 years of age, Trutch was a considerable force in the community. He had arrived in British Columbia in 1859, and pursued his career as an engineer and surveyor. Without a permanent position in the colonial service, he worked on government contracts. Through his substantial and wide-ranging surveying and road building work he learned where desirable land was to be found, and amassed substantial holdings, particularly on Vancouver Island.

Trutch soon became involved in colonial politics. He won a by-election in

Victoria District in November 1861, to become a member of the Vancouver Island House of Assembly. The Assembly was dissolved early in 1863, but thanks to his political visibility and contacts, in April 1864 he was named by Governor Douglas to the vacant position of Chief Commissioner of Lands and Works for British Columbia. As such he became, ex officio, a member of the Executive Council (Cabinet) of British Columbia. He also had responsibility for Indian policy, which he pursued with a remarkable lack of enlightenment.

Trutch and his wife Julia were prominent among the social élite of Victoria. Their home 'Fairfield House', on the city's outskirts, commanded a fine view of Juan de Fuca Strait, and was a centre of social life. He numbered among his personal friends most of the elite of the colony. The Attorney General, Henry Pering Pellew Crease, had been a friend since their school-days together. Peter O'Reilly, the Gold Commissioner, married Trutch's sister Caroline in 1863. It was known that Trutch's brother John would soon marry Zoe Musgrave, the sister of Governor Musgrave. Trutch was a bold, confident man, and a charming host.

He was known, unfortunately, to be less than keen about the idea of Confederation. His concern, shared by many senior government people in Victoria, was that their positions of authority would be eroded if BC were to become a province of Canada. A practicing legislature in the new province might even make them redundant or, at least, subject to the whims of an elected assembly full of men with uncertain pedigrees. Now, seated in comfortable chairs in a charming side room off the great room of Fairfield House, he sought Aleck's views on the Confederation question. This line of inquiry interested Aleck, as Trutch must already be fully cognizant of Aleck's views, having read of them in the newspapers, and listened to them at several meetings.

When Aleck had finished, Trutch said that the Confederation idea had concerned him for a number of reasons, but that his growing friendship with the new Governor had helped to allay some of his fears. He knew, for example, that Musgrave was determined that if Confederation did mean that some of the colonial officials would become redundant, he would see to it that they were properly compensated. That had been a major issue for him as there were many fine men who had served the colony well, and deserved to be treated properly, and not just tossed out on their ears. Aleck agreed – the evolution of governance should be smooth and fair to all parties.

On the question of responsible government for the province, Trutch said that he still had reservations about having a legislature full of elected men running things. Ottawa would of course always be there as the higher level of government, and the Crown would still have representation, but the idea of a bunch of uneducated farmers and merchants running the complex day-to-day affairs of the province gave him nightmares. What did Aleck think about it?

"I think that, as you say, Sir, the affairs of our province, when it comes to that, will certainly be complex, and beyond the competence of most farmers and merchants. Their interests are, for the most part, more mundane. But I stress 'for the most part', because there are some farmers and merchants whom I have met who are wise and honest, and might well make a real contribution to the management of our affairs. It would be hoped that the electoral process would find them out and bring them to the assembly. There would also be professional people interested in election. Our current Mayor is a good example – a doctor, and a fine Mayor as well. And then there are bankers and lawyers who have a broad and detailed understanding of the demands of public service. All in all, I am encouraged that if we were to place ourselves in the hands of an elected assembly, we would not be disappointed."

Trutch smiled. "Well said, Robertson. Of course, you are right. Tell me, you are one of those professional people you speak of. Would you consider running for election should the opportunity present itself? Does the idea interest you?"

The question confirmed to Aleck his suspicion that this was not a casual conversation. This important man had not taken him aside for a drink and some small talk. He was very close to the Governor, and very political himself. Perhaps Trutch was doing some scouting, laying some groundwork for the future. Aleck couched his reply carefully.

"That is a complicated question. Yes, of course, the governance of this colony, and of the province as and when it becomes one, is of interest to me. I have cast my lot with this colony, and I wish to see it prosper, and that involves good government. But that does not answer your question. Would I run for election? It is a very direct question, Sir, and I will give you a very political answer. Perhaps!"

They laughed. Then Trutch continued to wait for more of an answer, and Aleck was bound to deliver one. "I have pursued my profession with great vigour, and find it stimulating and satisfying. I do not relish the thought of changing my line of work, and I must admit I am not a natural politician. However, if the occasion arose wherein I felt that my services to the government would be truly required, and that I could do some good for the community, then I would accept the challenge."

"An excellent reply, Robertson. Spoken like a Prime Minister!" They both laughed and then, as if on cue, Julia Trutch tapped her husband on the shoulder, apologized to Aleck, and suggested to Trutch that he might like to come and greet the Mayor, who had just arrived.

Aleck moved across the crowded room to Maggie's side. When she broke away from her conversation with another guest, she asked him about his private chat with Trutch. "It looked terribly mysterious, darling. What was it all about?"

"I'm not entirely certain, but I think I'm being sized up for a political career. Heaven help us!"

22

THE CONFEDERATION DEBATE

Although Governor Musgrave's accident had been extremely serious, con-fining him to bed for several months, it did not stop him from working with his Executive Council to draft proposed Terms of Confederation for the consideration of the Legislative Council. Everyone knew that the pres-sure from London for BC to join Canada would be irresistible, but within that consideration it was important that the people of the colony have as much say as possible in the shape of the arrangement.

The Colonial Secretary, the Hon. Philip J. Hankin, presented the Governor's proposed 'Terms' to the opening session of the Legislative Council on February 15, 1870. Hankin said that to trifle with the Confederation matter further would be discourteous to Canada and to the mother country, and the Executive Council had therefore prepared draft Terms for the Legislative Council's consideration. In summary, the Terms proposed were as follows:

- Canada to assume the colony's debt, and BC to receive interest on excessive debt incurred by other provinces;
- the Dominion to make a yearly grant for support of the local gov-ernment of $35,000 plus 80 cents per head, to be continued until the population reached four hundred thousand, at which time the

subsidy would remain fixed;

- surveys for a line of railway to connect the seaboard of BC with the existing railway system of Canada to be commenced at once, and a wagon road across the Rockies to be completed within three years after Confederation, the railway to be commenced on the Pacific side within the same time, and not less than $1,000,000 to be spent every year thereafter on its construction;
- The Canadian government
  - to guarantee interest at five percent per annum on a loan of £100,000 for the construction of a graving dock at Esquimalt;
  - to provide fortnightly steam communication with San Francisco and regular communication with Nanaimo and the interior;
  - to build and maintain a marine hospital and lunatic asylum at Victoria and a penitentiary in the province;
  - to defray the expenses of the judicial, postal and customs departments;
  - to use all its influence to retain Esquimalt as a station for Her Majesty's ships;
  - to establish a volunteer force in the colony;
  - to pension those of the present officers of the colony whose services would not be required after Confederation;
- British Columbia to be allowed eight members in the House of Commons and four in the Senate, and to receive the same protection, privileges and immunities as the other provinces.

These Terms were tabled but not debated until Attorney General H.P.P. Crease moved on March 9 that the Council resolve itself into Committee of the Whole to consider the Terms. Ten days later the Terms were passed almost unanimously, with two minor changes.

Governor Musgrave had resolved the problem of having two Chief Justices in the combined colony by finding a new post for Joseph Needham, Chief Justice of Vancouver Island, as Governor of Trinidad. Needham resigned in March 1870, thereby leaving Matthew Begbie as Chief Justice of the combined colony. On March 11, H.P.P. Crease was appointed as the first puisne (new) judge of the Supreme Court of BC. Both judges resided in Victoria.

The next step in the process was to send a delegation to Ottawa to negotiate the Terms with the Dominion government. Governor Musgrave chose Dr. J.S. Helmcken and Joseph Trutch, both former opponents to the concept but now in favour, and Dr. R.W.W. Carrall, who had been an outspoken supporter from the outset. They were accompanied by Mr. H.E. Seelye, who acted as daily correspondent for the *British Colonist*, and was a watchdog to ensure that the concept of responsible government was fully honoured. It was Seelye who sent the historic telegram from Ottawa to Victoria on July 7, 1870:

Terms agreed upon. The delegates are satisfied. Canada is favorable to immediate union and guarantees the railway. Trutch has gone to England. Carrall remains a month. Helmcken and your correspondent are on the way home.

On August 9 the Imperial Parliament passed the 'British Columbia Act, 1870'. There were a few changes from the Terms proposed by the BC Legislative Council, including a reduction in BC's representation in Parliament from eight Members to six, and from four Senators to three. There was also an order-in-council passed constituting a BC Legislative Council of 15 members, nine elective and six appointed, to move the issue forward.

"You must agree, Robertson" said de Cosmos in one of their coffee meetings, "that things have gone well. Why, even if nothing else, we will now have a Legislative Council dominated by elective members rather than appointed. It almost sounds like democracy!"

Aleck did agree. "It does indeed, and I congratulate you on this amazing progress. You take considerable credit for it, to be sure. But of course, you will not rest on your laurels. There is still much to be done I am certain. What will be the next steps?"

"Well now, so far we have our Council approving proposed Terms that were agreed to almost intact by Ottawa – not yet by Parliament, but by government officials. The bigwigs in London approved of them in short order. Now we are instructed to elect a more democratic Council to consider the Terms once again, so that this time it will be truly the people of the colony accepting them. After that, I suppose it will go back to Ottawa for Parliament to consider and approve, and then, if they do, we will be confederated!"

"Bravo" cried Aleck. "Well done! It's a complicated process, but necessary, of course. I assume that you will run for this short-term Council?"

"Oh yes, I certainly will. And I must say I wish you would join us on the hustings. Your silvery tongue would serve well in moving the ship forward. But I understand that you may have other plans."

"I do, or at least I may have. That is something I wanted to speak to you about. As you know I have been approached by Dr. Powell, speaking on behalf of many of our Masonic colleagues, suggesting that I run for Mayor this November. I do naturally feel gratified with this display of support from my friends, but I hesitate, for two reasons. One is that I'm still not certain that I should be directly involved in politics. I have a very full agenda in the courts, and they pay well. I know that I could continue my practice if I were Mayor, but it would be a distraction that would be not altogether welcome. I do like to have some time for my wife and child, you know, and Maggie is about to produce our second child any day now.

"The other concern is that our friend and colleague Dr. Trimble is the incumbent, and is doing a very good job. I feel hesitant to challenge such a friend." He paused, and de Cosmos rushed in.

"On the first objection, I understand, but do not agree. Oh, I agree about taking time for your family, of course. But I don't agree that it is a bad thing to take a few hours away from your legal practice. Here, step back and take a look at yourself. You're a young man still, yet considered one of the most important lawyers in the colony. But how do you stay on top? I think that you need to have a high profile, and maintain it over time. Politics is the way to go about it. Get yourself in the Mayor's chair for a year or so. By then there will be a provincial legislature, and you might run for membership in it. You can keep your practice going through all of these distractions, and your name will be in everybody's mind then and into the future. The final icing on the cake is that some political exposure like that may actually be interesting to you. You would learn more about the law, and how it is cast, and how it is preserved."

Aleck tried to intervene, but de Cosmos was in full cry. "As to the second objection, forget it. By November Trimble will have had three years in the chair, and he could use a rest. I would add that change is a good thing in such positions. And, knowing him as I do, I would say that he would welcome a good fight, and shake hands at the end of it no matter how it comes out."

Maggie, meanwhile, carried on with her own busy life. She was certainly interested in the Confederation issue, if for no other reason than that it would bring them a railway direct from BC to Ontario. There were other reasons of course, which she understood and discussed frequently with Aleck, but her thoughts were dominated by family and social obligations.

In March she had announced to Aleck that she was pregnant once again, and due in September. She was convinced that this time they would have a girl.

From January to mid-August, when her condition finally forced her to stay close to home, she enjoyed a round of social calls and events, expanding and deepening her sense of community in Victoria. At the top of her list were the formal calls on the senior women in Victoria. Her call on the venerable Amelia Douglas, wife of the former Governor and founder of BC James Douglas, was a highlight. Mrs. Douglas was most friendly and interested, and then in the midst of their discussion over tea the great man himself came in fresh from his walk. Maggie was charmed by the interest he took in her. He had met Aleck on a number of occasions, and heard great things about his work. The colony was fortunate to welcome young couples like them. He heard that they had a son, and asked after him. What were Maggie's hobbies? Had she visited New Westminster yet?

Then there was Sarah Crease, whose husband had just been made a judge of the Supreme Court, and Julia Trutch at her lovely home. Susan

Beaven, Carrie Humphreys, Jane Dewdney, Caroline O'Reilly, Susan Robson, and the young Sophie Walkem – they were all lively and interesting, welcoming and helpful. She entertained a number of them on return calls, and also enjoyed the tea parties she occasionally hosted for her closest friends – Jenny Powell and Mary Finlayson, Emma Jenns and George Pearkes' new wife Mary. These were all occasions to show off the young Rockie, now a bouncing one-year-old.

Aside from these calls and small gatherings, she and Aleck attended numerous larger affairs, mainly dinners. There the conversation always turned, at some point, to Confederation and the state of the colony, and discussion of the promising new industries, the 'non-golds' as someone described them. In the summer there were picnics and several garden parties, including a lively event at Judge Begbie's residence, where he led his guests in croquet, wine and song.

They were actively involved in the church, and Aleck had his Masons. And then there was the shopping. Victoria was not a major shopping place by any means. It paled in comparison even with Chatham, and certainly with Toronto. But it had its charms, and Maggie enjoyed visiting the shops along Government Street, and the rather menacing but colourful shops in Waddington Alley between Yates and Johnson Streets. On several occasions Cecelia Powers took her in the buggy to country stores away from the city, which offered fresh produce and plants for the garden.

In early July she took Rockie with her to visit the Rev. and Mrs. Richard Lowe up in the Saanich area. They had been introduced by the Jenns when the Lowes came to Victoria the previous year. They had kindly invited the Robertsons to visit them at any time. Their guest cottage, 'The Parsonage', was comfortable, and their welcome most warm and gratifying. She vowed to return next year.

Later in July, Myla Holden came to live with the Robertsons as their maid. Aleck had met the storekeeper John Holden on one of his business trips to Nanaimo. In the course of their conversation, Holden had told him that his oldest daughter would soon be turning 13 years old. She was fully grown and very mature for her age, and should the Robertsons ever be in need of a live-in maid to help with the children, they would be pleased to send Myla. Aleck met the girl, and found her intelligent and articulate, and eager to leave Nanaimo and come to the city. With another baby on the way, they decided to invite her to come, on a trial basis at first. She would receive her room and board and clothing, and a small allowance. Now she was here, with her bed in the third bedroom awaiting the arrival of the new baby.

Maggie spent some time at her desk every day. She thought of her desk, beside the window in their bedroom, as her window on the world. She could sit there in the quiet and think about family and friends, make plans, and communicate with whomever she wished. She was an avid gardener, and the garden around the house was a joy. It was helpful to have Aleck and Brett to do the heavy lifting, and she studied the plants and flowers of the area, and took great care to plan and then plant and cultivate an attractive array.

In the warm days and evenings of spring and summer she and Aleck would often sit on their verandah, or on chairs right in the garden, sipping lemonade and discussing anything but Confederation. One of their favorite topics was how they were going to improve the house. It was comfortable, but too small. They would like to have at least four children, and with the live-in maid they needed more bedrooms. Their budget was still recovering from buying and furnishing the house, but that did not stop them from sketching out plans for some changes and additions in the future.

All of this notwithstanding, the big event on their calendar was the prospective arrival of their second child, and they were both greatly relieved and happy when Herbert Ewen Arden Robertson was born the morning of September 13, 1870. They had hoped for a girl, but were quite delighted when Herbie emerged, handsome and healthy.

A new mother once again, Maggie was out on long walks by early October, and a month later was fit and ready to withstand the rigours of her husband's budding political career.

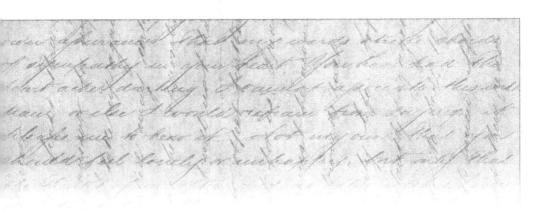

23

YOUR WORSHIP

Mayoral elections in early Victoria were rowdy political theatre. On nomination day the candidates would come to the appointed place with their supporters. A colleague would nominate a candidate, and another colleague would second the nomination. Depending on the circumstances and the candidates involved, there could be great cheering and noisemaking as the nominating proceeded. Once the nominations had been made, the presiding returning officer would call for a show of hands. If it was clear that one candidate was the favorite of the assembled crowd, he would be declared a winner, but subject to an appeal by the losing side for a formal vote. If such an appeal were made, then a voting day would be scheduled for very soon thereafter, usually the following day.

Voting was done on an open ballot system whereby a voter, having been duly approved as qualified (meaning, generally, he was a man who could speak English and perhaps owned a bit of property) would declare his vote in public. The sheriff would tally up the votes at the end of the day and declare a winner.

To date the only winner by show of hands had been the first Mayor, Thomas Harris. In the first mayoral contest in 1862 he had been accorded a wild welcome by the assembled crowd of over 600 people, and only five brave souls had dared to raise their hands in favour of his opponent, Mr. Alfred Waddington. Since then elections had gone to a vote every time. In November 1865 Harris nominated his fellow Mason, auctioneer Lumley Franklin to replace him. Franklin won in a vote by 78 to 73, and became the first Mayor of Jewish origin in British North America. He presided for just one year, and in the fall of 1866 the wealthy businessman William J. MacDonald opposed Arthur Bunster, a brewer. Bunster made it clear that he would serve only if it did not interfere with his business so, not surprisingly, MacDonald was elected.

The following year Dr. James Trimble, another Mason, decided to run against MacDonald, and defeated him by 236 votes to 137. Trimble was now nearing the end of his third year in office.

This was the process that Aleck faced if he decided to run for the office. The job of Mayor was by no means full time. He would chair the City Council, preside at official functions, greet important visitors, and represent the city as and when required. Some careful thinking and planning would always be welcomed, but Victoria was still very small. There would be plenty of time left over to pursue his profession without any hint of conflict of interest. On the negative side, he would have to face the public questioning and even criticism that was always the lot of politicians, and he found the prospect distasteful.

Maggie had similar concerns. On the plus side, politics would bring prestige to Aleck and, indeed, to them both. That would be nice, and would certainly be good for Aleck's career. On the minus side, doing a responsible job as Mayor, while at the same time trying to maintain his legal practice at a high level, might well put dangerous strains on him. She also knew that Aleck would find public attacks on his ideas or actions unsettling, possibly affecting his performance, and even his health.

After they had talked it through many times, all Maggie could do was to express her pride and her concerns in equal measure, and leave it to him to make his decision.

In late October the news was circulated that Mr. Lumley Franklin, the former Mayor, would be running for Mayor again. In a brief chat following a meeting of the Masons, the current Mayor Trimble had mentioned this development to Aleck. He was ready to step down, and had convinced Franklin to return to the chair. This made it easier for Aleck to opt for his profession and against politics, at least for the time being.

He took a brief trip to Somenos Lake, in the Cowichan region up the east coast of Vancouver Island, to relax and do some hunting – a respite from his work and his tiresome dilemma, now seemingly resolved. He returned to Victoria on October 26 and plunged back into his work, but the issue did not go away.

The British Colonist

October 29, 1870

> MUNICIPAL ELECTION – *the Clerk of the Municipal Council gives notice that a show of hands for a Mayor and six Councilors will take place at the Police Barracks at 12 o'clock, noon, on the 8th proximo; and that a poll following, if any, will be taken on the day following at the places indicated in the notice.*

~

> MR. A.R. ROBERTSON *was yesterday presented with a numerously signed requisition from citizens of Victoria, asking him to allow himself to be placed in nomination for the city; but Mr. Robertson, we are really sorry to say, declined the proffered honour, wishing to devote himself entirely to his profession.*

On November 3 it was announced in *The British Colonist* that Lumley Franklin had decided not to run for the mayoralty due to business commitments. This appeared to leave the field open, as it was thought that Dr. Trimble had decided to step down. Perhaps Aleck should reconsider?

Then two days later the following appeared.

The British Colonist

November 5, 1870

THE MAYORALTY – Dr. Trimble, it is believed, will consent to stand for Mayor again.

So it appeared that Trimble had been convinced that he should stay on and serve another term. Or had this been a ploy cooked up by Trimble and Franklin to forestall the entry of other candidates? Aleck sensed that it might be so. This annoyed him, and he returned to his state of uncertainty. Should he run against Trimble? In a conversation on November 6 with Dr. Powell, who felt strongly that it was time for him to be involved in politics, Aleck finally made his mind up to take the plunge.

Powell agreed to find a proposer and seconder to appear on nomination day, and to round up as many supporters as he could in the short time available. This nomination would come as a surprise to Trimble, but would add some spice to the proceedings.

The British Colonist
November 9, 1870

THE MUNICIPAL ELECTION – At the municipal hustings yesterday Councilor Carey nominated Mr. A.R. Robertson for Mayor. The nomination was received with cheers. Mr. McMillan seconded the nomination. Mr. Bishop proposed Dr. Trimble, present Mayor. The show of hands was in favour of Dr. Trimble and a poll was demanded for Mr. Robertson...

In the same edition of *The British Colonist* was a letter evidently copied to the paper the previous evening.

MAYOR TRIMBLE DECLINES A RE-NOMINATION

Victoria, V.I., November 8, 1870

To W.T. Leigh, Esq, Returning officer

SIR, - I hereby inform you although I was in nomination this eighth day of November, 1870, I decline to stand for the office of Mayor of the City for the ensuing year.

I am, yours truly, JAMES TRIMBLE

Also in that edition, the paper reported that, with Trimble withdrawn, Aleck must be automatically declared the new Mayor.

> THE NEW MAYOR – *By the retirement of Dr. Trimble from the contest, Mr. A.R. Robertson becomes Mayor of the city. Mr. Robertson is a gentleman in whose praise we need not speak. He is too well known to require a certificate of character from anyone. It is seldom that so young a man has been placed in so exalted a position; but, then, it is not often so young a man is possessed of those sterling qualities which fit Mr. Robertson for the office.*

David Higgins himself, editor of *The British Colonist,* arrived at the Robertsons' front door early on the 9th to deliver this newspaper with its unusual series of articles. Aleck and Maggie had gone to bed last night satisfied with the ceremony that had taken place – the nominations and calling of a poll for today. The thrill of the political battle was upon them, and Aleck and his friends had worked hard to raise a suitable number of supporters to likely win the vote.

But now what? Over breakfast they discussed this strange turn of events. Why had Trimble retired from the field so suddenly? Was Aleck really the Mayor now? He was not entirely certain how official Trimble's withdrawal was. It seemed to him that a vote had been called for, and then his opposition had written a letter to the returning officer. Did that really nullify the election – the need for one?

Aleck went with Higgins to the Police Barracks where the voting was to take place, and found that the poll had not yet opened, but the tables had been set up. The returning officer, Mr. Leigh, was in a quandary. The situation was unprecedented. Finally, early that afternoon of November 9 the poll opened, but there were no voters there. Later in the day Leigh decided that in light of the confusion surrounding the situation, the poll should be adjourned to the following day. He informed both candidates of this decision by messenger.

Aleck was naturally somewhat confused. What was actually happening here? Who had ordered that the poll go ahead after Trimble's letter had been printed? And who had made the decision to postpone the poll to the following day? Whatever the reasons, Aleck knew that he had better round up his supporters. He and Dr. Powell rushed to inform them that the poll would take place tomorrow, and to beg them to come out and vote.

The newspaper on November 10 reported on the confusion of the previous day, and included an open letter to the returning officer that showed that there was at least some support for having the poll, in spite of Trimble's announced withdrawal. It was written by Mr. John Gordon McKay, a loyal member of Trimble's City Council.

The British Colonist
<u>November 10, 1870</u>

A PROTEST

Victoria, November 9th, 1870

MR. W.T. LEIGH JR. ESQ., RETURNING OFFICER FROM YATES
STREET WARD:

SIR — *I protest against you, as Returning Officer, in declaring
that Mr. A. R. Robertson is Mayor of Victoria, in as much as
that a poll was demanded on nomination day, and that poll
was never held, and consequently there has been no election;
and furthermore no elector has had an opportunity to vote for
Mr. A. R. Robertson or any other person.*

JOHN GORDON MCKAY

Aleck saw at least two possible explanations for this turn of events. One was that Trimble may wish to withdraw, but at least some of his Councilors did not agree. If Trimble were to win the vote, but then resign later on, one of those Councilors would be appointed as Mayor without another election until the following year. Of course, the Councilors involved would have to retain their seats in the current election, but they would more than likely do so. So Aleck's opposition was really those Councilors rather than Trimble himself. The other was that Trimble did not wish to withdraw, and had laid down this protest as a smokescreen to confuse Aleck's supporters.

One way or the other, it didn't work. Aleck and Powell had done their work well, and next day's newspaper reported Aleck's success.

The British Colonist
<u>November 11, 1870</u>

THE MAYORALTY — *Pursuant to notice an adjourned poll was opened yesterday at 8 o'clock a.m., and continued until 4 p.m. The candidates were Dr. James Trimble and A. R. Robertson Esq. Very little interest was manifested, but about half an hour before the close quite an excitement was started and the voting became rather lively, and when the hour arrived to close the poll there were still three or four who wished to vote but were ruled "out of time". The vote at the close stood: Robertson 38; Trimble 30. Mr. Robertson was declared duly elected Mayor of the city of Victoria for the ensuing year. Mr. J. W. Carey, as the nominator of Mr. Robertson, thanked the voters on behalf of the absent Mayor elect, and the dripping electors dispersed to their homes.*

Aleck had been absent as he was required in court. When he arrived home later he was greeted by a beaming Maggie and the Powells, come to share a congratulatory bottle of champagne. "Well Robertson" cried Powell, "you have succeeded – and learned a few lessons along the way, I suppose. Politics is not for the faint hearted!"

"It certainly is not" said Maggie, "but at least it's over now, and my darling, we can all call you 'Your Worship."

Yet it still wasn't quite all over, for in the paper of November 11 some doubts were expressed about the legality of the election. But Aleck knew that he had won, for any legal challenge would be highly unlikely.

As he had expected, Aleck found that politics immediately took a lot of his time. He hoped that this would be a temporary thing during the early days, and then slacken off, leaving him more time for his practice. Even before he was sworn in as Mayor, he was introduced as such on November 12 at the nomination day for candidates for the Victoria City riding for the new Legislative Council, the one that would prepare the final Terms of Confederation for submission to Ottawa. He spoke at some length in support of his friend Henry Nathan Jr., a young wholesale merchant with strong political talents and ambitions.

The following day, Nathan and Dr. J.S. Helmcken won by substantial margins over the other candidates. In the same election de Cosmos won a seat in Victoria District.

On November 14 Aleck and his new Council were sworn in. The Councilors were George C. Gerow, William Heathorn, John Russell and Aleck's old employer and friend James E. McMillan. They soon found that if they had any doubts about the needs of the city, the press would not hesitate to remind them.

The British Colonist
November 16, 1870

SEWERS AND SIDEWALKS — *It may not be inopportune to call the attention of the new Mayor and City Council to the defective state of many of the sidewalks, crossings and sewers throughout the city. Now that the wet season is approaching it is most essential that matters should be attended to. We intend no reflection on the retiring corporation, for they indeed caused many improvements during the last year; but as we understand that the funds of the Corporation are in a flourishing state it would seem advisable and judicious to spend a*

*portion in repairing the sewers and crossings. The Sidewalk
Ordinance should also be enforced.*

It appeared that the actual work of the Council should not take up
much time, and with McMillan in the Council he felt that he could be away
for at least some meetings without too much bother. There would also be
formal duties such as ribbon cuttings to attend to, but all in all it should be
quite manageable. This estimation by Aleck proved to be quite correct.

On March 12, 1871 they received the sad news that George Pearkes, the
distinguished barrister who had been so helpful to Aleck, had died. Aleck
was a pallbearer at his funeral, and at the reception afterwards he met
Pearkes' partner, the solicitor Edwin Johnson. He had met Johnson before
and found him a pleasant sort. He wondered what Johnson would do now
that he had lost his important partner.

24

CONFEDERATION

The new Legislative Council opened on January 5, 1871. In his opening speech Governor Musgrave said the Terms of Confederation as agreed with Ottawa and by Parliament in London were the best that could be expected, and he trusted that the Council would accept them and pass an address to Her Majesty, praying for admission to the Union on those Terms. On the question of responsible government, he said that after the Terms were assented to, he would be prepared to submit a bill to constitute a new legislative body composed entirely of popular members, ready to come into operation immediately subsequent to the union with Canada.

The Legislative Council debated the Terms of Confederation starting on January 18. Their final product was an address to the Governor.

> "TO HIS EXCELLENCY THE GOVERNOR: *May it please Your Excellency – We, the members of the Legislative Council, in council assembled, having agreed to an address to Her Most Gracious Majesty, praying that her Majesty will be graciously pleased, by and with the advice of Her Most Honourable Privy Council, to admit British Columbia, under the provisions of the 146th section of the British North America Act, into the union or Dominion of Canada, on the basis of the*

terms and conditions offered to this colony by the Government of the Dominion of Canada, as in such address set forth, do hereby pray that Her Majesty's Principal Secretary of State for the Colonies to be laid at the foot of the Throne."

Governor Musgrave was thoroughly pleased with the work of the Council, and announced that from then on all members would be entitled to use the honourific 'Honourable' before their names. The address was passed by the House of Commons on April 1, and by the Senate on April 5. The Imperial Order-in-Council was issued on May 16, whereby Her Majesty declared that

"...from and after the twentieth day of July, one thousand, eight hundred and seventy-one, the said Colony of British Columbia shall be admitted into and become part of the Dominion of Canada upon the terms and conditions set forth in the hereinbefore recited addresses."

On July 19 the Governor assented to the *Constitution Act 1871*, under which a Legislative Assembly of twenty-five members would replace the existing Legislative Council. Vancouver Island was divided into six districts with 12 members, the mainland into six districts with 13 members. An Executive Council, or Cabinet, would be composed of not more than five members. The duration of the Assembly would be four years.

While these great events were transpiring, Aleck and Maggie decided that their budget was sufficiently back on track that they could upgrade their house. They were introduced to the builder Thomas Storey, who had a good reputation and was prepared to go to work for them immediately. Throughout April they met with Storey, surveyed the house, made drawings and plans and revised them several times until finally, on May 25, Aleck and Storey signed an agreement for the extension and improvements to the house.

The agreement was worth $1,243. It ran to six pages, and was full of complex legalese, as was to be expected in an agreement drafted by 'a fancy lawyer' as Storey put it to his friends. It called for raising the entire house onto a more solid foundation, changing some rooms, and adding a new bedroom and kitchen. When completed they would have a house with five bedrooms, which sounded like a lot, but would hopefully be needed over the years.

This planning distracted Aleck more than he would have thought. He found it both interesting and, in its own way, exciting. He enjoyed Maggie's excitement as well, and her many suggestions were useful. They made arrangements to move to Cecelia Powers' house when the work at their house made it unlivable.

Storey began his work on Thursday, June 1, and on that same day Aleck took his family and Myla by Williams Stage Coach to the Parsonage in north Saanich. They were met by the caretaker Mr. Clarke and, after settling in at the guest house, enjoyed tea with the Rev. and Mrs. Lowe. The family loved the place. It was simple but comfortable, close to the beach where the children could play in the sand. There were rough trails for walking, horseback riding, and fishing in the small boat operated by Clarke.

Aleck commuted to the Parsonage on many weekends, and back in Victoria stayed at Mrs. Powers' house. He and Maggie wrote brief letters to each other during the summer, often discussing political issues and rumours.

The expectation was that when there was an elected legislature, the Governor, or Lieutenant-Governor as he would be called, would appoint the Executive Council (or Cabinet) out of the elected members. But the existing Executive Council positions would have to be kept operating until after the election had been accomplished, so there might still be high profile positions to be had, albeit short-term. Aleck considered the possibility of seeking the appointment as interim Attorney General, but decided not to, and in the end the position was given to J.F. McCreight.

Aleck then accepted the invitation from the Attorney General to "take the Crown's business on the mainland". This would of course take him away from Victoria, but it was important business, and showed the respect in which he was held by officialdom.

On June 26 Aleck brought his family back to Victoria, and they moved into the Powers' house as their own was still a mess of unfinished walls, dust and open window frames. Two days later Aleck departed for the Cariboo with an unexpectedly large number of cases to attend to. For Maggie there was something terribly familiar about having Aleck far away in the hot summertime, writing him and awaiting his letters.

The newspapers on July 6 reported that the City Council, chaired in the Mayor's absence by Mr. McMillan, had appointed a very large committee of eminent people to prepare celebrations for Confederation Day, July 20. On July 7 came the announcement that the Hon. Joseph William Trutch had been appointed BC's first Lieutenant-Governor, to replace Governor Musgrave who was due to depart soon after Confederation Day.

Maggie commented to Aleck that this appointment would be questioned.

July 11, 1871

> *...Trutch's appointment is not satisfactory. I don't quite know whether he has enough finesse to try and govern popularly. My impression is that Robson will be Premier if the election follows the appointment of the Ministry. The Colonist has been lauding Trutch at a great rate. Will it go down with him? Or is he above it all?*

Aleck read this letter with great interest. Dr. Powell had recently told Aleck that he had been approached by the Governor to see if he would be interested in the appointment as BC's first Lieutenant-Governor. After due consideration he had declined, but had said that he would be grateful to be considered for a government position of interest and importance. Dr. Powell was busy professionally and in the education field, and also was soon to be installed as the first Grand Master of the newly formed Masonic Grand Lodge of British Columbia. He was a busy man, and did not wish to be removed from these many pursuits.

Aleck had heard about Trutch's appointment, and he was not surprised by it. Trutch was a successful and respected man in his profession of surveying and road building, wealthy and politically astute. His disdain for the aspirations of the native population was an issue that would, hopefully, be changed or at least moderated over time. He was known to be cautious about responsible government, concerned about the capabilities of ordinary men placed in positions of elected power. Thus he would clearly be very careful in the selection of his Executive Council, and might even want to participate in its meetings to be sure that it did the right things.

On the evening of July 19 the Powells invited Maggie and several other friends to late supper at their house. After the meal they left the house and walked out into the streets of Victoria. As midnight approached they found themselves in a growing crowd of excited people, everyone looking for the right place to be. They moved with the flow into Bastion Square, surrounded by a press of people waiting breathlessly for the midnight hour to strike.

And strike it did, loud and clear, marking the stroke of Confederation for British Columbia. The bells of the churches peeled, and there were explosions from the harbour where the anchored warships joined the celebration. Many people lit candles. There were handshakes and hugs and kisses on every side, great shouts of joy and congratulations. Powell formed his little group into a circle, arms entwined, and they jostled and cheered, laughing and chatting. Powell shouted "welcome to Canada everybody" at the top of his lungs, and then the circle broke, and the friends shook hands and hugged.

People were flowing in and out of the square, an increasing number carrying drinks and cigars. It was a joyful, noisy, important time, and they enjoyed it until their host gave a signal, and they retreated to the Powell residence for a glass of champagne. Maggie sipped her drink, still laughing and chatting with her friends, while at the same time thinking once again how typical it was – Aleck away just when he should be here!

Aleck, meanwhile, was going through more or less the same thing at Barkerville. He and a number of friends had enjoyed a wonderful late dinner at a tavern, and at midnight they joined the revelry in the streets outside. The beer was flowing. It was noisy and fun, but even as he was shaking those many hands in the street, he was thinking how typical this was – away from Maggie just when he should be with her!

In Victoria next morning, Cecelia Powers brought the newspaper to the breakfast table. "I have no doubt that you are looking forward to the official ceremonies today, Maggie? The ones arranged by that enormous committee set up by the Council?"

"Yes, I suppose so" replied Maggie, feeling somewhat subdued thanks to the Powells' late champagne.

"Ah, well then, let me read you this."

The British Colonist

<u>July 20, 1871</u>

> NO PUBLIC CEREMONY – *there will be no official ceremony today on the occasion of the taking over of the Colony by the Dominion...*

Maggie was startled. "Why my dear Cecelia, what on earth has happened? Surely the committee could come up with something!"

Cecelia laughed. "It seems not. Perhaps if Mr. Robertson had been here he would have made sure that something was done. But perhaps not. I suppose that this official inaction is caused by lack of money to pay for anything."

Maggie could only agree. In the event a salute was fired by the warship *H.M.S. Zealous* in the harbour, flags and pennants were waved, and businesses were closed for the day.

Aleck finished his business at Barkerville on July 22, and left immediately for New Westminster, where he had some work before he could take the steamer back to Victoria. While en route he received another letter from Maggie with some political commentary.

July 24, 1871

My darling husband,

…Mr. Robson called to express his delight, etc. at the Confederational union and we had a political talk. He tells me that nothing has as yet transpired to Mr. Trutch's intentions – only that Drs Helmcken and Carrall received telegrams from him – the latter whilst at New Westminster, but that Carrall utterly declined entering political life again. Having seen him I suppose this is stale news to you. As to Helm', the impression seems to be that he will be premier.

Mr. McCreight came up just before church last night and walked to St. John's with me, and he told me he does not expect to be A.G. for he does not know Trutch. From the way he said it I fancy his wife might have been the cause. He also said that if Musgrave had remained here he thought there was a chance of his getting that office – but not now under Trutch. He is so ingenuous.

They say the Hon. Hamilton Gray from St. John, N.B. is coming here to practice, and that he has been A.G. of N.B., and is clever. What chance has Walkem with Trutch?...

So Gray was obviously well considered by Ottawa. Interesting! Might he be the next new judge of the Supreme Court?

Aleck had given some thought to running in the first election to the BC Legislative Assembly, but it was still very much a decision yet to be taken after further consideration, and discussion with Maggie. Thus the July 28 newspaper came as a surprise.

The British Colonist
July 28, 1871

THE CITY REPRESENTATION – The question has been repeat-edly asked if the Mayor will be a candidate for the city repre-sentation. To this we would reply that Mr. Robertson will be a candidate, and, if the 'signs of the times' are to be relied on, a successful candidate.

He knew that this would perplex Maggie when she read it, and others as well. It was time to get home and start making decisions. He sailed home next day on the steamer *Enterprise*.

25

THE CANDIDATE

After Aleck's happy homecoming, Myla took over the boys and he and Maggie started their evening together with lemonade on the front veranda. They talked about the house and the garden, the weather and the repairs on their street. Aleck told her about his work in the Cariboo and New Westminster, and she told him about her busy life in Victoria. They drifted in to their dinner, kissing the boys goodnight on the way, and sat down to a special meal prepared by Chin for Aleck's return. It was a hot, muggy evening, so they moved back out to the veranda for their coffee. It was there that their conversation moved naturally into the political issue.

She told him that in her discussions with McCreight he had stressed the need for lawyers to become involved in the new provincial government. There would be, at the outset, a lot of real law-making to do, setting the province on a proper legal and legislative footing. They discussed the pros and cons of Aleck becoming involved, all issues that they had gone over many times over the previous year. In the end Aleck asked Maggie for her considered opinion.

"I think, my darling, that you should run for office. This is such an important time here in British Columbia, and you have already played a vital role in bringing us into the Confederation. But there is still much to do, and I just know that you will want to continue to be involved. I am so very proud of you, Aleck. I would even go so far as to say that British Columbia needs you."

Aleck turned away, a smile on his lips, and gazed out at the darkening street. "What about my practice? I could still take on some work, but it would mean giving up a substantial number of cases."

"Your practice will wait for you, my love. In the long run it will flourish, because you will be so well known – and not just here in British Columbia, but across Canada as well."

"What if I run for election and lose? What then?"

"Then I will love you every bit as much as I do today, and you will have many more profitable clients to heal your sorrow."

Aleck raised her hand to his lips and kissed it softly. "Then we have a decision. Thank you Maggie darling."

The British Colonist
August 4, 1871

MAYOR ROBERTSON *is suggested as a probable candidate for Ottawa in the Vancouver District.*

Aleck read this line with some amusement. He was actively involved as the Mayor of Victoria and interested in running for election in the BC Legislative Assembly, yet faced with a totally unfounded rumour that he would seek a seat in the Canadian Parliament! He wondered who would have started this rumour, as he had spoken to his friends only about the BC Legislature. Well, in politics it didn't seem to matter where rumours came from, or how true they were, they became facts when spoken through the press. At least the paper had used the words 'suggested' and 'probable'!

On August 11 a delegation of citizens called upon him in his Mayoral office and delivered a requisition calling for him to stand for election to the Legislature. He thanked them for their support, and said that he intended to abide by their wishes and run for office.

The British Colonist

August 12, 1871

Dr. Powell is spoken of as a probable candidate for the Commons in Vancouver District which comprises Sooke, Lake, North and South Saanich, Cowichan, Chemainus, Salt Spring Island, Nanaimo and Comox.

This was interesting. The doctor had not spoken to him about any intention to run for the Canadian Parliament, but then Aleck had not seen him for quite some time. He must call upon him soon.

Since early July, when Trutch's appointment as Lieutenant-Governor had been announced, the people of BC had been waiting for his return to Victoria to take up the office. Out of courtesy he had planned to delay his arrival until Governor Musgrave departed, which he did on July 26. Thereafter the newspapers followed closely the progress of Trutch's return, for until he arrived the province was effectively without government. He was delayed by bad weather, finally arriving at Victoria late in the evening of August 13. He was sworn in on August 14.

On August 19 Aleck and his Council members delivered a formal address of welcome to the new Lieutenant-Governor, and Trutch's reply was friendly, polite and constructive. That same day Trutch announced the members of his interim Executive Council. He appointed Anthony Musgrave Esq. (the former Governor's nephew) as his Private Secretary, Charles Good as Colonial Secretary, Richard Graham Alston as Attorney General, and Benjamin William Pease as Chief Commissioner of Lands and Works.

There were no surprises in this announcement. It had been widely assumed that the Lieutenant-Governor would appoint an interim Executive Council pending the election of a Legislative Assembly. This explained the 'acting' nature of the appointments.

Aleck had read this article on board the steamer headed for New Westminster. He was going to Yale for the assizes there, where he would be prosecuting. His travelling companion on this voyage was his son Rockie, now a rollicking two year-old.

Taking care of Rockie on the trip was more work and time-consuming than Aleck had anticipated, but he found it wonderfully satisfying. The assizes finished on the 27th, and on the 28th they travelled back to New Westminster and settled in at the rest house run by Mrs. Edmonds. The following day they went to the steamer terminal in the early afternoon and watched the *Enterprise* come into the dock. Rockie was thrilled to see the big ship, and even more thrilled when his Mamma came down the gang-plank and took him into her arms. After a wonderful cuddle and great cries of happiness, Maggie turned to Aleck to give him a kiss and found him in deep discussion with Judge H.P.P. Crease, who had arrived on the same sailing. Aleck was describing the assizes at Yale, but broke off to receive Maggie's kisses. They all had a friendly chat until the judge was called away.

Before he left, Crease took Aleck aside. "One final question, Robertson. Trutch will be calling an election soon. I have heard that you intend to run. Is it so?"

"It is, your Honour. I must admit I feel drawn to it."

Crease smiled. "That is good. Yes, indeed, very good. I can tell you that Trutch has his eye on you. You had better be ready for a call from him."

Lieutenant-Governor Trutch did indeed have his eye on Aleck. A week after the family returned to Victoria, Aleck received a note inviting him to attend upon the Lieutenant-Governor the following day.

Government House, also known as 'Cary Castle' after the man who built it, was a most imposing structure on Rockland Avenue. Aleck rode up to it in his mayoral carriage (Mrs. Powers' buggy, driven by Brett), and was greeted on the front steps by the Lieutenant- Governor's Private Secretary Anthony Musgrave. "Good morning, Your Worship. Welcome to

Government House".

"Good morning to you, Mr. Musgrave, and please accept my congratulations on your appointment."

Musgrave led Aleck into the building, and along to the Lieutenant-Governor's office. Trutch rose and came around his desk as they entered, greeted and shook hands with Aleck, and led him to comfortable chairs at the window. Musgrave established himself with note pad away from the table, and a maid appeared with a coffee tray. Comfortably settled with coffee cups in hand, Trutch began.

"Thank you for coming to see me so soon after your return from the mainland. Begbie tells me that the assizes at Yale went well."

"I believe they did, Sir. I was satisfied that the cases reached their correct conclusions, and I think the Judge felt the same way."

"Right. Now then, I understand that you have received a call from the citizenry to run for a seat in the Legislative Assembly, and that you have said that you would do so. Am I correct?"

"You are. I told them that I intended to run, and I have not changed my mind in the interim."

Trutch smiled broadly. "Splendid, Robertson. Well done. As you know, the first provincial Legislature will have a lot on its plate. We shall have to establish the legal and legislative machinery for the new province, so we'll need some strong legal minds in the House, and certainly in the Executive Council. Thus I'm delighted that you will run, and I'm hopeful that several of your legal colleagues will also run. This is not to say, of course, that we don't need members from other walks of life to give us the benefit of their various forms of wisdom, but lawmaking is a technical business requiring some real legal expertise."

"I agree, Sir." They sipped their coffee.

"Tell me, Robertson, have you considered where you will run – in what riding?"

"I have assumed that I should run right here at home, in Victoria. But I would be grateful for your views."

"That would certainly make sense – either in Victoria City or the district. But I do have another thought for you to consider. As you can imagine, there will be very strong slates of candidates in these ridings. This historic election will bring out all of the best people. I've been watching things carefully, and I fear that there could be a real dogfight for the Victoria seats. Now let me stress that I am certain that you would win a seat in such a fight. You are well placed, well known and popular.

"What that would do, however, is deprive some other worthy Victoria person of a seat. Too bad for him, but actually too bad for us all, as we need all the good people we can get. My thought is this. The riding of Esquimalt is lightly populated, and has no obvious choices for the election. There will be candidates, of course, but I think that a man of your capabilities and prestige would be an obvious choice for the voters there. Indeed, I think that they would feel privileged to have you as their representative. I would add that there will be two seats from that riding, so if you run in Esquimalt, there will still be a place for someone who actually lives in the district."

He paused, giving Aleck his chance to respond. "An interesting idea, Sir. I believe that the District of Esquimalt includes Esquimalt, Highland and Metchosin?"

"That is correct."

"Well, I have visited all of those places, and have found them beautiful and the people friendly and welcoming. I thank you for your thought."

Trutch smiled. "You are most welcome. And I must say, I will look forward to having you in the Legislature. Your experience as Mayor will stand you in good stead, I am sure."

The Lieutenant-Governor dropped the writ for the election to BC's first Legislative Assembly on October 2, 1871. Aleck prepared himself for nomination day in Esquimalt, scheduled for October 12, by visiting the region and meeting with friends there. The word spread quickly that he would be running in that district, and there was general agreement that having such a high profile man representing their community would be a good thing.

Nomination day dawned bright and sunny. A small crowd of men had come to the schoolhouse at noon to participate in the nominations in Esquimalt district. C.E. Pooley, the returning officer, worked to secure the temporary platform that had been erected on the front steps of the school. Then he turned to the crowd and called for nominations for the two positions of Member of the Legislative Assembly of British Columbia for the riding of Esquimalt.

First onto the platform was Mr. Fred Williams, who said that he was proud to nominate Mr. Alexander Rocke Robertson, currently Mayor of Victoria, an upstanding and widely respected citizen who would make a most admirable representative of Esquimalt. This was met with a good round of applause, and the nomination was seconded by Mr. Brockman. Nominations of seven other candidates followed, and the candidates all delivered brief speeches.

Pooley then said that there would be vote by a show of hands by those present. He called each candidate's name in turn, and as reported in the newspapers next day, the results were: A.R. Robertson – 10, Wm. Fisher – 6, D. Cameron – 5, H. Caulier – 4, C.B. Brown – 2, H. Cogan – 1, A. Pratt – 1, M. Gibbs – 0. The returning officer said that on the basis of this show of hands, Mr. Robertson and Mr. Fisher would be declared elected, but a citizen immediately demanded that there be a formal poll. Pooley said that in that case a poll would be held on October 26 at three locations, namely Esquimalt, Sooke and Parson's Bridge. He then called the nomination meeting to a close.

Similar meetings were taking place all over the province, and the newspapers were full of descriptions of them and summaries of the speeches of the candidates. Dr. Powell had nominated his friend Simeon Duck, the lawyer, in Victoria. Powell was, in fact very much in the news, for another reason as well.

The Mason community in BC, led by Powell, wanted to form a Grand Lodge of British Columbia, so that the lodges in BC could come under their own Grand Lodge rather than under the Grand Lodges of England or Scotland, as was currently the case. At a meeting on October 11 the Grand Lodge of British Columbia was formed, and Dr. Powell was installed as its first Grand Master. Eight of the nine lodges immediately surrendered their existing Charters and received new ones from the new Grand Lodge. It was an important time for this influential organization.

Between nomination day and polling day on October 26, Aleck made two visits to Esquimalt to attend candidates' meetings. Gibbs and Pratt had withdrawn their names due to the obvious lack of support they had received at nomination. At the other end of the spectrum he found that he was received with great respect and pleasure, his brief speeches warmly applauded. Between these two extremes was a loud and sometimes rowdy battle amongst the other contenders, fighting for the second seat in the riding.

It was during this time that the Robertsons finally decided to buy a horse and carriage. Mrs. Powers had been very kind to them, but they could not rely upon her good nature forever. As public life became increasingly important to them, so was having a conveyance that they could rely upon at all times. Aleck went about finding and purchasing a horse and carriage by the simplest of methods – he asked Brett to find them. In short order the young man had found a fine horse named 'Thunderer', and an acceptable carriage, used but in good condition.

On polling day, in the mid-afternoon, Aleck rode Thunderer out to the Esquimalt schoolhouse, the main polling station for the election in the riding. Fred Williams had been there all day to ensure that there was no interfering with those wishing to vote for his candidate. Aleck timed his arrival to be there when the polls closed, so that he could face the voters as his election was announced. The small crowd at the schoolhouse was not, however, treated to the expected announcement, as the results from the polling station for the Metchosin area, situated at Sooke, had not been received, and would not be available until next day.

Pressed by the crowd to at least give them the results so far, Mr. Pooley announced the following: Robertson – 68, Cogan – 33, Fisher – 29, Cameron – 26, Caulier – 9, Brown – 5.

David Cameron was known to have some support in Metchosin, so it looked like it would be a close race for the second seat.

The next morning, Aleck went out once again to the schoolhouse in Esquimalt. This time he had Brett drive him in his new carriage. There were around 40 men waiting impatiently as Mr. Pooley strode onto the top step, turned to the hushed crowd, and announced the final results.

"Gentlemen, the results came in from Sooke late last night. The final total votes are now as follows: Robertson – 74, Cogan – 34, Cameron – 31, Fisher – 29, Caulier – 9, Brown – 5. Therefore I declare that Alexander Rocke Robertson and Henry Cogan have been elected to the first Legislative Assembly of the Province of British Columbia, representing the riding of Esquimalt. Congratulations, gentlemen."

26

MR. SECRETARY

As the polls were completed around the province, Aleck found many familiar faces amongst his fellow members of the Legislature. Amor de Cosmos was in Victoria district, and Victoria City had elected Robert Beaven, Simeon Duck, John Foster McCreight and James Trimble – all personal friends. McCreight, who had been appointed acting Attorney General when Alston departed some time ago, headed the poll in the Victoria City riding. George Walkem was running, and would likely win, in the delayed election in the Cariboo. John Robson had won in Nanaimo.

On November 8 Aleck chaired the last meeting for the year of the Municipal Council. He would continue as Mayor until a new man was elected, but would not stand for re-election. The Councilors handed him a letter of appreciation, and he thanked his colleagues in return, spending a moment for a personal comment to each of them.

The next day Aleck attended a nomination meeting for the mayoral and councilor positions, and then proceeded to his office. To his surprise he found J.F. McCreight waiting for him there. His assistant Jonathan Courtiez had invited the recently appointed acting Attorney General to come in and wait, so McCreight rose and welcomed Aleck into his own office. Aleck called for coffee and then, with the door closed, asked his guest to what he owed the pleasure. McCreight went straight to the point.

"Trutch has invited me to head the government – the first government of this new province. As you may imagine, I am most flattered."

Aleck rose and came around his desk to shake hands. "My dear friend, please accept my heartiest congratulations! I am most pleased for you and, may I say, for the province. We will need a steady hand at the helm, and you shall provide it. Oh yes, well done!" He returned to his seat as McCreight, somewhat red of face, sat down and composed himself.

"The Lieutenant-Governor has asked me to consider whom I should select to join me in the Executive Council. Well, perhaps 'asked me' is somewhat liberal. Let us say he has made some suggestions, and asked me to consider them." They both laughed at this, as Trutch was known as wanting to have a say in everything.

"He mentioned you and said, quite bluntly, that he wanted you in the Cabinet. He appears to think very highly of you, as you perhaps know. And I must say, that feeling is rather broadly felt around Victoria, and I am pleased to share it. His feeling, which I also share, is that we should start with a very small, efficient Cabinet and get a large number of basic laws and statutes passed before the politicos – his word, not mine – take over and start slowing things down.

"So he would have me continue as Attorney General, place you in as Colonial Secretary, and then get Henry Holbrook in as Chief Commissioner, assuming that he is elected. That would give us a good man from the mainland. Then, as things progress, he would like to see another lawyer in, preferably one from the mainland, and I agree with him that George Walkem would be a good choice. The Cariboo elections are somewhat slow as you know, but I think he'll make it. We will probably put Walkem in as Chief Commissioner, and move Holbrook over to President of the Council. He'll receive no salary for that post, but it will give him good position, and he can be useful to us."

He stopped, and for several heartbeats there was complete silence in the room. Aleck sat with his face unmoving, but inside he was seething with excitement. He waited to see if McCreight had anything more to say, but he didn't. It was up to Aleck to respond.

"I am most flattered by your remarks, Sir. I admit that I am not a natural politician, but as a member of your Executive Council, I do feel that I could do some good work. Mr. Premier, I thank you for the confidence you have decided to place in me. I shall not let you down."

He leaned forward and they shook hands. Then it was time for practicalities. "There is obviously much to discuss" said McCreight, but I wish to get my thoughts in order first. Your salary will be $3,500 per annum. I trust that will be satisfactory." Aleck nodded, and McCreight continued. "We must of course keep this arrangement confidential until Trutch makes his announcement, but I will be in touch with you soon. Perhaps we could get together and plan our work so that we can be effective from the opening. Would that suit you?"

"It would Sir, and thank you again." They rose and shook hands, and he showed McCreight out the door. Then he returned to his office, closed the door, and strode around the room with a wide grin, clapping his hands with delight.

When he arrived home that evening, bursting to announce his news to Maggie, he found that there was even bigger news to be digested first. Herbie, now just over a year old, had finally produced his first tooth. Maggie greeted Aleck at the door, hugged him and then cried "we have a tooth, darling!" Aleck took the boy from Myla and, after giving him a big hug, opened his mouth gently with his finger and examined the evidence. It was tiny and surrounded by an angry red gum, but there was no question that, as Rockie put it loudly from ground level, "Papa, Herbie's got a toof!"

Then it was play time for the boys, and finally Aleck was able to tell Maggie about his appointment to the Executive Council. She was so excited she burst into tears and hugged his neck until he had to pry her arms apart to breath. "Oh Aleck, my darling darling, it has happened. Oh, I am so proud of you!" They discussed it briefly, but now it was time for them to start their preparations for the Lieutenant-Governor's Ball, the major social event of the year.

They started by having a short nap, then a light supper. Then it was into formal dress for the great occasion. Aleck shrugged into his white tie and tails, and Maggie stepped into her lovely blue dress. Blue was her favorite colour. It matched her eyes, and made her feel fresh and attractive. Aleck loved her in it, and for a moment, when she appeared dressed and ready to go, his heart missed a beat.

"Maggie, my dearest Maggie, you look splendid! You are truly magic to me." Myla, waiting at the door with their coats, was also swept up in the moment. "Oh Ma'am, you do look fine. So lovely! What a lovely color! Why, it even matches your eyes!"

Maggie took these compliments with an inner glow and the slightest of blushes. They left the house and climbed into their carriage, handed up by Brett dressed in his finest. At Government house there was a line-up of carriages, so they had to wait several minutes before it was their turn to alight at the front door. They left their coats with the maid, and joined the receiving line that consisted of Lieutenant-Governor Trutch and Mrs. Trutch, Chief Justice Matthew Begbie, Judge H.P.P Crease and Mrs. Crease, and the guests of honor, Admiral Sir Arthur Farquhar, RN and Lady Farquhar.

The ballroom of the mansion was ablaze with light from gas lamps and candles, and beautifully decorated with boughs and streamers. The orchestra played soft music as the guests strolled around, exchanging greetings and sipping their wine. The scene reminded Maggie of the comments her father used to make after he and Mary Bell had been to a major function in Chatham – "everyone who is anyone was there!" That was certainly the case here – politicians, judges and magistrates, lawyers, doctors and bankers, officials, merchants, hoteliers, brewers and manufacturers, and a lovely array of wives dressed in their finest. "There must be almost 200 people here" she said to Aleck between conversations with others. "What a wonderful party! I do hope you plan to dance with me, darling."

"I certainly will my dear – that is, if you can tear me away from all these other women!" He laughed as she smacked his arm, and then they turned to greet the new Mayor William J. MacDonald and his wife, a most distinguished couple. Maggie congratulated MacDonald on his election, and said that she hoped Aleck had left the office in good order.

They stopped talking as a hush fell over the crowd. The Lieutenant-Governor spoke words of welcome, and then called upon the orchestra to play the opening dance. The dance of honour involved two couples – Mr.

Trutch with Mrs. Crease, and Admiral Farquhar with Mrs. Trutch. They waltzed around the floor for several minutes while the crowd watched and chatted. The dance ended with loud applause, returned with gracious bows by the dancers. Then the orchestra struck up anew, and the dancing was under way in earnest.

Maggie danced with Aleck, and then was invited by McCreight. He led her smoothly around the floor, speaking quietly about how much he looked forward to working with Aleck in the Cabinet. Maggie returned his remarks with some of her own, and thanks for the confidence he had placed in her husband. Then, to her surprise, the Lieutenant-Governor himself asked her for a dance. As they waltzed around the floor he, like McCreight, spoke warmly of Aleck. "You are looking lovely this evening, my dear, and Mr. Robertson looks very fit. I am glad of it because he will soon have a heavy burden to carry. But I can assure you there is none better for the job." Once again Maggie expressed her thanks, and then was charmed when Trutch asked after her two boys. Were they healthy? Were they active? For one brief minute she found herself describing Herbie's new tooth to the most important person in the province of British Columbia!

Dinner was served at midnight – a fine dinner for the sea of guests seated comfortably around their tables, now thoroughly relaxed and enjoying themselves. The Robertsons' six tablemates were the Powells, a banker and his wife, and Dr. and Mrs. Trimble. They discussed no politics except the railway so long hoped for. Aside from that it was the weather, recent problems with steamships, prices in the shops, and the need for more schools. There were the usual toasts, and then the orchestra started up again.

Before they left their table, Aleck and Maggie were approached by the lawyer Edwin Johnson, the former partner of the late George Pearkes. Johnson had been the Solicitor and Pearkes the Barrister doing the work in court. They had done well, and Johnson clearly missed his late-lamented partner.

"Hello Mr. Robertson, Mrs. Robertson" he said, shaking Aleck's hand and nodding to Maggie." I have not yet had a chance to congratulate you, Sir, on your election to the Legislature. Please accept my congratulations now. It is a fine challenge that you have accepted, but I am sure that with your experience as Mayor you will find it to your liking. And to you, Madame, I understand that your two sons are doing well?" After a further exchange of niceties, Judge Crease came to invite Maggie to the dance floor, leaving Aleck to the conversation with Johnson.

"Tell me Mr. Robertson, will you be able to maintain your practice while you are serving in the Legislature? I ask because I would think that the government will take up a substantial amount of your time."

Aleck nodded. "It's a good question. The formal answer is, of course, that I can and will continue to practice as is permitted and is the custom. The practical answer is, however, that I cannot say as yet. I'll just have to see how much time I will have available outside of the Legislature, and set my case load accordingly. I must admit the issue has troubled me."

"Of course, Sir. Well certainly, time will tell. You may find, I think, that having a partner or colleague working with you at this most pressing time would help you to maintain your practice at a reasonable level. I would be pleased to discuss with you how I might assist you with this matter should you wish it. Please, Sir, do not hesitate to call upon me at any time."

"That is very kind of you Mr. Johnson. I shall certainly keep you in mind." They shook hands, and then moved into the melee of the dance floor, where the music played until well after 4 am. By then exhausted guests were departing in droves, and the Robertsons joined them. The call for their carriage was answered swiftly by Brett, who had enjoyed a long and profitable game of cards with other drivers, and several bottles of beer, and he whistled happily all the way home while Aleck and Maggie dozed.

The next day the writ for the by-election of six Members of Parliament was received from Ottawa, and announced by the Lieutenant-Governor. The elections would send BC's first official representatives to Ottawa. There were five ridings, all except Victoria representing huge territories. Victoria was to have two members, while Vancouver riding (all of the rest of Vancouver Island), New Westminster, Cariboo and Yale would have one each. The by-election was to take place on December 15.

On November 13 the Lieutenant-Governor made the announcement that everyone had been waiting for. He had asked John Foster McCreight to form a Ministry, and McCreight had selected Alexander Rocke Robertson of Victoria and Esquimalt as Colonial Secretary, and Henry Holbrook of New Westminster as Chief Commissioner of Lands and Works. The Premier would continue as acting Attorney General.

These appointments were met with general approval by the public, but many people were mystified by the formal procedures that then had to be followed. Because Robertson and Holbrook had been appointed to formal government positions, they had to resign their seats in the Legislature immediately, pending a by-election to make sure that their electors still wanted them. McCreight did not need to go through the same rigmarole, as his appointment as Attorney General was still 'acting', and the position as Premier was not a formal government position. The by-elections were scheduled for November 27, and both went off by acclamation, with no poll required. It was announced that the Legislative Assembly would hold its first session commencing on February 15, 1872.

Political issues were coming thick and fast now. There were these announcements, the by-elections to the federal Parliament, and the appointment of Senators to Ottawa. The Terms of Confederation had called for three Senators, and the announcement was made that William J. MacDonald, Dr. R.W.W. Carrall and Clement F. Cornwall had been appointed. MacDonald would have to resign his position as Mayor of Victoria to take up his new responsibilities.

The campaign for the seats in the House of Commons was a relatively low key affair lasting just over a month, with very few candidates entering the field. It was still acceptable under the law to hold seats simultaneously at both levels of government, and Amor de Cosmos declared himself a candidate for one of the federal seats in Victoria. Aleck was pleased to see that John Jessop, the educator who had done so much good work, but had struggled to find financing for the education system, was running on Vancouver Island. The issues in the campaign naturally revolved around BC's place in the Confederation. Would the government in Ottawa live up to the promises of the Terms – the railway, the graving dock, others?

Most of the candidates, but not Jessop, aligned themselves with Canadian political parties, and when the dust settled at the close of day on December 15, the Liberal-Conservatives of Sir John A. Macdonald had won three seats – Joshua Spencer Thompson by acclamation in the Cariboo, Hugh Nelson in New Westminster and Robert Wallace on Vancouver Island, edging out John Jessop. The Liberals of Alexander Mackenzie had the other three – Amor de Cosmos and Henry Nathan Jr. in Victoria, both by acclamation, and Charles Frederick Houghton, a farmer, in the Yale District.

Christmas season 1871 found a population in BC thoroughly satiated with politics, and ready for a good time. They had reason to feel satisfied. They had entered Confederation on generous terms, and had an elected Legislature and members in the federal Parliament and Senate. The economy was starting to show signs of recovery too. Gold was still important, with the Cariboo still producing, and promising finds at Omineca and Lightening Creek. More importantly, however, were the signs of other productive enterprise. The mines of Nanaimo were producing large quantities of coal, much of it going to the United States market. Whaling and salmon fishing were growing in importance, as was agriculture. New sawmills were springing up to serve the growing export markets for lumber, and there was now a nascent ship building industry. Victoria itself boasted breweries and distilleries, tanneries, a soap factory, a gas works and an iron foundry.

The first Executive Council of the Legislature was completed early in the new year, when George Walkem was finally elected in the Cariboo. On January 6 he accepted the appointment by Premier McCreight as Chief Commissioner of Lands and Works, replacing Henry Holbrook, who took on the unsalaried position of President of the Council. Like the other appointees, Walkem had to resign his seat and be re-elected. He did so on January 12, the day his appointment became effective, and was re-elected in a by-election on February 12, when he managed to return to the Cariboo after working in Victoria. He finally took his seat in the Legislature on February 23.

Aleck moved into his official office in the government office building, one of Victoria's 'Bird Cages' on the James Bay shore, in early January. His staff welcomed him, and he was impressed with them from the outset. He had an assistant named Hogarth, two secretaries and a records clerk.

Hogarth had ordered Aleck's official stationery, and almost before he knew it he was working at correspondence in the name of the Province of British Columbia. He had a broad range of responsibilities. The Colonial Secretary acted as the province's Registrar-General, and was responsible for formal documents and records such as licenses, birth and death certificates, land registries and surveys, business registrations and writs. As well, he was generally responsible for the administration of the civil service, and of elections. These duties naturally meant that he must be involved in the timing and substance of legislation, and in general with official correspondence between the government and the people.

At the first meeting of the Executive Council Aleck was not surprised to see the Lieutenant-Governor in attendance. He doubted that this was the normal practice. He could not imagine the Governor-General sitting in on Sir John A. Macdonald's cabinet meetings in Ottawa. But there he was, officially an observer, but never hesitating to participate and make suggestions. It was obvious that the Premier had expected it, as he showed no signs of surprise when he welcomed members of the Council.

Their task was to list the many issues to be faced by the government, to establish a list of legislation that they would like to see passed in the first session of the Legislative Assembly, and to plan the session and other government business and functions. At this early date, Aleck was already working on the structure of a proposed Public Schools Act which would put education firmly in the hands of provincial government action and finance. He had several private meetings with Dr. Powell and John Jessop to discuss the objectives and the substance to be achieved in the legislation, and it was readily accepted by the Executive Council in its list of legislation.

It was February 15, 1872, a cold and blustery day with a threat of snow in the air, when Aleck in top hat and Maggie in her finest coat and hat climbed into the carriage and rode in excited anticipation to the opening of the first session of the BC Legislative Assembly.

Arriving at the legislature building along with a crowd of other people – members and their wives, officials, newspapermen and onlookers – they entered the chamber and took their appointed seats. Aleck was in the front row along with his Cabinet colleagues. Maggie was also in the main floor area, seated next to Mrs. Trutch in a section reserved for wives and special guests. The chamber had a festive air to it, a sense of excitement and history. There was a heavy buzz of conversation until the Lieutenant-Governor, dressed in full dress uniform, entered the room and took his seat in the Speaker's chair.

The clerk read the roll-call and the statement of the rights of the Chief Justice to administer oaths. The Chief Justice then administered the oath to each member in turn, starting with the Premier. Aleck was second on the list, and Maggie listened proudly as his voice rang out clearly. The oaths completed, Premier McCreight rose and informed the House that His Excellency did not see fit to state his reason for summoning the Parliament until after the election of a Speaker. His Excellency would come to the House at 3 pm tomorrow to state his reason, assuming that a Speaker had been selected.

Lieutenant Governor Trutch rose and left the chamber, and in a ritual dance of sorts Dr. James Trimble was elected Speaker by acclamation. The Premier then moved adjournment, and the session was over. On the way out, Maggie whispered to Aleck "talk about 'much ado about nothing'". They were giggling as they climbed into their carriage.

The next day was much more satisfactory. The House was as crowded as it had been the day before, the ladies in their same seats. The Speaker gave a brief, highly appropriate welcoming statement, and then Lieutenant-Governor Trutch made a long, patriotic address. He left to great applause, and the business of the House began in earnest. It started with an unproductive debate over rules of procedure, then improved when the Premier gave notice of a large number of bills that would be introduced to the House over the next several days.

There was not yet a party system in the province, but the leanings and preferences of the members were generally known. Thus it was up to the government to rally sufficient support for every vote to be taken. This brought into play the personalities of the members and the rivalries amongst them. There was still the Mainland vs Island issue. The Mainland had a majority of one, with 13 members, so that could affect the direction of decisions over time. The overriding issue for the Legislature at this first session was, however, the strongly held public sentiment that the large slate of business was necessary for the new province, and the government should be allowed to get on with its work without disruption caused by contrary, political votes.

This served to hold in check the strongly political members such as de Cosmos, Robson and T.B. Humphreys, who were disappointed that this first Legislature should have been entrusted to the leadership of John Foster McCreight. He had previously been known as one who felt that the province was not ready for responsible government, so they doubted his ability or willingness to provide real political leadership. He was obviously a good legal craftsman, but not the inspirational leader that they felt was needed.

Thus with great debate and argument, badgering and catcalling, the first session worked its way through a veritable mountain of useful legislation. In the thick of the fray, Aleck introduced his Public Schools Act (1872), and guided it through the readings and debates until it finally received royal assent on April 11. As this process reached its conclusion John Jessop, with the support of Israel Powell and Aleck, was applying for the position of the first Superintendent of Education of the Province. Another well-qualified educator had also put his name forward, so Jessop had to lobby with the Premier and even the Lieutenant-Governor. With a salary of $2,000 per annum, this was an important appointment, one of the best-paid positions in the government service. To Aleck's relief, Jessop was appointed.

For Aleck this was a time of hard work and intense stimulation. He worked long hours at his office, and in Executive Committee meetings and Legislature sessions, and then filled in the spaces by keeping his hand in with several cases before the courts. There were, naturally, times when his schedules clashed, and he had to find which side would give in the more easily. In late April he found that he had to request postponement of a hearing in Begbie's court, as he had to attend a meeting of the Executive Council. The Chief Justice's reply showed not just his sense of humour, but also his friendly respect for this lawyer who had dared to stray into the political arena.

April 1872

Dear Mr. Colonial Secretary

(admire the cut of this note paper). I have just heard ambulando from Mr. Woods, that he has been informed by the messenger (Mr. Irving) that he (last antecedent) has been informed in the wayside by the Attorney General that you propose to make application or arrangement to postpone the hearing of the land squatting case which was last week fixed for tomorrow. I do not wish to put you to leave your work and come and make any such application personally – it is more work for the attorney (it is as yet lawful to notice the existence of attorneys) who instructs you. But I should like to be authoritatively informed whether my breakfast is to be hurried tomorrow or not.

As the matter has stood over now for 7 or 8 years, there is not immediately appearing any reason why it should not stand over for 7 weeks which will give you and your enemy (ad hoc) time to get over the session and have a leisurely fight over the piece or plot of land in question.

If this matter goes off, I shall certainly not be here tomorrow at 11.

Yours ever truly

Matt. B. Begbie

JOHN FOSTER MCCREIGHT, BC's FIRST PREMIER
COURTESY OF THE ROYAL BC MUSEUM CORPORATION, (D-04116)

AMOR DE COSMOS, BC's SECOND PREMIER
COURTESY OF THE ROYAL BC MUSEUM CORPORATION, (A-01224)

GEORGE ANTHONY WALKEM, BC'S THIRD PREMIER
COURTESY OF THE ROYAL BC MUSEUM CORPORATION, (A-01874)

Sir Joseph William Trutch, BC's first Lieutenant-Governor
Courtesy of the Royal BC Museum Corporation, (A-01705)

VICTORIA HARBOUR CIRCA 1870
COURTESY OF THE ROYAL BC MUSEUM CORPORATION, (A-08351)

VICTORIA LEGISLATIVE BUILDINGS "THE BIRDCAGES", 1862
COURTESY OF THE ROYAL BC MUSEUM CORPORATION, (A-02776)

MEMBERS OF BC's FIRST LEGISLATIVE ASSEMBLY
COURTESY OF THE ROYAL BC MUSEUM CORPORATION, (A-02559)

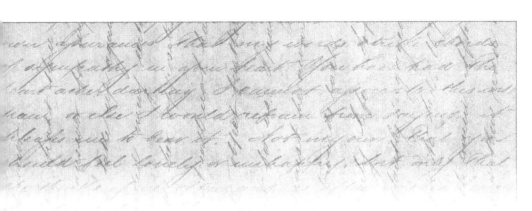

27

NON-CONFIDENCE

For a good part of 1872, Aleck had to face this hard schedule of work without the pleasures of family life. In January Maggie had started to talk about paying a visit back home to Chatham and Owen Sound. Aleck had dreaded the thought of not having his beloved wife and boys to hug each night, but he knew that she was right. He would be extremely busy with his two careers, so perhaps this would be a good time for such a trip. At the end of February he saw them off at the steamer terminal on their way to San Francisco, and the railway at Oakland.

Aleck's official duties were now taking up so much of his time that he realized that it would be useful to have a partner to help maintain some semblance of momentum in his law practice. He recalled his discussion with Edwin Johnson at the Lieutenant Governor's ball, and decided to sound him out further on the matter. Johnson was pleased to oblige, and they had a long discussion at Aleck's law office. Johnson was a Solicitor, so could handle all such business matters, and help in preparations for Aleck's court appearances. His work with Pearkes had given him valuable experience in office management. They agreed to meet again soon to discuss it further.

In early May Aleck invested as a shareholder in the proposed

'Inter-Oceanic Railway Company of Canada', one of two companies formed to bid on the charter to build the railway that was the key to bringing BC into Confederation. The company had been established by powerful business interests in Ontario headed by David Lewis Macpherson, and was headquartered in Ottawa with places of business across the country including Victoria. The company was formally incorporated on June 14, when its act of incorporation received royal assent. The prospect of being a part owner in this monumental new venture was thrilling, and stimulated Aleck's already strong interest in the railway question. Its competitor was called the Canadian Pacific Railway Company, promoted by Montreal tycoon Sir Hugh Allan.

On May 14 Aleck was back at the steamer terminal, this time to welcome Maggie's younger brother Melchior Eberts, who was visiting Victoria for the first time. Aleck was fond of Melchior, as was almost everyone who knew the personable young man, whose nickname was 'Buz'. Now 25 years old, Melchior had left school to travel extensively in eastern Canada and the United States. Recently, while living in Denver, he had almost gone into a mining venture in New Mexico. However, his mother Mary Bell Eberts had sent him several forceful letters telling him that it was a very bad idea. He would be better off going to British Columbia, which was much more stable and also had lots of mining going on. He had been persuaded, and here he was ready to seek his fortune.

With Melchior there Aleck's social life inevitably became more active. In response to Buz's questions about work opportunities, Aleck convinced him that he should study engineering, and take advantage of the jobs available on the survey work for the railway. He also introduced Buz to the survey officials.

In early June he received another house guest when his fellow MLA Robert Beaven moved in while his wife was away, and he had repairs going on in his home. Beaven was a businessman turned politician, rather quiet and distant. Aleck liked him well enough, and was pleased to help out.

June 11, 1872

My sweet wife,

…Buz will leave on Friday morning for Bute Inlet. He gets $60 per month. Tiedemann is in charge of the party he goes with. I am very glad of it because Tiedemann will endeavor to promote him, and instruct him in the profession.

At the end of June, Aleck had still to receive a letter from Maggie, so was starting to become concerned. His government work proceeded with its heavy load, and he found that the foundations of the government were shaky. Members of the Legislature were still going along with the government's proposals for legislation, but there was clearly unhappiness amongst many of the members, including de Cosmos, with having McCreight at the helm, no matter how good he was as a lawyer. McCreight, for his part, knew that there would be another judge appointed to the BC Supreme Court, and Aleck thought that he would likely accept such an appointment if it were offered to him. With this open secret before them, both Walkem and Aleck knew that they would be candidates for the Premiership.

July 2, 1872

My M

…We are on the eve of a change in the Cabinet. McC. I think will be made judge – this is private of course. Walkem is looking for the leadership I feel pretty sure. The Gov told me privately – he would like to see me Premier. Don't say a word of this to anyone. I don't know how it will turn out. I am afraid there may be a split in the Council – i.e. unless Walkem and I compromise in some way. We are on first rate terms, but I can see what he is looking out for…

On July 4 they learned that John Hamilton Gray, the lawyer and politician from New Brunswick, had been appointed to the BC Supreme Court, ending McCreight's dreams for the moment.

At the end of June Aleck had decided to go ahead with a partnership arrangement with Edwin Johnson, and on July 3 he and Johnson signed an Indenture of Partnership. Under its terms, Johnson would move into Aleck's offices and have responsibility for Solicitor work, research in support of cases, general correspondence and office management. It seemed like a good idea at the time.

On July 12, on his return from a trip to Nanaimo, Aleck finally received Maggie's first letter. It opened with the welcome news that she was once again pregnant!

A week later the federal election took place. Sir John A. Macdonald's Liberal-Conservatives were returned to power with a greatly reduced majority. BC now had four Liberal-Conservatives (Conservatives) and two Liberals. After the election Allan's Canadian Pacific Railway was awarded the contract to build the Pacific railway, on the assumption that he would divest himself of American control on his board of directors. Aleck was disappointed that he had invested in the wrong company.

The family arrived back in Victoria in early September, and on October 11, right on schedule, Maggie produced another boy. This was the next boy who was supposed to be a girl, but wasn't. But he was tiny and beautiful, and they loved him on sight, and christened him Percy Douglas Robertson.

One month later Maggie had regained most of her strength, and was able to pursue her round of social calls on the ladies of Victoria, and to join Aleck in social and recreational pursuits whenever possible. That fall she started to do volunteer work at the Royal Hospital, helping to raise funds and improve the amenities for the patients.

At an Executive Council meeting prior to the opening of the second session of the BC Legislature, there was general agreement that at this session there would likely be an attempt to bring down the government. They were fully aware of the strong forces against the Premier. There had been one productive legislative session; now those forces might decide to take up the political issue substantively.

The second session of the Legislative Assembly opened on December 17, 1872. *The British Colonist* article concerning the opening commented about the entry of the Executive Council members to this opening session, saying that they looked depressed and nervous.

Following the Speech from the Throne, there was a complex debate in which several members claimed that the Speech really contained nothing new. De Cosmos and Robson made a point of putting on notice that they would be bringing a large volume of issues to the house two days hence. This appeared to Aleck to be a ploy to show that if the government wasn't going to take sufficient action, then they must.

The second day's session was brief, taken up with a reply to the Speech from the Throne. Hon. T.B. Humphreys made the point, strongly, that it really contained nothing new.

On the third day Aleck noted that four members were absent, which was unusual for this early in the session. After some rather unpleasant debate, Hon. T.B. Humphreys moved a resolution:

That whilst entertaining the fullest confidence in that form of administration known as responsible government, still we believe that the administration of public affairs has not been satisfactory to the people as a whole.

So there it was, out in the open. There was further debate, but when the vote was finally held, the government was defeated by 11 votes to 10.

Four days later, after a weekend's reflection, McCreight resigned his post as Premier. His Executive Council colleagues also had to resign, so on December 24, Christmas Eve, Aleck awoke to the realization that he was now an ordinary member of the Legislative Assembly.

The Lieutenant-Governor immediately called upon Amor de Cosmos to form a Ministry. The editor of *The British Colonist* expressed the hope that de Cosmos had earned this position through honest means, and not by scheming. He also noted that the issue of de Cosmos' joint membership in the Canadian Parliament and the BC Legislature must be worked out.

De Cosmos appointed John Ash as Provincial Secretary, George Walkem as Attorney General, Robert Beaven as Chief Commissioner, and William James Armstrong as Member. *The British Colonist* completed its announcement of these appointments by noting that

It is understood that Mr. A.R. Robertson, ex-Provincial Secretary, was offered the position of Attorney General by Mr. de Cosmos, and that he declined to accept on the ground that he could not in honour do so. Mr. Walkem, it will be observed, afterwards accepted the portfolio declined by Mr. Robertson.

Maggie was surprised by this turn of events. "How could Walkem do such a thing, Aleck? Surely he must feel that he should leave with his Premier, as you did?"

Aleck smiled. "I think, my dear, that some of us, Walkem included, want to be active in politics more that some others. If that is the case, then they must stay in the game, no matter what. In any case, it is good that Walkem is there, as it will give the new Cabinet at least some continuity."

28

LIFE'S CHALLENGES

Starting at Christmas day of 1872, Aleck's life was much simplified, and enriched at the same time. He was still an elected member of the Legislative Assembly and active in committee work, but the burden of government was gone, and with it the long days of correspondence, document preparation, representation and Cabinet meetings. His high profile helped to ensure a steady flow of profitable legal business, smoothed by the steady presence and assistance of Edwin Johnson.

At St. John's Church he was now Superintendent of the Sunday school, a responsibility he took seriously. His music career, amateur but highly enjoyable, flourished with his new membership in the highly regarded 13-piece 'Victoria Amateur Band'. They played at social functions and dances around Victoria, to some of which he and Maggie were invited as guests. It inevitably amused their hosts when their high-profile guest left their table to take his seat in the orchestra.

On April 2, 1873 Aleck, McCreight and Walkem were appointed Queen's Counsel by Governor-General Sir Frederic Temple, the Earl of Dufferin. Aleck grinned as he showed Maggie and Melchior his new business card: 'Hon. Alexander Rocke Robertson, QC'. They were sitting in front of the fire with their pre-dinner sherry, the boys having gone to their stories with

Myla after a good romp with their father. Melchior had been with them for several weeks, following his wintertime stay back in Chatham and Ottawa, where he was courting the lovely Anna Burritt. He was preparing to head north once again with the railway survey. They enjoyed having him there. He loved the boys, playing with them and spoiling them terribly.

Melchior left Victoria soon thereafter and joined the crew doing the survey for the proposed railway route to Bute Inlet. The question of what route through the mountains the railway should take was at that time contentious and hotly debated. The main candidates were the Bute Inlet route and the Fraser Canyon route. In the former, the railway would come through the Cariboo region and emerge on the coast at Bute Inlet. From there a series of bridges over the spray of islands would bring it to Vancouver Island near Campbell River, from whence it would come south-east along the coast to Victoria.

The Fraser Canyon route would run farther south, bringing the railway down the Fraser to the coast at New Westminster, or beyond at tidewater. This would clearly make somewhere on Burrard Inlet the western terminus of the railway, rather than Victoria. Should this route be chosen, Victoria urged that at least the government should finance a railway from Victoria to Nanaimo in compensation.

The railway was very much in the news at the time, due in part to what came to be known as the 'Pacific Scandal'. Liberal Members of Parliament had brought to light the fact that Sir John A. Macdonald and his colleagues George-Etienne Cartier and Hector Langevin had solicited over $360,000 in campaign funds for the July 1872 election from a group of promoters that included Sir Hugh Allan. Some of the money had, it was now learned, been raised from American sources, contrary to the earlier promise to the contrary. Thus it was found that at least some American money had been used by Macdonald and friends to influence voters. The scandal had broken on April 2, and was now clearly headed for a Royal Commission to sort things out. The Canadian Pacific Railway Company collapsed, but the railway survey carried on as a government project.

Freed from the responsibilities of the Executive Council, Aleck decided that it was time for him to travel back to Ontario to visit his family. Letters from Chatham and Owen Sound were constantly begging him to come back to visit, and Maggie could only confirm that such a visit was overdue. His mother Effie in particular, living with the family in Owen Sound, evidently spoke of him all the time.

In planning his visit he decided that this would also be a good time to sound out his case for a judgeship. Visits to officials in Ottawa and London would be useful in his cause. He would leave at the end of July, sail for England in late August or early September, and should be able to return by the end of October.

He sailed for San Francisco on the steamer *Prince Alfred* on July 28, 1873.

In her determination not to be lonely, and in need of help with the children, Maggie invited several friends to come and stay with her while Aleck was away, especially when Myla went home to Nanaimo for a visit. Cecelia Powers was, as always, there to help when needed. Maggie found that she was unexpectedly nervous about Aleck travelling away from her, even though she had done the same to him quite confidently the year before. Her efforts to mitigate the loneliness did not work at all.

The loneliness continued, but Myla returned and Maggie started to feel better, so became more active socially. Seated at her desk at the end of August, gazing out the window, Maggie thought just how reliant she had become on having Aleck at her side. Her only comfort now came from the realization that by this time he would be in England, and almost ready to turn for home. She kept her ear to the ground on political matters, with a view to helping him stay up to date.

September 1, 1873

My sweet precious husband

…I must tell you something which Mr. James told me on Friday evening last – when he and Mrs. J. came over to see

me. Dr. Ashe told him that De Cosmos said that you were to be made a judge. He (De Cosmos) spoke as though it was a settled thing. I have no doubt that De C. would shelter you if he could in any way. It seems too good to be true, does it not? ...

I hope as you may have got off to England a little sooner than you expected, that you may be home by the last steamer in October. I do not think I can content myself for two months longer...

A week later she received a letter from Aleck dashing her hopes of his early return. He had decided to take a trip up the great lakes on a steamer with his brothers James and Tate. His letter came from a steamer docked at Sault Ste. Marie. Maggie consulted her calendar, and saw that Aleck's quest for adventure could cause a serious delay in his return, and might even harm his intention to press his case for a judgeship.

In his next letter to her he said that he would be going to England accompanied by his sister Margaret, also called Maggie. Throughout September she wrote letters every several days, giving Aleck the latest gossip and describing her active social life, which included several visits to Government House. Her letter of September 22 had an interesting line about Edwin Johnson.

September 22, 1873

"...Mr. Johnson tells me the business is getting on nicely and is increasing - & that he has as much as he can do. Mr. Jessop told me last week that Mr. Pollard says that your being away makes a great difference in the business, there being not nearly so much. I tell you what both say. You will be able to gauge the value of the two estimates better than I..."

In mid-October Melchior appeared at the house one day. After kisses all around and a great romp with the boys, he settled down with Maggie for tea and a talk. He said that he was visiting for a few weeks before heading up to Barkerville for the winter. He had been offered a temporary accountant position by the Bank of British Columbia there, and thought it would be a good idea to take it and save his money, rather than going home to Ontario for the winter.

On October 24 the city was seized by the news that Macdonald's Conservatives had not been able to survive the Pacific Scandal, and had resigned. The election was set for January 22, 1874. There was great concern in Victoria that if Mackenzie's Liberals were to come to power, they might threaten some of the Terms of Confederation, and in particular the promise to build the railway.

Melchior had been gone for several weeks when Aleck finally arrived home on November 17, bursting with good humour after his wonderful trip, and in good health as well. The boys climbed on him like a pack of puppies, and Maggie was not far behind.

As the year 1873 drew to a close, the Robertsons in Victoria had much to be thankful for, but Aleck's partnership with Edwin Johnson was an uncertain benefit. It had not in fact been that busy while Aleck was away, and now that he was not so busy in government, having a partner to mind the affairs of his law office was no longer as important. With the help of his assistant he had little trouble keeping up with his correspondence, and the work that came in was virtually all due to his own efforts and reputation rather than those of Johnson. It would, however, take more time to really see if the partnership was the right idea.

29

THE FEDS

The fire was warm on a chilly evening in January 1874 as Aleck and Maggie enjoyed a pre-dinner mulled wine. "Now then my dear, tell me about your day. I believe you were at the courts?"

"I was, but it was my luncheon with Powell that was the interesting part. Politics of course."

"Of course, dear. We seem to be surrounded by politics don't we? So, what did dear Dr. Powell have to say?"

"Well now, it seems that he had a session with the Lieutenant-Governor, and Trutch asked him to sound me out, informally, of course, as to my interest in being elected to a seat in the federal Parliament. Now that Nathan has decided not to run again, there is a vacancy to fill in the Victoria riding. Trutch said that if I wished to run, I would be assured of winning. I don't know what that means, but I suppose with his influence and the Masons and so on, I would have a strong chance."

"What did you tell him?"

"I told him that I would discuss it with you. And so we should right now, because if we decide to try for it, then time is short." He paused as he sat down beside her, and they both gazed into the fire. Then he spoke again. "Let me go first, as I've had time to think about it. I'll lay out the good and bad aspects for us to consider."

"On the good side, it would be a great honour to represent British Columbia in the Parliament of Canada. I would side with Sir John's Conservatives, I suppose, because he is the leader with the stronger vision of Canada as a nation. I might, over time, be able to achieve a position in the Cabinet. I would be there to push for BC's interests, and the pay would be adequate. On the bad side, I would pretty well have to give up my law practice, and I would be away a lot. We would have to continue to reside here, but my work would be in Ottawa, for the most part anyway." He stopped, but Maggie waved to him to continue.

"Those are the facts, darling. Now you want me to express my feelings, I suppose?" She nodded.

"Well, I must say I'm not strongly drawn to it. Politics is a great game, certainly. I enjoyed my time in the government, and still find the Legislature diverting and even occasionally stimulating. But as a long-term proposition I do have reservations, as you know. On the other hand, I do like the cut and thrust of the legal arena – dare I say the drama of important cases. I wouldn't like to have to put it aside for a long period of time. Nor would I like to have to be away from home for months on end, sitting in hotels in Ottawa while you and the family are here. Indeed, that is a consideration of prime importance to me. I get so very lonely when I am on my own, and I know that you hate it too. If I must be away, I would rather be on short trips to BC's magnificent interior than on long trips to drab old Ottawa." He stopped and looked at Maggie's smiling face.

"Oh Aleck, my sweet darling, you make a convincing case. No wonder you are such a good lawyer!"

That decision taken, they moved on to other issues raised by Powell at lunch. "As you know, de Cosmos is away in Ottawa right now, trying to get more funding for our projects than was included in the Terms of Confederation. He'll be back soon, and will probably announce some success, but that raises a danger. If Mackenzie and his Liberals are elected on the 22nd, they will likely be far less happy with the Terms than is Sir John. If so, they might take this as an opportunity to open up the Confederation agreement for further changes, and that might threaten

our promised railway. I cannot think of anything so dangerous as that particular course of action. People out here would be furious, and the idea of
annexation to the United States would raise its head again, probably even
more forcibly than in the past."

"Oh my dear, what a terrible prospect! What can be done about it?"

"Well, the election out here is being postponed until February 20, so
nothing can really happen until after then. But it's up to us, the members of
the Legislature here in BC, to put all possible pressure on the federal government, no matter which party is in power, to leave the Terms as is. They
are good, and they are agreed. So with that in mind, I'm already speaking
privately with a number of colleagues to start lobbying and speaking on
the subject, and raising such a row that Mackenzie would not dare to make
such a move".

"Who are involved?"

"We have McCreight, Robson, Bunster, Humphreys, Smithe, Mara and
myself in a sort of informal committee. Amongst us, we have many good
contacts in Ottawa, and can claim any number of platforms here in BC to
spread the word. As to de Cosmos, I believe that he will resign his seat in
the BC Legislature to run again for the Canadian Parliament. Trutch will
have to decide who will replace him as Premier, and my guess is he will go
with Walkem. The Lieutenant-Governor seems to like having lawyers in
charge of making laws."

Dr. Powell's predictions turned out to be accurate. Mackenzie's Liberals
were voted into power in the election at the end of January 1874, and the
issue of the Terms of Confederation was raised almost immediately. Amor
de Cosmos, who retained his seat and was on the Liberal side, had done his
best to secure some increased financing for the province, but now the threat
of more changes in the Terms became real, and Aleck's group had to work
hard to fight against it. The centerpiece of their work was a public rally on
the evening of February 7, 1874 at which over 800 people gathered to agree
upon a resolution stating that the BC government should not agree to any

change in the Terms of Confederation unless it was first put to the people.

The crowd then swarmed into the BC Legislature to press their point, forcing the Speaker to leave the chair. This event, generally referred to as the 'rebellion', showed how strong the feelings were in BC concerning the proposed railway. In the end they did not succeed in gaining assurances that there would be no changes in the Terms (the funding changes could proceed), but they did succeed in gaining assurances that the changes in funding arrangements would not affect the railway or other clauses of the Terms, or be considered as a waiver of any rights of the province. Any changes in the original Terms of Confederation would have to be put to the people for a vote. The railway as a national policy seemed safe, except for the inevitable and substantial bickering over financing, the route and timing. As it turned out, it was anything but safe.

Amor de Cosmos did resign his seat in the Legislative Assembly, and the Lieutenant-Governor did appoint George Walkem to replace him as Premier.

A large formal banquet was held at the Driard Hotel on March 9, 1874 to thank the group that had worked so hard to maintain the Terms of Confederation. Dr. Helmcken chaired the gathering, and they were treated to some lengthy, detailed and fine speeches. Aleck spoke for well over half an hour.

Less than a week later the 'Texada scandal' erupted into the headlines once again. Back in 1873 it had been reported that several prominent politicians including de Cosmos, Walkem and Beaven were owners through nominees of valuable mineral properties on Texada Island. It appeared that they had used their government positions to help them gain these investments. In response to the public outcry, Lieutenant-Governor Trutch appointed the three judges of the BC Supreme Court, Begbie, Crease and Gray, to conduct a formal investigation into the affair. The hearings commanded the rapt attention of the citizens of BC. When the report was finally issued in October, it stated that while there were some suspicions surrounding the deal, there were not sufficient grounds to believe that any member of the late de Cosmos government, or the present Walkem government, had acted in a manner prejudicial to the public interests.

For Aleck and Maggie, the year proceeded with happy family life, good legal business, one visit to the interior by Aleck to assist with cases, and another pleasant summer retreat at the Parsonage at Saanich. Maggie reported that she was once again pregnant, due in late February 1875.

Melchior Eberts continued to be a welcome and jovial family visitor. In mid-May he arrived in Victoria after his winter of banking in Barkerville. There were some delays in the railway survey due to the change of government, but by mid-July he was on his way north again to join his crew. He returned to Victoria in late November, and on November 30 he left by steamer to go back to Ontario for Christmas. He visited Chatham, of course, but the real object of this visit was Ottawa, for Anna Burritt lived in nearby Easton's Corners, and Anna's family welcomed him for a stay.

In early September Johnson departed for a family visit to England, a visit that he said would be brief. However, just before Christmas Aleck received a letter from him saying that he had decided to stay on for a while as he was courting a lovely lady, and hoped to marry her. Aleck was pleased for him personally, but thoroughly annoyed professionally.

The work of the Legislative Assembly was overshadowed throughout the year by the railway issue. Premier Walkem could not agree with Prime Minister Mackenzie's government concerning proposed modifications to the Terms of Confederation to make the project more palatable to the central government. Walkem was tied in to the obligation to go to the people with any proposed changes to the Terms. In effect, it would mean an election.

Late that summer the Premier went to London to argue the province's case before the Colonial Office. Lord Carnarvon, head of the Colonial Office, finally took it upon himself to present a compromise set of Terms concerning the railway that might be acceptable to both sides. These then formed the foundation of further bickering back in Canada, and great trouble for Premier Walkem, who seemed not to have lived up to his promise of taking such issues to the people first. While the politicians bickered, the people of BC fumed.

30

JUDGES, POLITICIANS AND REAL LIFE

Harold Edwin Bruce Robertson, Aleck and Maggie's fourth son, was born on February 26, 1875.

Following his decision not to pursue a seat in the House of Commons, Aleck moved quickly to the personal decision that he would not seek re-election in the BC Legislative Assembly in the elections scheduled for the fall of 1875. He had his sights still firmly fixed on the prize of a judgeship, and perhaps even the position of Chief Justice. And then there was the tantalizing prospect of a seat on the new Supreme Court of Canada.

Maggie was happy with his decision, and questioned him on the prospects.

"I've been so out of touch with having dear Harold. Tell me darling, has there been any progress in the judgeship question? I remember you mentioned that there was a great fight between Ottawa and Victoria over appointing judges, but I've forgotten the details."

"Oh yes, there's a battle alright – the sort of quiet but vicious war of words that legal people love." Aleck went on to explain that the dispute was over the structure and administration of the courts in BC: the division of powers between the Supreme Court and the County Courts, and the roles of the federal government, the provincial government and the judges themselves in paying for and administering the system.

"If it is agreed that the Supreme Court can take over the functions of the County Courts, as I believe it can and should, then the issue comes down to the question of who will actually run the affairs of the Supreme Court – the judges themselves, or the provincial government? Our current government is inclined to want to tell the Supreme Court where and when it should operate, just as they do with the County Courts. The Supreme Court Judges who are, after all, appointed and paid by Ottawa, fear that if this is allowed, then local politics could harm the Supreme Court. They might, for example, insist that a Supreme Court Judge preside at assizes at inopportune times in difficult places, in effect hounding the judge involved to seek other pastimes. So Begbie and Crease feel very strongly about the need for judicial independence, and several attempts by our government to have their way have been denied by Ottawa.

Maggie rose from her chair. "Well my darling, I support your idea, and I will assume until proven otherwise that when the Supreme Court of this province is enlarged, you will be appointed to it. Then you will no longer be 'Your Worship' or 'Mr. Secretary', but 'Your Honour'. Whatever your title – come to dinner."

When Edwin Johnson arrived back in Victoria in March, he found Aleck working very hard at his cases, while still being involved in some work at the Legislature. Johnson was full of good humour, but his partner was not. To Aleck, a junior partner who felt that he could disappear for six months in the current circumstances lacked the wit or the responsibility to continue in partnership. It was clear to him that Johnson was pleased to ride on his senior partner's very substantial coat-tails, without being able or willing to come up with his side of the bargain.

In early April, therefore, he sent a note to Johnson suggesting that they terminate the partnership as of July 1. He stated that he was working even harder than before without requisite return, accounts were in arrears, and he saw no need to increase staff as proposed by Johnson. There followed an annoying exchange of notes in which Johnson spoke of changing the *modus operandi* of the partnership, the need for more staff, and how well Aleck was actually doing, without even acknowledging the fact that his partner had called for a dissolution of the partnership. He was an elusive target for Aleck, who did not wish to bring the matter into an open, public dispute. He eventually let the partnership struggle on, generally avoiding Johnson, and minding his own cases and clients.

Melchior arrived back in Victoria in early May, later than expected as it had taken some time for the survey authorities in Ottawa to make up their minds how to proceed. He was welcomed by the Robertsons like a wandering son come home, spoiled by Aleck and Maggie and worshipped by the boys. He told them that Ottawa had been the highlight of his trip east, as he was now madly in love with Anna Burritt, and hoped to ask her to marry him some day if he could only save some money. "This sounds rather familiar" said Aleck, winking at Maggie. "But take my advice Buz, don't leave it too long. Money is not, after all, as important as love." Maggie guffawed, and they all chuckled. Two weeks later Melchior left for the interior to join his survey crew.

The summer of 1875 was a pleasant time for the Robertsons. They retreated once again to the Parsonage in Saanich, with Myla along to help with the children. Aleck commuted on the weekends by horseback, enjoying the freedom of having Thunderer at his disposal.

Melchior's occasional letters were always welcomed because they were interesting and amusing. In a letter written from the Homatcho River he described the work as being very rough. Then he said something that, just for a moment, made Maggie's blood run cold. "I had a narrow escape on a bluff on Tatlarco Lake, which I will tell you about on return."

"Just how dangerous is this survey work?" she asked Aleck. "Have you heard of accidents?" Aleck brushed it off. "It's rough work I am sure, but those crews are used to it and very strong and skilled. I doubt that there is much danger."

All through the summer Aleck had been receiving letters from his family back in Owen Sound, telling him of the worsening health of his mother Effie. Although only 57 years old, Effie had been ill off and on for several years, so much so that Aleck had agreed with his brothers James and Tate that if she should show signs of serious deterioration, they should send him a telegram summoning him to her bedside.

On Saturday, October 2 a telegram did arrive from James saying that Effie was ill but stable, and he would keep Aleck and Maggie informed. The situation of her health was, however, uncertain, so he may wish to come. Aleck immediately booked a steamer to depart Victoria on October 12. Then, early on October 12 itself, a messenger arrived at their door and handed a telegram to Maggie. She read it, and then turned to Aleck, tears streaming down her face. "Oh Aleck my darling, I am so sorry" she cried as she handed it to him.

It was from James, saying that Effie Robertson had died at Owen Sound that very day. They sat together in the parlour, quietly in tears while the household moved softly around them. It was the bleakest of news. Aleck could only be happy that he had visited his mother just two years before. So now his trip back to Ontario was cancelled, and he plunged back into his work, with several evenings spent in personal correspondence with his grieving family in Ontario.

The election for the second Legislature proceeded that fall, with Aleck happily on the sidelines. Walkem and his colleagues were still in serious trouble due to the ongoing dispute over the railway, but they nevertheless managed to survive the election with what appeared to be a majority of two supportive members. The new Legislature was scheduled to open on January 10, 1876.

Late in December Judge Begbie returned from a year-long visit to Ottawa and England. He sent a note inviting Aleck to a private meeting, ostensibly to discuss some cases that would be arising in January. Aleck attended at his Victoria residence, driven by Brett in the brand new phaeton that he had recently purchased from a company in Ontario. Upon being ushered into the great man's study his first words were of congratulations.

"My warmest regards, Sir Matthew, on your knighthood. I am delighted for you, and for the honour it brings to you and, indeed, to our province. It seems that London is still aware of us!"

Begbie exploded in mirth. "By Jove they are, Robertson. Oh yes, they are! Indeed, they hear far too much about us sometimes, I fear. They are thoroughly wearied of railways, graving docks and the like, and of course of judges trying to do their work with independence. But thank you for your good wishes. Come, have some coffee."

They sat, and for a while the judge regaled Aleck with stories of his trip. He had spent considerable time in Ottawa meeting with friends, and also lobbying with the Justice Department concerning the 'judges' dispute'. He felt that they understood clearly the side of the issue taken by him and his colleagues on the bench, but he also knew that officials in Ottawa were anxious to show as much understanding as they could to the new government in Victoria.

"But tell me Robertson, what are your views on the dispute? Should we have County Courts around the province, or can our Supreme Court, duly strengthened, do the legal work required? And should we be able to decide our own rules and run our own system?"

This was hardly a trick question, and Aleck was well prepared for it. He had his own strong opinions on the subject – the need for a strengthened Supreme Court – as he had explained to Maggie in their previous conversation. The judge was smiling as Aleck expounded on the subject.

"Well said, Robertson. I can see you are on the side of the angels, and wisely so. Now then, on my trip I also took the occasion, in both places, to raise the subject of you, your current status and prospects. I had the presumption to suggest that you were rather clever at your law, and respected in the community. I trust that you don't find this disagreeable?"

Aleck blushed. "Not at all, Sir. I am complimented."

"Not really, Robertson. I was just being realistic. You have proven yourself in our courts as well as in your positions in front of the political hounds. You have done well, and I congratulate you. But now then, where to from here? I'm sure that you would like to carry on in your practice and become rich as Croesus, and have a wonderful estate and many servants. But there are other duties to be considered, should you wish to do so."

Aleck sat forward on his chair. "Sir?"

"I speak, as you may guess, of a judgeship. We will at some point require the services of one or two additional fellows on our bench. I don't know when. We'll have to sort out our differences with the government before any more appointments can be made. But it will happen sooner or later, and when that time comes I think you may expect to hear from the Attorney General. Tell me, how would you consider it?"

Aleck's exuberance, his lack of hesitation, made the judge smile. "Why Sir, I would be most honoured! I cannot deny that I enjoy arguing in front of you and your colleagues, but to join you on your side of the bench would give me the greatest pleasure."

"Good, Robertson, good! Now of course, I am not promising anything, but I do suggest that you keep the prospect in mind." He rose. "Well now, I mustn't keep you from your family in this happiest of seasons."

31

THE GOOD YEARS

Maggie would always look back at the period 1876 to 1880 as the ideal time in their lives – a time when life moved on in an active but gentle way, when Aleck was doing so well, and when the family was growing and playing and delightful to behold. Victoria was coming of age, and the new province of British Columbia was starting to show signs of its future prosperity.

Lieutenant-Governor Trutch retired from his post when his initial five-year term was up in 1876, and was replaced by the Canadian lawyer Albert Norton Richards. Trutch went back to England to seek another imperial appointment, and the one that eventually arose was back in BC. He returned in 1880 as Dominion Agent, with responsibility to supervise the construction of the railway in BC.

The Legislative Assembly continued its rambunctious ways when it opened on January 10, 1876. The railway dispute was still in full force, and the Walkem government was defeated due to it. Walkem resigned on January 27, to be replaced by A.C. Elliot. The Governor-General of Canada Lord Dufferin and Lady Dufferin had a long, wide-ranging visit to BC in August and September of 1876. The message that they received everywhere was naturally "where is our railway?" Lord Dufferin proved to be a diplomat of the highest order, succeeding at least to some extent in convincing the people that the project would precede.

George Walkem returned to the Premier's office in the May, 1878 provincial elections, capitalizing on his continued, determined opposition to A.C. Elliot. That August the Legislature passed an historic resolution calling for the secession of British Columbia from the Dominion, with substantial compensation, should the Dominion government not live up to its promises concerning the railway. This startling action was, however, nullified by the federal election later that year. Defeated in his usual Ontario riding of Kingston, Sir John A. Macdonald had a second chance as the federal election in BC ran later than in the rest of the country. He ran successfully in the delayed election in the Victoria riding. Once his Conservatives swept back into office the railway project was assured, and went ahead with the CPR almost immediately.

On October 4, 1879 the government made its final decision on the route of the railway through BC. It would come through via the Fraser River, terminating at Burrard Inlet. Granville's [Vancouver's] future was assured. The dispute over construction of a railway on Vancouver Island went on for some time.

Removed from the direct glare of these political events, Aleck proceeded with his legal career with great vigour, generally recognized as the leading lawyer in the province. He continued to act at assizes around the province, and his expertise in the courts was such that he was commissioned by the government of British Columbia to advise them on the drafting of the *Better Administration of Justice Act*. This act, which was passed by the Walkem government in 1878 and accepted by the Dominion government, formed the basis of settlement between the two governments concerning the management of judges in the province. It:

1. Authorized the Governor General to appoint two more Supreme Court judges.
2. Provided that these judges were to preside in the County Courts as well as the Supreme Court. When in County Court they would be County Court judges. Appeals to the Supreme Court must be heard by two Supreme Court judges.

3. Required no less than three of the five Supreme Court judges to reside on the mainland.

Aleck played such a substantial role in the drafting of this bill that Judge H.P.P. Crease referred to it as 'Mr. Alexander Rocke Robertson's Bill'. Crease himself was not in favour of the bill, as he saw it permitting the provincial government to tell Supreme Court judges what they should do, and where they should live. This dispute would carry on for several years, but the act itself was in place, and would have a major impact on Aleck's life.

In 1879 he was appointed Legal Agent in British Columbia for the Dominion of Canada.

His private practice continued to be haunted by the dispute with Edwin Johnson. They had occasional exchanges of letters, but Johnson was clearly not interested in dissolving the partnership. Eventually Aleck moved for impeachment of his partner, and the partnership was finally dissolved in January 1880.

While this sorry affair was heading to its conclusion, Maggie's younger brother David (Dide) came to BC to pursue his career in the legal profession. He had come first in 1876 for training in Aleck's office, and then in September 1878 he arrived and settled in to article and study for the Bar. Dide, like his older brother Melchior, was a friendly, open, happy man, devoted to his sister and a great admirer of Maggie's famous husband. He settled into rooms in Victoria, and was a frequent and popular visitor at the Johnson Street home.

Melchior also came to establish himself in BC, and in an even more substantive way. In May 1876, working back in Ottawa, he was formally appointed by H.J. Cambie as an engineer on the railway survey. He came out to BC immediately, and was soon toiling once again on a crew in the interior. Back in Ontario that winter, Melchior married Anna Burritt on February 26, 1877. Their son William was born on March 2, 1879. Melchior finally received his formal posting to BC in early 1880, and he and his family moved to Victoria. The railway project was now being launched, and that winter he was summoned to work in the interior.

Aleck and Maggie's family continued to grow and prosper. Always hoping to have a girl, they produced two more boys over this period: Herman Melchior was born on September 2, 1876, and Tate McEwen on December 24, 1878. They still did not decide to give up, in spite of the jibes of their friends that they were clearly determined to field a family cricket team.

Aleck visited Ontario in late 1876, feeling drawn to his family members who were still grieving over the death of their mother. He continued with his business visits to the mainland, pursuing both private and government business, and sport when he had the time. He often travelled in very good company, and sometimes he took his older sons with him for the enjoyment of their company, and to teach them how to fish. The family also continued to enjoy summer vacations at Saanich and the Cowichan area.

In 1880 Aleck was aware that his name was under consideration for a judgeship. He also knew that an act called the Judicial District Act was being considered by the BC Legislature. Under this act there would be four judicial districts in BC – Vancouver Island, New Westminster, Clinton and Cariboo. A Supreme Court Judge should reside in each district, with two on the Island. This was not popular with Begbie, Crease and Gray, but it moved ahead anyway.

On November 26, 1880 two new appointments were made to the Supreme Court of BC: Alexander Rocke Robertson, QC was appointed to the Clinton District, and John Foster McCreight, QC was appointed to the Cariboo District. The appointments were greeted with general approval, although *The British Colonist* of December 1 stated its concern that Aleck, a political star with a great future, should be shelved by the appointment.

Aleck knew that this opinion was held by many influential people. Some felt that Premier Walkem had orchestrated these appointments to get two very powerful lawyers out of the way, so that they would not be a danger to him politically, and would also not interfere with his own plans to be appointed to the bench in Victoria when he left politics. But the situation was still fluid, and Aleck was still young, and he was convinced that he would not be living in Kamloops, the centre of the Clinton district, for very long. In any event, for the moment, Aleck savoured the appointment.

McCreight and Robertson received the congratulations of the Law

Society of BC, and were entertained at a dinner by the members of the Bar at the Driard Hotel on December 29, 1880. Premier Walkem presided, and the chair was occupied by Mr. M.W.T. Drake, then one of the leading counsel in the province, and afterwards also a Justice of the Supreme Court.

PART 3
1881

Tragedy

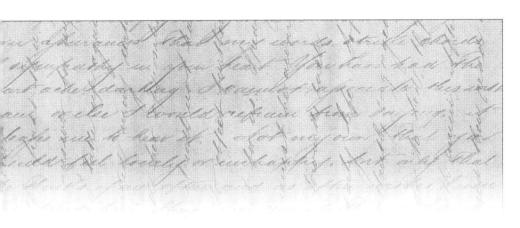

THE NEW JUDGE

Congratulations flowed in to the new judge, but this exciting, happy time was interrupted by a terrible tragedy.

Melchior Eberts enjoyed a brief Christmas season in Victoria with his wife Anna and son William. The family – Aleck and Maggie, their children and his brother Dide – had taken them into their hearts, so it was a joyful family celebration made even more auspicious by the fact that Anna was pregnant, and due to produce their second child in late February. Shortly after Christmas, Melchior was called back to work, and left Victoria in the first week of January.

He died near Spuzzum, BC on January 15, 1881.

The Inland Sentinel, Yale, B.C.

<u>Thursday, January 20, 1881</u>

Sad Accident

The melancholy and terrible death of Mr. D.M. Eberts, of the Canadian Pacific Engineering staff, has shocked our community, as it will doubtless shock his numerous friends throughout Canada, when the sad news shall have reached them. On Saturday last Mr. Eberts was crossing Alexandria

Bluff, near the Alexandria Bridge, in the performance of his duties, when, by some means, he lost his footing and fell a distance of over two hundred feet, until he was thrown against some stumps, which alone prevented his being plunged into the river, from which his body would in all probability never have been recovered...

The accident was investigated immediately, and no fault or blame was allocated. It was simply an unfortunate mistake made by a popular man.

It was the worst possible news for the Robertson family in Victoria. They brought Anna and William to their home, and assembled in tears for the funeral at their church. It was so sad that the irrepressible Buz, that most joyful of men, should be gone from them. Anna was in a state of numbed disbelief, struggling with her pregnancy, while the love that had been her joy and her strength had vanished from her forever.

Aleck brooded in his library, pacing back and forth, wringing his hands and talking in low tones to Maggie who sat nearby, dabbing her eyes. "It is so ironic, is it not, that this terrible thing can be traced to what seemed to be sound advice from your mother and from myself? She convinced poor Buz to come to Victoria rather than to New Mexico, and then I urged him to take up engineering and introduced him to the railway people! Oh my God, so many good intentions, and all gone wrong!"

"Oh Aleck, you mustn't blame yourself. It was good advice, and this terrible accident was, well, just that – an accident. I suppose we could say it is the will of God, although I really do wonder. I know I must not...'

It was time for the family to start considering Kamloops as a place of residence. Considering, yes, but Aleck learned though discussions with his new colleagues on the bench that there was no rush to make such a move. There was still a lot of politicking and maneuvering to take place on the question of locating Supreme Court judges away from the capital, before it would be fixed in stone. Did it really make sense to have a judge located in Barkerville and one in Kamloops, with very little to do and circuits that they could carry out almost as easily from Victoria?

The old lay County Court Judges were retired on January 14. Their work would now be performed by the Supreme Court Judges. But Judge Gray, who was to be posted to New Westminster, said that he refused to move there, so there were still large gaps in the situation. That being said, Aleck took his instructions seriously. With his love of adventure and the outdoors life in the interior, he was not repelled by the idea of living in Kamloops. It would not be as good for Maggie and the children, but it was unlikely to last for too long.

The newly strengthened Supreme Court held a full session early in the year, and then Aleck proceeded to take long trips to the interior to establish his credentials in his district, administer justice, and begin the task of locating living quarters for his family. Once again he and Maggie were back to writing letters, and they were, as before, long and passionate. Maggie was again pregnant, due in early December.

Life was exciting – more so for Aleck than Maggie, who was kept busy in Victoria with her young boys. In late August she enjoyed a brief visit by her husband, in Victoria to attend at the birth of their seventh child. He was another boy, whom they named Alexander Septimus Rocke in honour of his position in the family.

Maggie worried about what would happen when the time came to move to Kamloops. She knew that there was a church there, and some interesting people, a few of whom she had met and liked, and there were some facilities for educating the boys. She was not an adventurer like her husband, so the prospect of long hikes and rides, hunting and fishing, was not a positive one for her. On the other hand Aleck was clearly happy in that environment, and would thrive there. A few years in Kamloops would be just fine.

McCreight, older and less flexible than Aleck, did not view his posting to the Cariboo in the same philosophical way. It was clear to him that Premier Walkem's strategy was to move two legal stars, McCreight and Robertson, as far away from Victoria as possible so that, when he eventually stepped down (or was voted out) as Premier, he would have a judgeship right at home in Victoria. Having pondered over it throughout the summer, he made his feelings on the matter clear to Aleck.

Sept 17th 1881

Private

Dear Robertson

I am glad to hear Mrs. Robertson is as well as you can expect and sincerely sympathize with you in being obliged to live so much away from your family. I have also my letter directing me to reside in the Cariboo District.

I do not see that a Full Court can be of any practical use or at least very little till the 28th section of the Admin. Of J. Act/81 is repealed. Any business that crops up after the one sitting can't be dealt with under the Act. I can't find words to express my disgust at the selfishness which has carried out the legislation in question. Having drawn the Bill which G.A.W. wangled into the present Act for the purpose of carrying out his own schemes, the whole affair is transparently clear to me. Neither you nor I will ever leave our respective districts till G.A.W. has secured to himself an eligible judgeship if he can compass it.

And I doubt that the G.G. would appoint him a Judge. One sitting is all the Act will allow. People will see at last G.A.W.'s game. There is nothing G.A.W. would more dislike than our going to Victoria to stay the winter and he can and will prevent it by "what do you think of the final Monday in each month for a County Court at Kamloops and ditto at Barkerville"?

Try to fix anything you can! The admin of justice will be sacrificed as long as he is A.G. As you say "his idea you fear will be to keep us at our stations during the winter."

After 2 or 3 winters at our stations it will be open to him to "regret that we must have grown a little rusty" and are not as eligible as a certain member of the Profession to wit G.A.W. for any possibly occurring vacancy in a central place. Again the Profession will forget us!...

HON. MR. JUSTICE A.R. ROBERTSON, 1881

33

WOUNDED KNEE

A warm August breeze gusted across Kamloops Lake as Aleck and the two boys, Rockie and Herbert, stripped to their bathing trunks and headed for the cool water. The summer had been remarkably cold and wet, but now it had returned to its more usual state, and what a blessed relief it was to escape from the oppressive heat of late summer! As usual the boys rushed across the sandy beach and plunged in. Aleck was slower, enjoying the scenery before he waded in.

As they continued their play, he swam for a few minutes along the shore, and then headed in to the beach. While wading through the shallows, now up to his hips, he blundered into a submerged log. Cut down long ago and now limbless and waterlogged, the tree trunk still had sharp stubs of its former branches, and he hit one of them in a spot just below his left knee.

He waded quickly ashore, and found that the wound was a sizeable puncture just below the ball of the knee. It hurt a lot, and was bleeding profusely. He called to the boys, who came out of the water reluctantly. Their disappointment changed to concern, however, when they saw their father bent over, clutching a reddening towel to his leg. "Oh Papa, what have you done? Are you alright?"

He assured them that he was fine, that it was just a small wound. But it was still bleeding, so he tied his handkerchief around his leg to protect it, and they withdrew quickly to the carriage, and thence to their rooming house. Mrs. Wren, the landlady, clucked over Aleck's wound, sat him down in a chair and administered to it. It did not heal quickly, however, so the next day they called for the doctor, who applied several stitches. There was no further bleeding, although the wound, and indeed the knee itself, remained tender.

Aleck received a note informing him that his assizes would convene in Clinton on October 17, and then Kamloops on November 3. When he was in Victoria in mid-September, Maggie was alarmed to see that Aleck was walking with a cane, favouring his left knee. Within half an hour of his arrival at home she had him sitting on his bed in his nightgown, the doctor summoned. The doctor's diagnosis was no surprise. The wound had become infected, so he must take great care and keep it clean, and of course eat well and healthily.

When he returned to Kamloops in early October and resumed his duties in the region, his knee was no better. It was very sore, and he had to keep it firmly bandaged and walk with a cane. Hot baths were a great comfort to him. Mrs. Wren prepared for him a lineament of beef's gall, turpentine, vinegar and cayenne pepper. It actually helped to ease the pain for a while, but it did not make the wound heal.

Aleck presided at the assizes in Clinton, but it was a painful experience. He strove mightily to hide his affliction from the courtroom, and for long periods on the bench he dared not move his body at the risk of igniting the pain that would start at the knee itself, and then move quickly to consume the entire leg.

Immediately following the assizes in Clinton, the knee took a turn for the worse. The wound was glowing, swollen and angry, and the pain constant. It was now so bad that he could not work. The doctor was alarmed, and told him that he must go to Victoria for treatment. Aleck had to agree, and informed Victoria by telegram that he would not be able to sit at the

November assizes in Kamloops. Judge McCreight was appointed to do so in his place.

Aleck returned to Victoria on November 1 to seek the help of Dr. Powell and Dr. Helmcken. Dide met him at the steamer terminal, and took him straight home. Maggie and Dide helped him to his bed, where he collapsed in exhaustion, calling for brandy to fight off the pain. Maggie sent Brett with a note to fetch Dr. Powell.

The doctor's prognosis was not optimistic. He said that the infection in the knee had set in strongly, and seemed to be spreading. There was little that he could do aside from prescribing complete bed rest, and whatever would work to relieve the pain. Aleck managed to carry on some limited correspondence, mainly with family, but otherwise slept a lot and had quiet, composed conversations with Maggie, Dide and the boys and immediate friends.

Maggie knew that her beloved man was dying. Dide agreed with her – there was clearly very little hope. In a brief, private and very sober discussion they agreed that Dide would look into their financial and business affairs to ensure that there would be no problems arising upon Aleck's death. The basic assumption upon which they based their approach was that when Aleck died, Maggie would sell up in Victoria and take her seven children back to Chatham, where she would have the support of her family and many old friends.

Dide paid calls on Mr. W.C. Ward, the Manager of the Bank of British Columbia, the Hon. H.P.P. Crease, Supreme Court Judge and close friend and associate of Aleck's, and other business contacts. Ward assured him that should Aleck die, his family would not perhaps be wealthy, but would certainly be comfortable. Judge Crease said that he was already looking into the question of a pension for Maggie.

As Aleck's crisis worsened, Maggie gave whatever attention she could spare from nursing him to her family. She had two groups to deal with. The four older boys – Rockie, Herbie, Percy and Harold – were fully aware of the trouble their father was in, and insisted upon seeing him and asking about him. The younger group – Herman, Tate and Septimus – were a different case. Having just turned five, Herman was certainly aware that there was trouble in the home, but Maggie described the trouble in vague terms, and asked him to give special attention to his younger brothers, so that he was diverted to be captain of that young and vulnerable team.

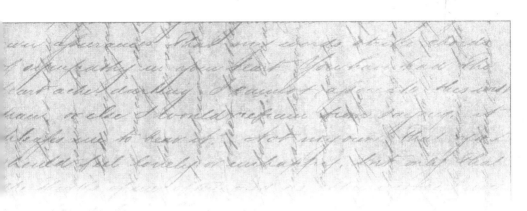

34

THE END

On Saturday, November 26, after a feverish night, Aleck was in terrible pain and shock. Maggie sent a message to Dr. Powell, and also to her friend Sarah Crease accepting Sarah's standing invitation to take the young ones off her hands during a crisis. Within an hour Sarah arrived in the Crease family coach, accompanied by her young maid Emily, who knew the boys well from previous visits. They bundled the three youngsters into the coach, where Emily set Herman and Tate in place and held the baby. Maggie gave Sarah the details of the wet nurse she had arranged, and after a fierce, tearful embrace the women parted, Sarah to the coach and Maggie to her sad duties.

Soon thereafter Dr. Powell arrived with an ambulance carriage and attendants. They carried Aleck into the kitchen and laid him on the table. The doctor examined him and bound up and splinted the leg as firmly as he could. Maggie assisted by applying ether with a dish cloth to ease Aleck's pain. Then they put him into the ambulance and took him to the Royal Hospital, where they operated on him that afternoon – Dr. Powell, Dr. Helmcken, Dr. Davie and Dr. Matthews.

Aleck was in serious but stable condition in the following days, sleeping for the most part. The doctors believed that he was recovering, and on November 28 they permitted the family to take him home, where they could care for him more directly and personally. Maggie nursed him throughout the day, and engaged a nurse to watch over him at night. The doctor visited each morning, knowing that there was little he could do except attend to the dressing on the leg and administer sedatives.

Aleck's condition was the subject of great concern throughout Victoria. It seemed to be on everyone's lips – the impossibility of such a young and dynamic person being in so much trouble.

November 29, 1881

My dear Mrs. Robertson

We are all very anxious to know daily how Mr. Robertson is getting on, but then everybody feels ashamed to pull the bell and worry the person who answers the summons with the same question for the 20th time daily. Would it be too much trouble to get Mr. Eberts to hang out fresh bulletins, dated, as the doctors announce them – with a small box for cards?

Pray give Mr. Robertson my best remembrances and believe me.

Yours very truly.

Matt. B. Begbie

On that very afternoon Aleck became flushed with a high temperature, and was incoherent and clearly in pain that no drug could control. That evening and the next day and night passed in a cloud of misery and exhaustion. Foul weather kept the boys from venturing outside, so they huddled in their room, Rockie leading them in reading and quiet play. Myla kept them clean and fed, and Maggie visited them occasionally to try to keep up their spirits, although in reality seeking the solace of their love and concern. Whenever the opportunity arose she would release them individually or in twos to peek into their father's room, or perhaps come to his bedside and gaze at him for a few moments.

When he was home, Dide kept an eye on everything, with particular attention to his sister. She was amazingly strong, dealing with the children and Myla with a voice and demeanor that was almost normal. But not quite. He saw within her the gray, rasping seeds of despair, and he did what he could to support her with words and help, and comforting embraces. The night nurse released them all for a few hours of sleep.

During the evening of November 30 Aleck lapsed into a coma. On the morning of December 1 it was clear that the end was near. He was no longer in a coma, but was sinking into himself, dreamy and far away. Maggie sent for the three youngest boys, and Sarah Crease delivered them at noon, giving Maggie a brave hug before leaving. Holding the baby in her arms, Maggie spoke to the boys sitting in a circle around her, telling them what was happening, and preparing them for their last meeting with their father. Percy, always the most sensitive one, reminded her that they must be sure and tell their grandma and all the other relatives about what was happening. She agreed, and said that she would need all of her boys' help to do so.

Aleck died at 3:40 pm that afternoon. It was Thursday, December 1, 1881.

December 1, 1881

Telegram

David Eberts (Victoria) to Hermann Eberts (Chatham)

Aleck died this afternoon from shock after operation on leg. Wrote yesterday. Maggie bearing up wonderfully. Inform family.

Percy Robertson (age 9) to Mary Bell Eberts, his grandmother
December 3, 1881

My dearest Grandmamma

I hope you are quite well and Grandpapa too. Oh dear Grandmamma I suppose you heard the news of our sweetest darling there ever was. We have lost our dearest our darling father. I have cried over him and over him again.

But oh to see the beautiful bright eyes sink into the gloom of death. He did not struggle he died peacefully and he said before he died I shall tell you the words he said. Peace gentle peace. Thank God for that peace, but he said them so peacefully and so beautifully that it made me cry when Mamma said Percy do you promise your father you will be good to your mother and I said I would and I will try by God's help if I can.

Dear father was always prepared to die and died with God and he was so beautiful when he died he was looking up towards heaven all the time he looked like if God had come to help him and died with all of us around him and when before he died dear Uncle Dide came in the room and said Aleck do you know me and he said with a smile in his face said how Dide can I ever forget you, and after a little time Mamma came in the room and said Aleck do you know me and he said – why Maggie my wife, and Mamma kissed him and every time she kissed him he kissed her back.

We have lost a precious soul a soul that we cannot see again but once when I cannot tell you all about it because I must help dear Mamma. He has suffered a great deal from his leg and now he is lying in his coffin and will sleep in the narrow grave where he was prepared for.

(ends)

[This letter breaks off in mid-sentence and is unsigned. It was never mailed, but Maggie kept it.]

35

DECEMBER 3, 1881

11 o'clock on a chilly Victoria morning. A sharp wind was rushing up from the harbour, and brief showers of icy rain caught the bundled visitors under their blowing parasols and hats as they moved quickly from their carriages to the Robertsons' house in Johnson Street. The event was the christening of their latest child, Alexander Septimus Rocke Robertson.

The visitors were greeted at the door by Dide Eberts. He shook hands, welcomed them in quiet, somber tones, and passed them on to the maid who took their coats and hats, and directed them to the parlour.

A christening should be a happy event, but this day was anything but happy. The six older boys sat clustered around their mother except for the oldest, 12 year-old Rockie, who stood by her side, bravely holding onto her arm to support her. Maggie herself was dry-eyed but severe and unsmiling, save for occasional gracious nods to visitors. As the brief service started, Dide moved through the visitors to stand behind Maggie and Rockie.

Reverend Jenns spoke briefly and in low tones, and the visitors stood with heads bowed, the women dabbing eyes with their handkerchiefs, the men with stern, crowded eyebrows. The cause of this unhappiness, on what should have been a joyous occasion, lay in state in a casket on a raised platform on the other side of the room – Maggie's husband, the late Hon. Mr.

Justice Alexander Rocke Robertson, dead at the age of 40.

Yesterday and this morning the important people of Victoria had come through this room to pay their respects to the family of the departed judge. Lieutenant-Governor Clement Francis Cornwall and Mrs. Cornwall had visited, accompanied by Premier and Mrs. George Walkem. Aleck's old colleagues Chief Justice Matthew Begbie and Justices H.P.P. Crease and John Foster McCreight had been through. Earlier today Maggie had greeted Victoria's Mayor John Turner and Mrs. Turner, and so it went – friends and colleagues expressing their sadness and condolences.

To all of them, and especially to the family, it was inconceivable that Aleck should be dead at such a young age. Indeed, lying there with his eyes closed, he looked as if he might jump up at any moment and welcome them, and perhaps play them a piece on his violin. But of course he would not, and the flags of the city flew at half-mast, and the military ball was postponed, and the newspapers bemoaned his untimely death.

Maggie, his beloved Maggie, mourned Aleck with a passion of unimaginable depth and strength. She and Aleck had loved each other from their earliest times together. They were fated for each other, and had clung together through endless letters for those years before they were finally able to marry, and through his many absences. Their family life in Victoria had bounced with happiness.

And now Aleck was gone, and she was on her own in Canada's wild west, far from her old family home and friends in Ontario. She had seven boys to raise in the proud traditions of their families, and no Aleck to help her – bounding up the walk at the end of the day to play with the boys and help solve the problems of the day and oh, most important of all, to love her in every way.

'Oh Aleck, my darling, darling Aleck – how can you leave me like this? Stay with me Aleck. Pray for me and for the boys. Watch over us!'

POSTSCRIPTS

The Eberts and Robertson families were distraught over Aleck's untimely death, and Dr. Duncan William Eberts took a lively interest in the matter. What exactly were the doctors treating? How could he die from a simple wound in his leg?

The British Colonist said

> *The ailment from which he is suffering is a rare and formidable disease, which has developed itself in the head of the tibia or large bone in the leg called osteo (or bone) aneurism. So rare, indeed, that very few instances of it are recorded by the best surgical authorities.*

This presumably came from the doctors interviewed following his death.

The *Dominion Pacific Herald* was perhaps more perceptive in saying that

> ...the *exact nature of his disease does not seem to be well understood.*

Whatever the real nature of the disease was, *The British Colonist* noted that Aleck underwent a long and painful operation, and that the shock of the operation (presumably combined with the force of the disease) seems to have killed the patient. Operations are not usually painful if the patient is properly anaesthetized. Was he?

There was no mention of amputation. They were trying to save the leg.

Dr. Eberts' conclusion was that Aleck did not die from complications arising from his swimming injury, but rather from a serious cancer that was exposed through his body's inability to recover normally from a minor injury. Without the best and most accurate medical care involving immediate amputation of the leg, he was doomed. Even with such care, he might well have died soon anyway.

The newspaper reports of Aleck's death and official messages of regret and condolence were widespread throughout BC. The following brief excerpt from the lengthy account in *The British Colonist* of his funeral provides, in a most dramatic way, a sense of the respect in which he was held.

The British Colonist
December 5, 1881

Funeral of the Late Hon. Justice Robertson

The last sad rites to departed worth were performed on Sunday afternoon over the remains of the universally-esteemed judge of the Supreme Court of this province just deceased. No single demise in British Columbia has excited so much genuine regret, and probably no funeral yet held has been attended by such a number of sympathetic mourners... the whole procession (extended) fully three-fourths of a mile, and (took) twenty minutes to pass a given point while en route to St. John's Church. Here a vast assemblage of people were in waiting, while the church itself was crowded to its utmost capacity long before the procession arrived...

Excerpt from 'BRITISH COLUMBIA from the Earliest Times to the Present', Biographical Volume IV, The S.J. Clarke Publishing Company, 1914

In an enumeration of those men who won honour and public recognition for themselves, in a conspicuous way in the legal and judicial history of the province of British Columbia, and at the same time honoured the province to which they belonged, mention should be made of the Hon. Alexander Rocke Robertson. Taking precedence as an eminent lawyer and statesman, he was a man of high attainments, occupying a unique position during the early epoch in the history of British Columbia, in which connection he bore himself with dignity and honour as to gain the respect of all. Distinctively a man of affairs, he became connected with many phases of pioneer life as it existed here under early conditions, wielding wide and powerful influence in his day. His strong mentality, invincible courage and determined individuality so entered into his make-up as to render him a natural leader of men, and fitted him for the high position which he occupied in the province and as a member of the provincial Supreme Court.

True to her word in her discussion with Dide, Maggie sold the house and furniture, packed up her family and left Victoria in early January 1882, heading back to the family haven of Chatham. Dide helped her on her trip, and then returned to Victoria and took over Aleck's practice.

Maggie managed to acquire the old Robertson home 'Heatherdale', and brought up her boys there, surrounded by her parents and other family. It seemed, however, that British Columbia was in the blood of her family, for one by one they returned. Rockie came to Victoria in 1891, and was employed in a County Court office. Unfortunately his health failed, and he returned to Chatham in 1895, where he died in May.

Herbert and Harold both returned to Victoria as lawyers. Herbert moved to the Yukon, and was appointed a County Court Judge in Prince George, and eventually Senior County Court Judge. Harold was appointed a Justice of the Supreme Court of British Columbia, and eventually of the

Appeal Count.

Percy died in 1887 from an attack of appendicitis, thought to have been brought on by a blow in the abdomen from a cricket ball.

Herman and Septimus both became medical doctors who served in the First World War. Herman became President of the Canadian Medical Association.

Septimus pursued a distinguished medical career in Washington State, and it was to him that Maggie entrusted the letters that have formed the foundation of this book.

Tate was the only businessman in the family. He worked mainly in the United States, in the investment banking field.

Maggie was unable to withstand this reverse flow to Victoria, and moved back herself in 1897. She lived with Harold and his family until her death from pneumonia on January 9, 1912. During that stay in Victoria she was active in society and volunteering, and her death was noted with interest and sorrow.

One anonymous tribute printed on January 16, 1912 said in part:

> *The passing to her eternal rest of the late Mrs. Rocke Robertson was an event of more than ordinary interest – it was the removal from our midst of a great and noble woman who had endeared herself by her fascinating personality and goodness of character to all that had the good fortune to call her 'friend'. She was a rare combination, possessing the charm of a most tender nature with an indomitable will, and tenacity of purpose that inspired her projects in life and carried them to a successful completion.*

Over four years after Aleck's death, in a letter appearing in the weekly *Colonist* on March 23, 1886 signed by "Lex", a regular commentator on legal affairs, it was said:

The most brilliant and successful lawyer the province ever had was the lamented Mr. Justice Robertson, who was one of the advisers of the crown in the first ministry after confederation. During that time how many criminal cases did he defend? The answer is, every one of any importance. His forensic talent commanded for him the cream of the criminal business.

BIBLIOGRAPHY

Letters

The letters between Aleck and Maggie, and between them and relatives and friends, were the core of the reference material.

Books and Published Documents

The following were the main reference works. Many others were consulted briefly.

British Columbia – From the Earliest Times to the Present, Volume II; F.W. Howay and E.O.S. Scholefield; The S.J. Clarke Publishing Company, 1914

British Columbia – From the Earliest Times to the Present, Volume IV Biographical; F.W. Howay and E.O.S. Scholefield; The S.J. Clarke Publishing Company, 1914

The Eberts Family – Official Records, Traditions, Reflections; Edmond Urquhart Melchior Eberts; Boarish Press, 1944

The Pacific Province – A History of British Columbia; Hugh J.M. Johnston,

General Editor; Douglas & McIntyre, 1996

The Struggle for the Supreme Court: Law and Politics in British Columbia, 1871-1885; Hamar Foster; *Law & Justice in a New Land: Essays in Western Canadian Legal History*; Louis Knafla, ed.; (Carswell 1986), pp. 167-213

Victoria Historical Review – Centennial Celebrations; City of Victoria, 1962

An Act to Incorporate the Inter-oceanic Railway Company of Canada; Assented to 14th June, 1872

No Ordinary People – Victoria's Mayors Since 1862; Valerie Green; Beach Holme Publications, 1992

Victoria – A History in Photographs; Peter Grant; Heritage House, 1995

Private Papers

Biography of Alexander Rocke Robertson, QC; Hon. Mr. Justice Harold Bruce Robertson; undated

The B.X. Express; Kirsten Parsla Barnard Robertson; undated

Web Sites

The following are the main web sites visited for research purposes. Wikipedia was consulted many times; www.wikipedia.org; key sites are noted below.

An Act Respecting Public Schools, 1872; www.viu.ca/homeroom

Albert Prince; Wikipedia

Archives of Ontario; www.archives.gov.on.ca

BC Archives – Royal BC Museum; www.bcarchives.gov.bc.ca

The British Columbia History Internet/Web Site; http://victoria.tc.ca/Resources/bchistory

Canada Gen Web – British Columbia; http://bc.canadagenweb.org

Canadian Information Pages; http://cyber-north.com/Canada

Canada in the Making; www.canadiana.ca/citm

Canadian Election Results 1867-2008; www.sfu.ca~aheard/elections/1867-present

Chatham, (C.W.,) Canada Directory; www.accessgenealogy.com/scripts/data

Victoria: The Capital of British Columbia – Proud History, Bright Future; www.victoria.ca

The British Colonist – Online Edition: 1858-1910; www.britishcolonist.ca

Dictionary of Canadian Biography Online; www.biographi.ca

The first newspapers on Canada's west coast: 1858-1863; http://hughdoherty.tripod.com

First Transcontinental Railroad; Wikipedia

NYTimes.com – Free Articles from December 1864; http://spiderbites.nytimes.com

Henry Nathan Jr.; Wikipedia

The Homeroom – Timeline of education development in BC; http://viu.ca/homeroom

Electoral History of British Columbia 1871-1986;
http://elections.bc.ca

Freemasonry in BC; www.freemasonry.bcy.ca

KJA Vintage Posters, Maps and Prints; www.rainfall.com

List of Ghost Towns in BC; Wikipedia

List of Mayors of Victoria; Wikipedia

Law Foundation of BC; www.lawfoundationBC.org

Miners at Work – a History of BC's Gold Rushes;
www.empr.gov.bc.ca/mining

The Canadian Encyclopedia – Rupert's Land;
www.canadianencyclopedia.com

The St. Albans Incident; www.rootsweb.ancestry.com

Supreme Court of Canada – Creation and Beginnings of the Court; www.
scc-csc.gc.ca

The Cariboo Gold Rush (1858-1865) – Historical context, economic
impact, and related links; www.canadianeconomy.gc.ca

The Times Magazine – Windsor's First Mayor Samuel Smith Macdonell
(1823-1907); www.walkervilletimes.com

Upper Canada Chronology Pre-1791-1842;
www.uppercanadagenealogy.com

Vancouver, BC Timeline; www.garvick.com

ABOUT THE AUTHOR

With a B.A. from McGill University and an M.B.A. from Harvard, Ian has been writing all his life – in business and government, and now as an author of historical creative non-fiction. His inspiration has been the substantial collection of family letters, diaries and documents that have told exciting stories dating from the early nineteenth century to 1950. From the chaotic politics surrounding the creation of British Columbia as a province of Canada (The Honourable Aleck) to the bloody battlefields of the

Second World War (While Bullets Fly), his books bring human, passion-ate insights to historic times and events. Ian and his wife Bonnie grew up in British Columbia and lived in Toronto, Ottawa, West Vancouver, Boston, Philippines, India and Singapore before settling on Vancouver Island in 2003.

See http://www.ian-b-robertson.com

INDEX

CPSIA information can be obtained at www.ICGtesting.com
Printed in the USA
LVOW06s0333101013

356201LV00001B/18/P